May, 2004

Laura

PS Scouting for Boys it isn't!

INDIA CALLING

CORNELIA SORABJI

INDIA CALLING
THE MEMORIES OF CORNELIA SORABJI

BY CORNELIA SORABJI

Edited by Elleke Boehmer and Naella Grew

TRENT EDITIONS

Published by Trent Editions, 2004, with the permission of Sir Richard Sorabji.

Trent Editions
Department of English and Media Studies
The Nottingham Trent University
Clifton Lane
Nottingham NG11 8NS

Printed in Great Britain by Goaters Limited, Nottingham.
ISBN 1 84233 077 2

Contents

IV Success: Some Problems Of The Way

V The Last Lap

Acknowledgements

The editors are grateful to Sir Richard Sorabji, Cornelia Sorabji's nephew, for the permission to reprint *India Calling* of 1934, together with our Editorial Apparatus and Introduction. We should also acknowledge his kind help and generosity as regards the loan of Cornelia's books, making her papers available to us, and sharing his memories of her. We are grateful to Jon Stallworthy for putting us in contact with Sir Richard Sorabji, and for his enthusiastic encouragement throughout the process of editing this book.

E.B. and N.G.

Editors' Introduction

Cornelia Sorabji (1866-1954), the Bombay-born pioneering lawyer, imperialist, and woman of letters, embodied some of the most potent contradictions of empire of her time. Oxford University changed by decree its examination regulations to enable her, a scholar of distinction, but a woman, to write for the B.C.L degree: it was a measure unprecedented for the period with respect to any woman, British or non-British.[1] 'Brought up English', and grateful to the English ruling classes, with whom she formed close personal ties, because of the doors they opened for her, she remained throughout her life a Tory imperialist in her values, an admirer of imperial effort, and a follower of English high society. However, she worked for many years in India in the self-made role of Advisor to the Court of Wards representing women in purdah and securing their rightful legal entitlements – essentially as an innovator in her field. Whilst privy to the injustices that women suffered in their state of confinement, she was even so an opponent of women's suffrage and a supporter of tradition over modernization for orthodox India, as her career memoir *India Calling* and its companion volume *India Recalled* both demonstrate.[2]

With her conservative beliefs yet respect for Indian traditions, both Hindu and Muslim, and with her anti-nationalist and yet relatively progressive woman-centred values, Cornelia Sorabji can probably be seen as one of the most successful if internally divided Indian mediators of her time. Cherishing a conviction cultivated from her childhood to 'help India', especially Indian women in purdah, she was typical of that deracinated, 'in-between' class instituted by Macaulay's 'Minute on Indian Education' of 1835 (q.v.) in all but her gender.[3] It was her gender, however, which not only motivated her strong identification with 'her' *purdahnashin* but which (along with her Christianity) also ensured the special status which she was accorded as a student in England, at the same time as it furnished the central grounds on which she experienced discrimination. As such her gender is fundamental to the several contradictions which cut to the heart of her often controversial achievements.

She was born into a large Parsee family, the fifth of eight children (seven daughters and a son) who survived into adulthood, and was named for her mother's adoptive mother, the Englishwoman Lady Ford. Marked out by their Zoroastrian faith, Persian cultural origins, and success in business and civic life, the Parsee community of Bombay had traditionally been favoured by the British in their efforts to impose their authority in India.[4] Sorabji Kharsedji, Cornelia's father had, however, achieved a distinct notoriety within the community by adopting the Christian faith at age seventeen, and remaining a Christian despite concerted persecutions by the community fathers, as Cornelia evokes them in 'Therefore', her memoir of her parents.[5] Having severed connections with the Parsees, and set up a Church Missionary Society station in Nasik in the Western Presidency, her father married a Christianized and anglicized 'tribal' woman of the Nilgiri region, Francina Santya, who had been adopted as a girl by Sir Francis Ford and his wife Lady Cornelia. In their different ways both Sorabji and his wife, Francina, represented minorities within minorities (Christianized groups within Parsee/tribal groupings): this special if somewhat beleaguered position would inform and reinforce Cornelia's self-perceived outsider status. It also possibly accounts for the tenacity with which she clung to the social trappings of English high society (its autograph books and calling cards; the name-dropping in *India Calling*; her delight in being presented at court; her fond, scented reminiscences of Oxford). It was in England alone that her specialness had afforded more public approbation than discomfiture.

Brought up with English values and at a distance from the Parsee community, Cornelia indeed saw herself as only nominally Indian, as the description of her childhood in Part I of *India Calling* makes plain. Although she undoubtedly remained proud of her Indian origins, she saw herself as 'Parsee by nationality' (10), yet 'taught to call [herself] Indian' (12). Her Christianity, along with her earliest formative experiences – English nursery tales, games, and discipline, English as the Sorabji lingua franca, 'English' meals and table manners – aligned her with the British at a time when culture and religion were inextricably linked. Circumscribed by the 'invisible circle' (12) within which her family was exiled, she was from the outset cast into the role not only of outsider but more precisely of objectifying observer, even of voyeur, vis-à-vis India. Schooled on Western thought and literature she continued in later years to contribute to the construction of India as a romantic and orientalized space to which, moreover, as Advisor to the Court of Wards, she had special access. Her perception of the country can be seen as, effectively, a cluster of images drawn from the colonial archive and reinforced with local knowledge. The opulence, decadence and superstition of the *zenanas* she describes are mirrorings of the *Arabian Nights*, as she herself acknowledges (47).

Along with the British in India, her family shared preoccupations with religious, educational and social reform, self-improvement, and a belief in duty and civic responsibility – the 'good' or 'useful' work for India to which Cornelia remained so committed. The family's creed, as articulated by her mother, was to "[share] with others the Gospel as she knew it, the Good News – of Christianity, of Health, of Education, of Sanitation" (16) – in other words, the blueprint of the imperial civilizing mission, of the 'white man's burden'. Cornelia and her sisters devoted their lives to continuing their mother's good work, under the motto which Cornelia attributed to her educationalist sister Susie, yet herself fundamentally shared: 'One Flag, One Throne, One Empire'.[6] Her extensive knowledge of Indian faiths and customs was used as a tool to achieve greater compliance from women in purdah in order to modify those very customs, or, as she writes, to proceed 'from the known' to 'the unknown' (153). At the same time, however, her time at Oxford gave her some insight into the narrowness and prescriptiveness of missionary ideals, and she steadfastly resisted efforts by Church missionaries to enlist her as a standard-bearer for their cause: it is one of the significant instances of fracture in Cornelia's self-construction.[7] She also tried to promote the appointment of Indians in education, despite the tide of English opinion against this.

Revealingly, as if describing her own personal ideal, Cornelia would later underline that there was no '"join"' in her mother's hybrid cultural makeup. '[S]he did English lessons and learnt English ways of usefulness; and she did Indian lessons, and was encouraged to learn all that she could about the people of India and their faiths and customs', so embodying the best of the West, while remaining proud of India (*Therefore*, 43-4). She 'assimilated', Cornelia wrote, without 'displacing', she was 'unifying' (*Therefore*, 55), as if justifying thereby the processes of cultural accretion through education which she herself had undergone, yet which never caused her to deny her own cultural origins outright, as a more conventional colonial 'mimic man' might have done.[8] The Victoria High School which her parents founded, she further remarked, was presciently based on what would now be called child-centred Montessori and cross-cultural principles: this was because 'nothing but an English and Indian *combination* could save the country and help its truest development' (*Therefore*, 58; emphasis added).

Yet this personal fantasy of a seamless cultural and religious 'combination' masks any number of fissures in Sorabji's writing, and is certainly contradicted by the evidence of her life. Excluded by race as well as gender from complete assimilation into English society, and divided by religion and culture from her fellow Indians, Cornelia was, to quote from her own self-description, 'homed in two countries' (5), yet at home in neither. Throughout, she restlessly distinguished herself from a broad cross-section of Indian and British society, from the 'England-returned' Indian civil servant to other pioneering Indian women; from the shabbily-dressed woman reader at the British Library to the suffragettes.[9] Constructing herself as a citizen of empire, she effectively found herself at the intersection point of any number of faultlines in the colonial establishment. As this Introduction will go on to show, both affiliation and isolation were central themes that informed her life: her identity was constituted within the tensions of their interplay.

Cornelia Sorabji's deep dependence on the approval of her family, her Oxford mentors, and her English audience (both in her education and work, and in her writing), betrayed throughout her life a strong need for affirmation. Even the text of *India Calling*, written at the end of her career as a lawyer, seeks to display and confirm, through its enumeration of connections and professional successes, her exceptional status. In India her dependence on such forms of approval, which, lacking social connections, she continued to invoke, inevitably separated her from the Indians for whose improvement she so tirelessly worked. Indeed, it was probably due to the fact that Oxford – a think-tank of imperial ideas and a training ground for imperial officers – granted her favoured status, both socially and academically, that it occupied such a special place in her memory. A place of possibility and fulfilled dreams, the University was the one place where she felt at once unreservedly accepted and respected. She became, essentially, its graduate in spirit as well as in name, setting out, with the blessing of Benjamin Jowett (q.v.), to fulfil its mission of social responsibility as a civil servant of the Empire.

At the same time, however, the role of contented, assimilated Indian was one that Cornelia in all likelihood also strategically manipulated in her dealings with her English mentors.[10] As Antoinette Burton and Suparna Gooptu both point out in their studies of Sorabji, her private correspondence from England, as well as India, reveals frustrations, differences of opinion, and anxieties which the public persona did not betray. In relation to the Church Missionary Society, for instance, which funded her mother's Pune school, she took care at Oxford to play the diplomat and to seem the malleable Christian, even while questioning this approach in her letters.[11] Interpellated as Indian, she carried out the role in Britain and on her European travels with finesse and even cynical delight, down to her preparedness, albeit reluctantly, to demonstrate how a sari was worn by stripping before a group of disbelieving Italian Customs Officials (36-7). Yet back in India, too, while setting herself up as a *pukka* (though for years unofficial) Indian Civil Servant in the British mould, she experienced repeated bureaucratic setbacks as she negotiated over various issues relating to her service conditions, and complained about these in private. As is recorded with pain in her long correspondence with Eleanor Rathbone, she had to face entrenched 'layers of gender and racial discrimination' concerning pay, pension, chances of promotion, as well as the possibility of her post being renewed after her retirement.[12]

Annoyingly for her many nationalist opponents, Cornelia Sorabji pursued throughout her career a gradualist, step-by-step approach to social reform, especially as regarded the legal and political status of women. The narrative of *India Calling* itself, thus fittingly, traces the steady chronological progress of the social and legal pioneer-'pilgrim' Sorabji as she faces, and usually overcomes, the obstacles to her work as a woman, and disseminates to women not thus advantaged advice at once insightful and sensible. From the formative moment of encounter with the Kathiawar Rani as a child, this is the pre-scripted path along which India has called her.

As she records in Chapter II, she was, in 1885, the first woman student to graduate from Pune College. 'Topping the Presidency', she obtained a Government of India scholarship to study at a British university, but was prevented from doing so because she was a woman. Later, despite obtaining a LL.B. degree from the University of Bombay on her return to India from Oxford (46), she was prevented as a woman from working as a *Vakil* or lawyer, and spent the next ten years as a 'roving practitioner of law'. It was finally in 1904 that, cannily finding a niche for herself as, necessarily, a woman representative for women in purdah, she authored her own job as Ladies' Legal Advisor. Barred from working as a lawyer, she thus strategically turned her attention to breaking through another barrier, that of purdah. She had however to work hard to convince the authorities of the usefulness of her position, and had often to stand upon her status as a colonialist-favoured-by-colonialists. Significantly, in *India Calling*, her self-justificatory rhetoric of improvement in favour of the women in purdah is often allowed to mask the ambition which, equally, inspired her professional fervour. (Throughout, she retained a keen awareness of the rival achievements of other prominent Indian women, such as Sarojini Naidu, and felt considerable ambivalence with regard to her own sister and fellow writer, Alice, or Ailsa, (later Pennell), who trained as a doctor, a profession to which Cornelia felt strong attraction despite her romanticized sense of legal calling.)[13] It was as long as five years later, in 1909, that her job was at last made permanent, though based on a non-European salary scale.[14]

However, even if her ideas of social and educational reform, inspired by her mother, were woman-centred, Cornelia Sorabji was, as already indicated, no supporter of political emancipation for women, or indeed for India more generally. She believed, like her imperial mentors, that traditional women had always first to be introduced to the benefits of modernity – instruction in social service, hygiene, literacy – as the essential groundwork for other reforms. In relation to the *purdahnashins*' primitive helplessness or their superstition-bound obedience, as she saw it, she styled herself as, by contrast, their masculine practical helper: the '"Man of Business"', the 'one-who-might-help' (56), even the 'Magic man', adapting rather than contravening *zenana* rules to their advantage, as she explains (150). Feminist 'Progressives' she simply labelled 'hysterical' (54); Congress workers, as the penultimate chapter on Gandhi and the Indian National Congress makes very plain, were at best socially disruptive, at worst terroristic and oppressive to the poor. Freedom, she fundamentally believed, had to be earned, not bestowed. Such views worked directly against the nationalist groundswell of the time, and earned her the vilification of her countrymen and women. Her reputation touched its lowest point in 1927 when she favourably reviewed the American Katherine Mayo's controversial book, *Mother India*, in which the 'crime' of child-marriage was laid at the feet of Indian men. It is an incident that *India Calling*, not surprisingly, omits to mention.

Overcompensating in these ways for her own secondary status as a woman, and a non-European, Cornelia Sorabji lived out a paradox through which she reproduced certain of the patriarchal and colonial views which had frustrated her own work and promotion as a lawyer. She recreated, in other words, the structures of imperial authority even as she contested them – as Suparna Gooptu, for instance, points out. Such contradictions developed particularly complicated inflections within the context of the *zenana*, her chosen place of work. Locating herself in *India Calling* as an often patronizing outside observer in cahoots with a like-minded European audience (86-7, 93), she seeks to penetrate the innermost sanctum of Indian domestic and spiritual life, the most highly mythologized space in the orientalist lore of the East.[15] She adopts, that is, the all-seeing eye of the imperialist, playing to the scopophilia, disguised as reforming interest, of her Western audience, whilst also exploiting her privileged status as female observer. Where high-caste women traditionally concealed, she chose to reveal, in ways reminiscent of the sari incident on the Italian border. It is noticeable that the vocabulary of her descriptions is almost deliberately titillating, highlighting the mystique and the subterfuge, as well as the courage and devotion, which defined life behind the veil. Yet, in as much as Cornelia Sorabji speaks of the 'simple' *purdahnashin* as pawns of unscrupulous men and tradition, the question that might be asked is to what extent she herself, as a compliant reporter for the West, acted as its peon.

In recent years, the critical attention which has focused on postcolonial 'mixedness' and cultural syncretism has forged new ways through which to read, in retrospect, Cornelia Sorabji's writing, and the considerable achievement which it marks. Culturally and politically exiled from the Indian motherland she sought to claim as her own, she effectively found herself caught between two 'imaginary homelands', in Salman Rushdie's description. On the one hand there was the hidden India she interpreted very much like a Victorian traveller, though with the benefit of vernacular knowledge, and, on the other, the England of her rosy student memories, where she eventually settled and died, in a mental hospital. Along with her short stories, tales for children and other memoirs, *India Calling* intentionally makes a contribution to colonial knowledge of the other, to a colonial discourse. Yet this was from a writer who was herself often othered and patronized by her benefactors, whose career was moulded in directions which they favoured, and whose financial accounts as well as work reports were laid open to their scrutiny.

With its vivid character sketches, and a narrative that is curiously at once modest and self-pleased, *India Calling* records, 'between its lines', the intense friability despite outward appearances of Cornelia Sorabji's self-construction as India's first woman lawyer and pro-woman non-feminist. Reprinted at a time when she is, after many years of disapprobation and neglect, attracting new academic interest, the memoirs moreover form an important document of a period of immense social and political change, in Britain as well as in India.[16] Many of its representations are plainly of interest to those taking up postcolonial viewpoints, but this is not the only source of relevance for our time. Cornelia's view of Indian history as a depth of layered accretions corresponds to a view to which contemporary Indian writers frequently refer. Her ideas about modernization feed into a debate on India's participation in nationalist and internationalist developments that has continued across the twentieth century, extending from Rabindranath Tagore and the Brahmo Samaj, to the rise of the Bharatiya Janata Party (BJP) in the 1990s. Moreover, Cornelia Sorabji believed passionately in the transnational links that might be built between women within the framework of the Empire. In a post-imperial world, her imperialist beliefs have been discredited, yet the bid for cross-cultural solidarity between women, to which *India Calling* testifies, and which the book itself enacts, may also command a particular attention from women readers internationally today.

A Note on the Text

India Calling: The Memories of Cornelia Sorabji was first published in 1934 by Nisbet & Co. Ltd., London. The text printed here is from that edition.

Throughout this edition, superscript Roman note numbers refer to Sorabji's own footnotes (included in the text). Arabic note numbers designate the editors' explanatory notes. Asterisks alongside names indicate individuals appearing in the biographical notes.

Elleke Boehmer and Naella Grew 2004

Notes

1. (p.ix) See *India Calling*, 23-5, 79-80, below. As a woman Cornelia could not however be admitted to the degree or called to the English Bar until 1922. Due to work commitments in the early 1920s, she missed the distinction of being the first woman so called.
2. (p.ix) On the debates over women's reform in India, see Geraldine Forbes, *The New Cambridge History of India: Women in Modern India* IV.2 (Cambridge: Cambridge UP, 1996).
3. (p.ix) Thomas Babington Macaulay, 'Minute on Indian Education', in *The Postcolonial Studies Reader*, eds. Bill Ashcroft, Gareth Griffiths and Helen Tiffin (London and New York: Routledge, 1995), 428-30.
4. (p.x) See Eckehard Kulke, *The Parsees in India: A Minority as Agent of Social Change* (New Delhi: Vikas, 1974).
5. (p.x) Cornelia Sorabji, *'Therefore': An Impression of Sorabji Kharsedji Langrana and his Wife Francina* (Humphrey Milford: Oxford University Press, 1924).
6. (p.xi) Cornelia Sorabji, *Susie Sorabji: Christian-Parsee Educationist of Western India* (Humphrey Milford: Oxford University Press, 1932), x-xi.
7. (p.xi) Antoinette Burton, *At the Heart of Empire: Indians and the Colonial Encounter in Late Victorian Britain* (Berkeley: University of California Press, 1998), 138-9.
8. (p.xi) Homi Bhabha, 'Of Mimicry and Man', in his *The Location of Culture* (London and New York: Routledge, 1994), 85-92.
9. (p.xi) See Burton, *At the Heart of Empire*, 135.
10. (p.xii) For example, the Hobhouses who put up the money for her 'substituted scholarship' (20), Benjamin Jowett, the solicitous Master of Balliol, and also the Church Missionary Society, which funded her mother's educational efforts back in Pune. See Burton, *At the Heart of Empire*; Suparna Gooptu, 'Cornelia Sorabji 1866-1954: A Woman's Biography', Unpublished Ph.D. Thesis, St Antony's College, University of Oxford, 1997.
11. (p.xii) Burton, 139 and 124.
12. (p.xii) Gooptu, 19-20, 123. Little of this frustration filters into *India Calling*, though see 180-1.
13. (p.xiii) See her account of the story of Rukhmabai, *India Calling*, 54. See also Burton, 117, 120, 122-5.
14. (p.xiii) Gooptu, 115.
15. (p.xiv) See Inderpal Grewal, *Home and Harem: Gender, Nation, Empire, and the Cultures of Travel* (London: Leicester University Press, 1996).
16. (p.xv) See her inclusion in Susie Tharu and K. Lalita, eds., *Women Writing in India: 600 B.C. to the Present* (New Delhi: Oxford University Press, 1991), 1: 296-309.

Further Reading

Bhabha, Homi. *The Location of Culture*. London and New York: Routledge, 1994.

Brown, Judith. *Gandhi: Prisoner of Hope*. New Haven: Yale University Press, 1989.

Burton, Antoinette. *At the Heart of Empire: Indians and the Colonial Encounter in Late Victorian Britain*. Berkeley: University of California Press, 1998.

Chandra, Bipan. *Nationalism and Colonialism in Modern India*. New Delhi: Orient Longman, 1979.

Chatterjee, Partha. *Nationalist Thought and the Colonial World: A Derivative Discourse?* London: Zed, 1989.

Forbes, Geraldine. *The New Cambridge History of India: Women in Modern India* IV.2. Cambridge: Cambridge University Press, 1996.

Grewal, Inderpal. *Home and Harem: Gender, Nation, Empire, and the Cultures of Travel*. London: Leicester University Press, 1996.

Heehs, Peter. *The Bomb in Bengal: The Rise of Revolutionary Terrorism in India, 1900-1910*. New Delhi: Oxford University Press, 1993.

Khilnani, Sunil. *The Idea of India*. London: Hamish Hamilton, 1997.

Sarkar, Sumit. *Modern India 1885-1947*. New Delhi: Macmillan, 1989.

Sorabji, Cornelia. *India Recalled*. London: Nisbet and Co., 1936.

Sorabji, Cornelia. *Love and Life Behind the Purdah*. London: Freemantle and Co., 1901.

Tharu, Susie and K. Lalita, eds. *Women Writing in India: 600 B.C. to the Present* vol. 1. New Delhi: Oxford University Press, 1991.

Chronology of Key Events

1757-1857	British Rule in India under the East India Company.
1846	Treaty of Amritsar gave the predominantly Muslim valley of Kashmir to Maharajah Gulab Singh, the Hindu ruler of neighbouring Jammu, in recognition of his help in subduing a Sikh uprising.
1857	The military Mutiny or Rebellion, also sometimes known as the War of Independence.
1858	Following the Mutiny, India was absorbed under the direct control of the British Crown, and the Indian Empire (British India) was created.
1879-1880	Land reform controversy in Ireland
1882 & 1893	Irish Home Rule controversy.
1885	Indian National Congress (INC) founded.
1896	Fashoda incident between Britain and France.
1898-1905	Lord Curzon Governor-General (Viceroy) of India.
1899-1902	Anglo-Boer or South African War.
1896-1900	Period of plague and severe famine in India.
1905	Curzon's Partition of Bengal triggers Swadeshi movement of Indian resistance.
1906	Muslim League founded.
	Liberal party triumph in British elections.
1909	Morley-Minto Reforms. Widely considered to be the seeds of communal representation in India, these Reforms eventually contribute to the Partition of the country.
1914-1918	World War I.
1915	Gandhi takes over as leader of the INC.
1916	Lucknow Pact between the Muslim League and the INC.
1917	British Parliament promises responsible government for India.
1919	Montagu-Chelmsford Reforms permitting partial self-government.
	Rowlatt Acts permitting imprisonment without trial of individuals suspected of subversion.
	Amritsar Massacre.
	Dominions receive greater autonomy within the Empire.
	Achievement of women's suffrage in Britain.
1920-1921	INC adopts Non-Cooperation.
1922	Abortive Civil Disobedience movement replaces Non-Cooperation.
1923	Swaraj (own rule or independence) party formed.

1926	Balfour's clarification of Dominion Status for colonies as complete independence in internal and external affairs. India is not explicitly included in this provision.
1928	Simon Commission, set up without Indian representation, to consider the constitutional reforms of 1919.
1929	INC declares complete independence as its goal.
	Irwin Declaration recognised eventual dominion status for India which, having already been defined by Balfour (see above), signified a milestone in the unravelling of the Indian Empire.
1930-31	Civil Disobedience movement starts in earnest, ceases and then resumes in 1932-34.
1932	Award of communal seats in legislative assemblies.
1939-1945	World War II.
1940	Muslim League demand for a separate nation-state.
1942	Cripps Mission.
	'Quit India' resolution by the INC.
	INC leaders jailed.
1945	Negotiations for independence begin.
	Elections held.
1946	Interim government formed.
1947	Partition of India, Indian independence and creation of Pakistan.
	Nehru appointed first Prime Minister of India.
	Jinnah appointed Governor-General of Pakistan.

Chronology of Key Events in Sorabji's life

1866	Born at Nasik, in the Bombay Presidency.
1883	Enters Deccan College, Poona.
1889	Takes up place at Somerville College, Oxford.
1892	Takes the B.C.L examination, following a special decree permitting her to do so.
1894	Returns to India and takes up a post in the Native State of Baroda, investigating the impact of primary education.
	Initiates self-created role as roving *Sanad* representing *purdahnashins* in the Native State of Kathiawar and in the Agency Courts of Indore (Central India). Cases concern inheritance, succession, and maintenance allowances.
1904	Takes up formal post as Advisor to the Court of Wards in Bengal. Acts as interface between secluded women and the Law designed to protect their interests.

xix

1919	Women admitted to the Bar in England.
	Sorabji admitted to the Rolls, Allahabad High Court.
1922	Sorabji formally takes her B.C.L degree and is called to the Bar. Awarded the Kaiser-i-Hind Medal of the First Class for Public Service in India.
1923	Returns to India and enrols in the Calcutta High Court.
1929-1931	Speaks at several venues in the USA in favour of British Rule in India.
1944	Sharp deterioration in health. Undergoes eye surgery in the USA, in an attempt to save her sight. Returns to England.
1945	Mental health deteriorates.
1947	Hospitalised in Britain.
1954	Dies in Britain.

INDIA CALLING

THE MEMORIES OF
CORNELIA SORABJI

First published in November 1934

INDIA—1857—1947

Scale of Miles

British India

Territories Permanently Administered
by the Government of India

Native States and Territories

To
E.

my Friend, greatly beloved

Introduction

At one of the many delightful visits which I paid in my youth to the Grant Duffs at York House, Twickenham – Sir Mountstuart said of me, making a necessary introduction, "A Friend who has warmed her hands at two fires, without being scorched." … Yes – it is true that I have been privileged to know two hearthstones, to be homed in two countries, England and India. But though it is difficult to say which "home" I love best, there has never, at any time, been the remotest doubt as to which called to me with most insistence…. Always, early or late, throughout the years, it has been "India Calling." …

And it has been such a happy life that, before I begin to try and tell what can be told in words, I want to glance back over my shoulder and savour it … patches of dappled sunshine lying all along the road from the very beginning – sunlight scented with rosemary and lavender. I inhale the Past in great whiffs. The eyes of my Mother, whatever her mood: my Father's laugh: the clearings in the woods near our home and the many games we played as children: the branches of the forest trees on moonlit nights as we swung from one to another: the stars hanging like lamps out of an indigo sky reaching immeasurably: the thrill of knowing that no one could rob me of dying, and the thrill of the "pretend" slipping out of my skin to go tiptoeing from star to star, as I meant to do when I was dead: the smell of the earth after the rains: the wonder of thunder and lightning: camping in India and waking in the dawn hour to sniff the sour-sweet mango blossom and hear the lovely sounds of a camp astir. The fun of cross-country journeys by palanquin or elephant, in canoe or dug-out…. Dawn at Darjeeling with the snows coming alive with colour: early morning rides in the hills, the trees dripping dew – "And all growing things I offer, thus, before the World has soiled them" …

Sunsets – flaming gold and red-gold: or bruised and blue: or pale mauve and primrose: the deep shadows on the hills, folds in the broidered mantle of God: gold mohur trees trailing bloom: the green paroquets at Budh Gaya: the blue wood-smoke in an Indian village. A thrush in an English garden, his throat swelling with song: the dark wood of trees in early spring bursting with swollen buds, or powdered with blossom: chestnuts alight: sheets of bluebells set in woods of grey beeches. Somerset, and the view from my window – old trees and flower-beds and sloping fields where the quiet cattle grazed: a dinghy on the

Cher: Bagley Woods and fritillaries: tramps in Oxfordshire or over Welsh hills, or in the Riviera: and always and always the Earth springing flowers.

Burnham Beeches aflame at Autumn's ending: beeches again in the New Forest; the lovely brown leaves on the browner earth and the feel of crushing them as you walked. Scotland and the look of heather in the distance, and the feel of heather when you lay upon it: and the little streams in Scotland and in Cumberland, with the stones showing through, held so safe and cool among the peat of their green-and-brownness.

London, and the way it caught one's heart, first seen . . . the feeling of standing at the core of the traffic, one morning at the Exchange, and knowing one's self utterly insignificant and alone, yet alive and perfectly companioned. My first robin: my first fall of snow: the ache when snow melted and got dirty: the Irish crossing-sweeper with her bonnet awry, who smiled at me – "One must keep up one's speerits, and one's appearance!": the exhilaration of London fogs: dream cities: the Towers of Westminster in a white mist: the lion in Trafalgar Square with whom I shared all my jokes and my anxieties – the one nearest the Strand: tiredness after work done: many an apt phrase heard or read: special loves in Books and Music and Pictures. Venice and Assisi: things seen, loved, felt, admired: and best of all, Friendships everywhere, and the faces of little children.

No! The goodness and happiness of it all can never really be gathered up to be bound into a book; it spills too much elusive golden grain, which only the heart remembers and recognizes.

But the Giver will know, and will take this for my inarticulate *Te Deum*.

I "FAITES VOS JEUX!"

ME – IN MY SETTING

I was born into a post-Mutiny world in the Bombay Presidency, at Nasik, a town of pilgrimage to the orthodox Hindu.[1]

India, under the Crown, was in the throes of reconstruction: the English machinery of administration, of education, of development of the resources of the Country, had not only been set up, but was in working order. In the north of India a wave of anglophobia centring in Ram Mohun Roy* and the Reformers (an impulse which indeed justified, if it had not inspired, Macaulay's* famous minute about the English Language and the World of our new Civilization) was affecting thought, aspiration, domestic detail, and even our dress.

The Pundits who had in 1813 refused to advise the Government to sanction the education of women, because "if women are educated, they will no longer admire and worship men, as is their duty", had been confounded by the Englishwomen – wives of the early missionaries and civilians – who had themselves started the education of girls in schools opened in the courtyards of mosques and temples: had toiled at these laboriously in the heat of the Plains, unrelieved by ice or punkahs, or journeys to the Hills: had had to learn the language in order to teach it, and to help compile the first vernacular "primers".... Nothing dynamic had happened in the Indian home as a result of this.

Orthodox Hindu women continued to live in subjection to their husbands, and to cook their dinners, as theretofore: Moslem women remained in purdah: *puja* and the response to the call of the Muezzin, continued to punctuate the hours.[2] Indeed the Indian schoolboy had said to his English masters in the government schools – now established all over the country – "Make our women like your wives and mothers." And it was probably this – the male opinion of the future – which had given the Government courage to finance the Department called "Female Education" in the year 1859.

In 1857 Universities were established in Bombay, Bengal and Madras – examining Universities on the model of the London University – and my Father was instrumental in securing a resolution of the Governing Body of the University of Bombay to the effect that women were, equally with men, admissible to all degrees and honours of that University.

A like interpretation had been given to the Acts of the other Universities. And in Calcutta, as far back as 1849, an Englishman, Drinkwater Bethune, had left his fortune for the foundation of what eventually represented the first Women's College in India, the Bethune College of Calcutta.

I am not prepared to say what effect all this had on the way of living in Indian homes generally during my infancy and girlhood.

I am Parsee by nationality: and I belong to that small community, numbering only about 110,000, which migrated from Phars in Persia, in the seventh century – Pilgrim Fathers setting sail for an unknown destination – in order to protect the Zoroastrian religion and their sacred fire against compulsion to Islamism by the Moslem conquerors of their country.[3] Driven by adverse winds into the Run of Cutch on the western coast of India, they landed, and made a treaty with the then overlord. The emigrants were allowed to stay in the country, and to retain the religion of Zoroaster: but they had to part with the Persian tongue and the Persian dress, in favour of what Guzerat had to offer.

This is understandable. In days when inter-tribal warfare was common, no potentate could allow a body of foreigners to consolidate itself in visible apartness. The treaty has been faithfully kept to this day; but the interpretation given to the taboo about dress and speech has nevertheless helped the "apartness" as a community, which our origin, temperament, and habits of life had made inevitable. Our women wear a sari certainly, but it is of silk, and draped differently from the Hindu *sari* (over the right ear, behind the left); while the Guzerathi spoken by the Parsees is "*Parsee* Guzerathi" – a debased form, but our own, of the language of the part of the country where we settled.

For the rest, the ruler of the seventh century need have had no fear. Parsees have shown no desire to compete with Hindus or Moslems for sovereignty in India. They have, like the British, helped the development of trade, and being, as a community, rich, prosperous and generous, have been responsible for many public benefactions in the cities where they dwell; giving the lead, indeed, in these directions to native Indians themselves. We have lived in isolation, but in real friendship and understanding with all races and communities in India. In the early days, we did, I believe, in individual homes, adopt some of the customs of the country; but our women have never been secluded, and the Zoroastrian religion made no exactions upon human relationships. Parsees have no social customs to which the West would take exception – unless, indeed, the disposal of the dead – exposure to a swoop of birds in a Tower of Silence – be counted as one such.

There is no parallel among us to the Hindu caste system: Parsees are one body. The Zoroastrian temple is devoid of idols. It is in fact rather beautiful – a spacious hall, furnished with an Altar, at which a white-robed priest burns sandalwood, night and day, without intermission – the prayers of the people ascending to God on the sweet-scented incense.

At ages usually between nine and eleven, Parsee children are made disciples of Zoroaster; sitting cross-legged before the priests in the Temple to be invested with the Sacred Thread (*Kusthi*), made of 72 strands of lambs' wool – 72 for the names of the Angels; and with "the Garment of the good and the beautiful way" – fine white vest (*Sudra*) without seam, and woven like the *Kusthi* by the wives and mothers of the Priesthood. The child takes the vows of Charity and Chastity, knotting the thread in token thereof; and there is always an extra knot which has been interpreted as "the vow not revealed", the vow which the wearer finds suggested by some special temptation.

When the girl-child grows to womanhood, she binds her head with a white fillet (*Mathabana*), explained by the generation of my aunts as a sign of subjection to man (tho' in truth, I believe, merely a useful expedient for affixing the *sari* to the head!). In these latter days the *Mathabana, Sudra* and *Kusthi* have disappeared in outward observance; but investitures still take place and the old-fashioned still scrupulously follow the old rule. In my immediate Family, to the isolation of our community was added the very real isolation of ourselves. In his youth my Father – Sorabji Kharsedji, of the house or lineage of Langrana – had in the manner of the Early Martyrs of the Christian Church, at peril of death, changed his religion to Christianity. That story has been told elsewhere;' ['*Therefore*, an impression of Sorabji Kharsedji Langrana and Francina his wife, Oxford University Press, 1924] but it has emphasized our great heritage as descendants of those who are able to sacrifice all for a conviction; and a conviction *of the Spirit.* My Father's ancestors did that, when they set sail from Persia; he did the like when his personal conviction compelled the course he took, in glad fearlessness and with thanksgiving – to the very end.

There is one circumstance, then, in my life, of which I may boast, unashamed – and that is my inheritance, the fact that I am the child of my Parents. For there are no two people in all the world whom I would have chosen as my parents, if choice had been given me, save just my very own Father and Mother. Of my mother also my book *Therefore* has told in detail. She had a very special type of courage, an intuition and understanding in heart and mind, which made her free of all things created, whether in trouble or joy, which made the wounded turn to her instinctively, whatever their race or creed; an intelligence which anticipated the needs of a progressive generation; and gifts of construction and organization which were unknown among the Indians of her day. I came fifth in a family of seven girls and one surviving boy. (Two boys had died in infancy.) My brother is the youngest but one of us, and, save for the passing of a beloved sister in 1931, we are still intact in this generation.

We had a perfect home and a joyous childhood – full of fun, and of love and the expressions and usages of love.

I have spoken of isolation as a Family; but I do not mean to imply that we were without contact with others. Never was there a home of those days to which more people came, of every race and condition, nor between which and other homes and people there was more traffic.

But there was an invisible circle drawn round it which brought us very close to one another, and which made it untypical of the Indian home of the period. My Father owed his personal thinking in an orthodox Parsee family to his English tutor, George Valentine. My Mother owed her education and ideals to her adoptive mother, Lady Ford, the wife of Sir Francis Ford,* an Englishman in command of a regiment stationed during her childhood at the place in the Hills where her parents lived.[4] We were therefore "brought up English" – i.e. on English nursery tales with English discipline; on the English language, used with our Father and Mother, in a home furnished like an English home. But – and this is where the Parents showed their wisdom – we were also compelled to learn the languages of the Peoples among whom we dwelt. We were told tales of our ancestors in Persia, and of our forbears and immediate family in the Parsee community in India. We were made proud of that community; but from our earliest days we were taught to call ourselves Indians, and to love and be proud of the country of our adoption: while the history of our Parents made us love also the people and country to which George Valentine and Cornelia Ford belonged.

Thus had our Parents conceived, and built upon, a unity which did not at the time exist in India: and which was also (and indeed till fifty years later) outside even the conception of the body which came, in the fullness of time, to represent Political India.

We moved from Nasik, where my Father had a little property, when I was a baby, to Belgaum, and then to Poona – going in the summer to a cottage in the Lanowli Woods, also owned by my parents. These homes of my childhood were like any house inhabited by the English community – single-storied bungalows with deep verandahs, set in gardens of flowers and shady trees. I remember chiefly the *Champak*, white-limbed, adorned with the exquisite ivory-petalled flower that held a golden secret in the bottom of the cup; and the tall straight teak trees beside our tennis-court, lighted with spiral candles when in bloom. And among "garden-people" my favourites were the red hibiscus, pink ragged-robin, stephanotis, jasmine, heliotrope (beloved of my Mother), mignonette, *quisqualis*, a tangle of pink, red and white, the blaze of tomato-coloured flowers in crisp bunches, the Indian honeysuckle which grew along the wall beside my room, the "Elephant-creeper", great bell-shaped lilac flowers which covered the wide porch (I would steal out to look at this, under the moonlight, and never knew why it squeezed my heart) – with croton bushes and the sweet-scented geranium and verbena that one crushed between the fingers.

The houses of our Parsee friends were furnished English (and Early Victorian) like our own. We ate in the English manner off English plates, and with English adjuncts, and our diet included meat. Nothing is taboo to the Parsee, except pork – the difference was in the cooking. Our meals were sometimes on the simpler (duller) English pattern: sometimes Parsee – luscious stews flavoured with pineapple or preserved mangoes, the sweet "motif" beloved of the community: or *pulaos* and *dhansak*. On Festivals, our Zoroastrian, Hindu and Moslem friends never omitted to send us the special ceremonial sweets and dishes that religious custom required. So that we were as cosmopolitan in our diet as in our general upbringing.

Other household garniture was also of the age – lamps, no electricity, no running water, baths in zinc tubs, water heated first on the kitchen fire, and later on the excellent zinc "boilers", which are still in use in India. Cooking was done effectively on fireplaces built of bricks and earth. When stoves were available, my Mother had our kitchen fitted with these; but it took a long time to make conservative Indian cooks use the stove. I remember how our old cook, discovered cooking in the old way by my Mother on her daily inspection of the kitchen, would run to the neglected stove, beaming all over his wrinkled face – "See! it's here, intact. I keep it safe and clean!"

Our nearest neighbours were Zoroastrian Parsees – very special friends. There was a wicket gate which connected our gardens, and we children were always running to and fro.

Sometimes we spent the summer with these friends in their Mahableshwar home, and it was there that my elder sisters learnt to ride, taught by our friend, who owned many horses. Something of our lives as children I have told in the book about my sister[ii]; [*ii Susie Sorabji*, Oxford University Press, 1924] but our days were spent in much the same way as those of children in England, except that we had more variety in contacts, and in out-of-door opportunities.

Hindu and Moslem children of the eighteen-seventies lived in houses in the older part of the city. Often these were of beautifully carved wood with courtyards, the architecture conforming to custom, based on religion. For the Hindu there was "the Outside" where the men lived, and "the Inside" (or *Zenana*) for the women, with their special courtyard in which grew the *tulasi* (basil) plant that the women watered, on waking, as they greeted the Earth Mother.[5] In the Moslem courtyard, the *Maulvi* (priest) would teach the children from the earliest years to recite the Koran in the Arabic tongue. Of furniture in these houses there was little; the beauty of the dwelling was in the walls and pillars. The Moslems sat on carpets often of exquisite Persian workmanship: the Hindus on mats finely woven, or on carved stools: and in the *baithk-Khanas* (sitting-rooms) of both there would be great bolster-divans, against which they leaned. The Hindu house of the period contained the Sulking Room (Boudoir), to which the woman of the house might retire to sulk until she coerced her husband to her wishes. Since she cooked his dinner, this practice of inaction in seclusion was not bad diplomacy. But the Sulking Room is not to be found in the modern Hindu house.

The difference between our home and the homes of other children lay chiefly, I expect, in education and discipline. Indian children of the period were terribly spoilt, never doing a thing for themselves, stuffed with sweets and overfed indiscreetly from infancy. A boy-child often ruled the household: of play there was little; of learning, except in the poorer homes where children went to the Mosque or Temple School, almost none. Here and there the child of the leisured classes would have, when the University began to turn out graduates, a tutor who taught him to get by heart pages of stuff. You might see him (you certainly heard him) any morning established on the verandah of his house, sitting on his haunches swaying back and forth as he chanted his reading lesson or his tables; or, for a punishment, holding the lobes of his ears, in hands that were crossed, and doing *uth-bais* (stand-sit) so many times, without remission – a torturing practice.

When Government Schools had crystallized, the children of all classes attended them.[6] There was at no time any snobbishness as to status in India.

But, I doubt if in these early days the children of the "Untouchables" went or wished to go to any but the Mission Schools which alone served that class. I do not mean to suggest that there were not Mission Schools, and later Colleges, which served the highest castes. Education owes everything to the enterprise of the Christian Church in India, as orthodox Hindus, Moslems and Parsees are never backward in acknowledging. At the present time 14,000 of the 100,000 Undergraduates in India are said to be members of Mission Colleges.

In our family we were severely disciplined, taught to do as much as we could for ourselves, and to be polite to the servants. Our servants worked for a wage. In Hindu and (sometimes) Moslem houses, they worked for their keep with gifts of garments at the religious festivals, and were mostly an untrained lot, bullying their mistresses if the mistress were gentle, and wrangling if she tried to be "mistress in her own house". It was in no small measure due to these servants that the children were so badly spoilt and so inadvisedly dressed and fed.

The well-ordered servants, the open windows and regular hours in our home were often commented upon by my Mother's Indian visitors; and not a few tried to imitate her in these respects.

The games we played, in origin as well as in fact, were also representative of a League of Nations. These were an Indian hop-scotch and an Indian hide-and-seek, *ánk-mu-chani, attia-pattia* (a version of "salts"), with Western varieties of games of the period taught us by the Parents' friends. Later, we played tennis and badminton, and a bowdlerized American baseball, while cricket and football were rapidly gaining popularity among boys and men. The garbas, folk-songs and games of Guzerat, were not in my childhood common as they now are among Parsees. In sharing our family games and in teaching other Indian children to play at all, we were, I suppose, pioneers. Differences of religion made as little cleavage between us as differences of race.

That will be hard to explain to Westerners. I suppose it was because, even as children, Easterners are conscious of a-tie-that-binds, of the *practice* of religion. Indeed, the fact that we also, individually, were tied-and-bound, was a link between us. Our child friends knew that we had obligations as to prayers, and church, and rules of conduct. The Moslem child had a creed, in like manner, and an exacting rule of prayer, albeit in a language foreign to him. The Hindu child said no prayers, and had no book of Ethics, but from the earliest years was initiated into his Book of Leviticus, the things which would outcaste him…. We grew up in amicable tolerance of one another's "must- (or must-not) be-dones".[7]

I have referred to discipline and education as experiences written in rubric in the Book of the Sorabji Home.

To this must be added the teaching that we, as individuals, were our Brother's Keeper.

In an age when Social Service was unknown to Indians my Mother cared for the sick and poor around her. There were great excitements in store for the child who was allowed to accompany her on her visits to the villages, and to see how airless huts were cleaned and readjusted at her asking: how she dealt with child and woman, whatever the trouble, or with the whole village if an epidemic were afoot. And then, to sit beside her as she gathered the villagers together under a tree, and spoke to them of the ideals and hopes she held in her heart for them – that was indeed great! Everyone loved her: and to me it was ever a marvel, as I grew to think about what I saw, how one who held very decided views of her own – a Zealot, in fact – could yet be broad-minded, and comprehending of the very different point of view of others; could be persuasive while assertive; and always and always loved and sought, and revered. She was never tired of sharing with others the Gospel as she knew it, the Good News – of Christianity, of Health, of Education, of Sanitation.

The gospel of Work she got very securely into our minds at home from the very earliest years. We were in the world to serve others. She was proud of having seven daughters, in a country where the birth of a daughter was considered a calamity: because "they were women that India wanted, just then, for her service". The ways in which we could serve our country were many; gradually we learnt what they were. She could not direct us what to choose. There was one bit of work which was our very own, no one else in all India could do it just that way: we must find it, and prepare to do it at whatever cost. And all self-discipline, however trivial, was to this end and was glorified thereby. I remember, for instance, when I was eight years old, realizing for myself that I was the slave of a story, and deliberately practising shutting down the book when I had got to the most exciting point. That was salutary, as I know now, when I am not always as drastic with myself. Personal adventures, such as this, were never breathed to a soul. We had our code of the "*pukka Sorabji Sahib*". But of course we were not abandoned to hazards. The family saw to that in delivering us to the care of elder sisters. My sister was an expert in regeneration, and in punishments to fit the crime. I gave her opportunity galore! There was, for one thing, my red-hot temper: and she never betrayed her rigid standards.

Again, responsibility for others began within the walls of our home; we must make no mistake about that. The application of right doctrine was apt to be crude in the beginning. I can recall more than one laughable waste of good worry or of officious energy. But things adjusted themselves as the years sped by.

We loved the visitors who came to see my Mother. She knew endless things about the customs of the different races, their religions, and their legends. And she never disappointed the enquiring child. It was one such visitor who set my own feet on the path that I have chosen.

She was a Guzerathi Hindu, who came in a *dumney* (waggon) which was all tied up in embroidered covers and drawn by two little white bulls wearing bells and blue bead necklaces and embroidered saddle-cloths. I loved the equipage, and the lady who had a gentle face, and big sad eyes with deep lashes. She was dressed in a cotton *sari*, and wore a tight little bodice, tied across her back with tasselled laces. Her back was bare, and the bodice was really only a breast-support. There was a hiatus of person between it and her waist-line.

When she arrived I was reading, lying on the floor at the end of the room, back up, my head between my hands. The ox-bells disturbed me, and the visitor fascinated me. She began talking, rapidly, crying often, my Mother comforting her. The story she told, as I learnt later in detail, was this.

She had owned, as a widow, a considerable estate in Kathiawar. As she was secluded, and could not manage her property, she left everything in the hands of her man-of-business. He was the son and grand-son of a long line of such officers and, as he had grown up in the service of the family, she was able to transact business with him freely, without breach of custom – with him, but with no other.[8] Her part was to give verbal instructions and to sign *blank papers* to enable him to carry out these instructions. She could not write, but was taught to make the hieroglyphic which represented her name. All monies, and the disbursement of monies, were in his hands.

There came a day when she instructed her man-of-business to build her a house in British India. She had once been on pilgrimage to Nasik and had taken a fancy to a place *en route*. "I will live here, part of the year," said she.

"Ha! ji! – certainly," was his answer. "But the necessary blank papers must be signed, in order that I may make the requisite arrangements."

"That, of course" – and she signed the papers.

When she came to see my Mother, she had just discovered, thirty years after the house had been occupied, that she was penniless. The man-of-business had filled in over her signature a deed of gift to himself of all her *stridhan*, the woman's property of which she could dispose absolutely at will: and she had for those thirty years been paying him a nominal rent for the occupation of her own house. The accounts were all in order. He had safeguarded himself legally, and was in secure possession beyond her capacity to dislodge.

I had crept to my Mother's knee, while the *Thakurani* was speaking, and when she had gone, my Mother said to me, "Did you understand what she said?"

"Only that she is in great trouble," said I (as my Mother reminded me in later years), "and even you cannot help her."

"That is so," said my Mother. "There are many Indian women in trouble in that way. Would you like to learn how to help them?"

I said, "Oh! I should!"

"Then, when you grow up and are able to choose the special thing you want to learn, ask to study *the Law*. That will show you the way to help in this kind of trouble."

And that was her secret and mine, fostered openly from time to time, when we talked of careers. I was going to be a Lawyer: and my littlest sister was equally determined to be a Doctor.

So thus early – I was between eight and nine – my feet were set joyously on the pilgrim's way, in gaiety of spirit, in love with work, and with whatever "taking the way" might entail; and fearlessly – because a lesson learnt also from my Mother since childhood's days, *vis-à-vis* every hazard, whether of unseen "dragons" to be fought, or of very real and visible plague and pestilence, was that – "there was nothing to fear – but Fear".

PREPARATION AND EQUIPMENT: IN INDIA
AND ENGLAND

The education I got as a girl, I owed to my Family – to my Father and my elder sisters, helped out by masters and mistresses for languages, mathematics, music and drawing. After passing my Matriculation I was still too young for admission to a College in England.

To exhaust possibilities in India seemed the only course. There were no Colleges for women in my Presidency, but the Parents had ascertained that I could be admitted to the Men's College in our Town. I could live at home and drive the five miles out and back daily.

They put the problem to me. Would I care to do this?

That was how it came to pass that I became a member of the Deccan College, Poona. I will not say that I was not scared of the hundreds of Hindus and Moslems in the big lecture-rooms; but there was home, when it rang to Evensong.

To my surprise I topped the Presidency in the final Degree Examination, and automatically obtained the Government of India Scholarship for a course at an English University – a handsome scholarship, including travelling and other expenses. In spite, however, of the University Constitution declaring that women were as men, I was not allowed to hold my scholarship. The test had been the same, and all conditions were fulfilled; but the Authorities said, "No!" – It was in fact impertinent of any woman to produce circumstances which were not in the mind of the Authorities as a possibility when they dangled a gilded prize before eyes that should have been male eyes alone!

The attitude of the Parents was a cheerful – "Hard luck! but the goal is still there. A way will open!"

And it did. A Men's College in Guzerat was deprived of its English Principal. I was offered a short term Fellowship in English Literature – to cover his duties in this direction, till arrangements could be made to replace him.

I decided to take it, and so help towards replacement of my lost scholarship.

A professorship at eighteen, in a Male College, was solitary and (inwardly) terrifying; but the students and the professors – Parsees, Hindus, Moslems – were kind. And it was quite good fun from the point of view of hard work, and of absurd authority – of dealing with ragging, and making quick decisions.

There is only one story of this period which I will tell, and that, because Jowett of Balliol* loved it, and because it is illustrative of the atmosphere in which I worked.

There was then no communal feeling, as we now know it, in India; but Undergraduates were more insistent upon observance of Religion than they are now.

It was recess, and I was in my room glancing at my notes for an afternoon lecture.

Two students asked to see me – a Parsee and a Hindu. The Parsee told his story. He was a resident student: a mad dog had got into his room, and he had told one of the College messengers to remove it. The Hindu lived next door, and had objected. – "Consider," said he, "the Soul of my Ancestor might be in that dog.' It's an indignity." Would I please settle their dispute?

I said that the beliefs of all students must of course be respected. That it was surprising that the Hindu should claim that the soul of his ancestor could inhabit a *mad* dog. But that at any rate, in that belief, filial obligation was not the Parsee's. The dog must be out of the compound before the afternoon session. The students must deal with their problem themselves.

Looking out of my window, ten minutes later, I saw the dog at the end of a long rope being led out of the compound by a College messenger!

By the time that my "locum" job came to an end, friends in England and Somerville College, Oxford (Lord and Lady Hobhouse* and Miss Madeleine Shaw Lefevre being the ringleaders in this conspiracy of kindness), had offered me a "substituted scholarship" which, with what we could add to it, made the English adventure immediately possible.

Of my time at College I do not propose to write in detail. I can never forget Oxford, seen for the first time in the October term with the reds and russets and tawny-greens of the virginian creeper against the grey worn stone: nor can I forget the kindness of everyone, from the Somerville student – A. M. Bruce – who "adopted" me as her special Fresher, and taught me the ropes, to the Heads of Houses themselves.

Through the Hobhouses, Jowett, then Master of Balliol, kindly came to call on me immediately.

When he went, the Warden took me in her arms and said, "My child, this is a great honour." And in my ignorance I wondered if that were a traditional Oxford custom when aged cherubs with white hair were polite to foreigners. I was not long in realizing what she meant; and the Master of Balliol added to his marvellous kindnesses to the end of his life. He used to take me walks, when my chief difficulty lay in matching my steps to his little ones. Happily, I did not realize that I ought to be awed – I chatted as I would to any companion. And he gave me staccato wisdom – in words that were unforgettable.

During his week-end parties, the kind Master always found room for me at the Lodge dinner-table.

It was there that I met for the first time Gladstone* and Balfour,* Alfred and Neville Lyttelton,* Mr. Asquith,* Margot Tennant,* Lord Bowen, Lord Coleridge the Chief Justice, Mr. Justice Wright* and Sir Henry Cunningham; Sir Mountstuart Grant Duff,* Sydney Owen, Max Müller,* Froude* and Freeman*, Mrs. Humphrey Ward* and Miss Braddon*, old Lady Carlyle, Lady Stanley of Alderley, Stanley the Explorer,* the Percy Wyndhams, Sir John Herschell, the Romanes, the Toynbees, Barnetts, Rowland Hills – High Churchmen, Broad Churchmen and Congregationalists, and many others of importance in the Public Life of the time. The Master had a genius for bringing together opposing forces in thought and action, and giving them the opportunity of finding common ground. From all I met, I breathed in what was of infinite value. They led me to an observation point, as it were – from which, in the fullness of time, I was enabled to study English politics, and the then new comradely attitude towards the East End; the freedom of thought as to Religion, together with the loyalty to standards of rectitude inspired by Religion – so characteristic of the moment; the growing recognition of the rights of women; the definition of Culture and its changing interpretation from just "breed" alone, to what an old friend of mine used to call "breed and feed" – though I knew also that Breed must ever prevail over Feed . . . (in India we knew about Breed but nothing whatsoever about Feed). Best of all, I learnt that difference of opinion need not affect friendship or personal appreciation: and that one could be a zealot and yet open-minded . . . could gain in breadth without losing in intensity. In short, I was hearing good talk, and getting England into my bones, without realizing how much I was learning, or how greatly I was privileged. I know now that it was this last fact which prevented self-consciousness, and helped me to savour my experience at its best.

With several of the friends met thus, contact was maintained in their country houses. Mr. Justice Wright and his charming wife, the Max Müllers, Margot Tennant, the Grant Duffs, among others. The Wrights had a ritual, the observance of which not even Jowett was allowed to escape. The men guests put out the candles after dinner with the words "boiled pork"! The master, spectacles on nose-tip, and not enough "blow" to produce even a flicker, was a delicious sight. And the Judge, superior in his "boiled" proficiency, would sternly insist: "No! at it again! we can't help you." And Jowett would go on seriously pumping at the bellows. I believe he really enjoyed amusing us thus.

Margot at Innerleithen in a vivid scarlet costume, playing football with the footman, "to assert her allegiance to Mr. Gladstone", is another unforgettable picture. Her guests – a woman or two of us to a galaxy of distinguished men – applauding from the slopes, overlooking the field. Margot has always been wonderful to me, however many the years which lie between our meetings. I admired her selflessness towards her parents, and rejoiced in the brilliance of her conversation.

With the Max Müllers I often stayed – even to his seventieth birthday, which he described as "the last day of his youth". His modesty, when asked how many languages he knew – "I hope I know my mother tongue, I may be acquainted with a few others" – he explained by telling a story. "An individual came to see me and addressed me in an unknown tongue. I said, 'What might that language be?' And the man huddled himself up on the floor and wept. 'All my life I have worshipped you', he said, 'as the greatest living authority on Sanskrit. I speak a simple greeting in that language and you do not understand me.'" It was, of course, only the difference between the spoken and the written word, but Professor Max would never allow that excuse.

At Sir Mountstuart Grant Duff's there was always good talk: and there were always people whose names one knew on paper. It was there that I met Lecky, looking like an early Dutch madonna.

If I dined at Balliol on a Sunday, the Master would ask me for my arm up the steps to the hall – and during the Concert, when I sat beside him (how it all comes back as I write – the young faces of the packed audience, the Master leading us to our seats, the sudden hush; Farmer walking up and down, taking snuff violently, or glaring at anyone who whispered during the Music), he would translate the words of any German item in the programme because I once told him that I knew no German. "I like you the better for confessing what you might have concealed," was what he said.

I remember too how the Undergraduates who had come in to coffee before the Concert would sit trembling at the end of a sofa when Jowett tried to set them at their ease. One day he said to me, of one such, "I am far more shy of him than *he* could ever be of me."

I had asked to read Law when I went up – and was told that no woman might read Law. Whereupon I said it was indifferent to me what I read, and our Warden was directing me to the then most popular School for a nondescript, when the Master asked me why I wished to read Law. I told him – and my programme of work was immediately changed. I was sent to lectures in Law, chiefly to Sir William Markby's, attended by both the Junior and Senior Indian Civil Service men up at Oxford; and to Professor Bryce on Jurisprudence.

The Warden only laughed when I asked her questions about my mysterious course – and I was too happy to want to dig deeper.

Mystery thickened when I was told that I would do the Term's "Collections" in the Warden's room, supervised by herself. She produced a sealed envelope, and Sir William Markby called to retrieve my Papers.

I said how jolly it was of them to give me the feeling of a real examination over these "pretend" terminal tests, and thought no more about the matter – till the day when I was sent for to the Warden's Room. Dear old "Marker" was there, looking benevolent and happy, and he said, "You may read for the Honour School of Jurisprudence next Term. Ilbert has marked your papers very high."

I knew the Ilberts at the House of Commons, but could not imagine what Sir Courtney had to do with Somerville Collections. The Warden explained that they had made me do the I.C.S. Law course and examination papers as a test. And it had been successful.

I won't try to say what I felt. It was such amazing luck.

My lectures were chiefly at Balliol and All Souls, and among my Professors were Sir Frederick Pollock, Corpus Professor of Jurisprudence, Mr. A. V. Dicey, Vinerian Law Professor, Mr. Thomas Raleigh of All Souls, Dr. Grueber of Balliol, Mr. Montague of Oriel. Mr. Raleigh was my Tutor-in-Chief, coaching me in Real Property; Dr. Grueber tutored me in my special subject in Roman Law, Mr. Montague in Criminal Law, and Mr. Dicey in Private International Law, which he induced me to take as a special subject for the B.C.L., because, as I gathered, he was writing a book on Private International Law, and I could have the benefit of the overflow. "Besides, it would be interesting to compel the University to set a Paper specially for you," he added, with his head on one side. (The men of my year were taking Criminal Law.)

Boldly, under the advice of Sir William Markby, my course had been changed after a year from the Jurisprudence School to the B.C.L. – "the best that Oxford had to give." And the hazard of this found me looking into the barrel of a pistol at the most crucial of moments.

The week before the final Examination I was dining quietly with the Master, and he said to me, "Would it make any difference to you if you did the B.C.L. papers sitting at your College, supervised by Miss Maitland" (the Warden)? I said, "Indeed it would. It would not feel like a regular University Examination; and some day when women are allowed to take degrees mine might be withheld because I had not sat in the Schools with the men. Why may I not sit with them?"

He said, "Because the London Examiner for the B.C.L. Examination refuses to examine a woman. But if you feel like that, we must get the University to pass

a decree that you are allowed to sit for the Examination."
And, being Vice-Chancellor, he took the necessary steps.
It was an exhausting experience waiting for the verdict. And the kind V.C.
said he would send me instant news from the meeting which was held on the
eve of the opening Examination day. M.A.s had been cited to vote on the
proposition:

"That Cornelia Sorabji be allowed to sit for the B.C.L. Examination."

The Master's letters to me were always written on minute paper in his minute,
incisive hand.
"Congregation grants you your decree," was what his letter said. I received it
at about 4 p.m. Soon after, my Roman Law Tutor was to be seen walking up the
drive towards the West Building where I lived. He was greatly excited, his red
beard shone in the sunlight and his red hair was flying in the wind; he carried
his hat in one hand and a badly-rolled umbrella in the other. I was in the garden
with my special College friends, who were rejoicing with me at the conclusion
of an anxiety which they had shared, and I remember wincing, as at a false note
in music, at the colour of Dr. Grueber's hair against the pink spirals of the
chestnut trees – a terrible disharmony.
"Miss Sorabyi" (as he always called me), said he, "you need not sit for that
Examination."
"But why?"
"You have your decree. That is enough for a lifetime. You need go no further.
The University of Oxford" (and the thrill in his voice was awesome) "to pass a
decree *like that!*..."
To whatever cause it was due that the result of my finals did not "copy fair
the past" – was, in fact, very bad indeed – it was not due to any lack on the part
of others. I had overwhelming excuse for doing better in the teaching and
opportunity given me. I had far more knowledge than I'd had for any of the
examinations in which I had gained Alpha-pluses. But there it was!
And I pushed my disappointment in myself away. For, whatever my label, I'd
got my equipment, and had had my fun! The lure and the delight of reading for
a School which branched out in so many directions was that one was always
going off the beaten track, pursuing enticing scents. Balliol and All Souls, as I
have said, were the Colleges I attended for my lectures, and the Warden of All
Souls, Sir William Anson, had kindly made me free of the Codrington Library,
that exclusively male preserve. It was there that I spent my days between lectures
in the little Ante-Room where Ethlinger, the Librarian, who was afterwards

translated to Lincoln's Inn Library, supplied me with books on the nail, and seemed to think that I must always be cold. The kind man used to have a rug for my knees, which he pressed upon me even in the Summer: and on the closest of days he would call to the boy in attendance as I entered the Library – "Pile on more coals, Horsley!"

Long years after I had gone down, I was revisiting Oxford and met Sir George Trevelyan.* A Life of Sir William Anson was in preparation and Sir George told me, teasingly, that there was going to be just one joke in it.

"Did Sir William Anson ever jest?"

"No! he winked only once in his lifetime. He winked at Miss Sorabji!"

The basis of this was the fact that when, after my time, History Students from Somerville asked to be allowed to read at the Codrington, Sir William would solemnly reply, "Certainly: if you can prove that you are Miss Sorabji!"

It was in June 1892 that I did my B.C.L. Examination. It was not till after the War that women were admitted to degrees. I took my degree of B.C.L., formally, in the Convocation of 1922 – the earliest moment at which I could get back from my work in India to take it.[10]

It was a good life, being up. Kindness and spoiling, feeling after one's powers, meeting people who thought, and people who talked clever nonsense: and finding companionship outside my family for the first time.

My College friends (the names of the chief of whom I cannot resist rolling upon my pen – Alice Bruce, Eleanor Martin, Mary Summers, Grace Player, Gertrude Latham, J. M. Atkinson, Chris Marshall, "Pat" Herbert, "Fritz" Paton) and those others passed beyond sight, whose names are written in my heart and whose ideals are still my standard of conduct – were all utterly and undeservedly good to me. Then Oxford itself in every mood, how I loved it: if not perhaps as later I learned to love London. Oxford is to me the place in which to get ready for life; not, unless your work lies there, in which to live it. But Oxford had and has its very own niche in one's being – the river, the Towers, the Meadows, College gardens, ghostly Long Wall Street (down which a Welsh Professor was said to slink when he wanted to invite the right mood in which to write about Machiavelli). College chapels – Magdalen and its music ("Like *that!*" said Farmer of Balliol. "Why, it's only a soul shampoo!"): the Sunday afternoon Services at the Cathedral – Oh! a hundred memories, from which one must turn with firmness, or one would never end fingering the sweet-scented rosemary.

Of Jowett, however, I must record one more memory, before I turn to the world outside Oxford. When living in London I often went back on visits to Oxford: and the Master would ask me to *tête-à-tête* breakfasts or lunches at the Lodge. He had given me an introduction to Miss Florence Nightingale, and had asked me to write and tell him about my visit. And I wrote, no doubt garrulously, of the little old lady with rosy cheeks in a frilled nightcap whom I saw in bed, surrounded with flowers, her birds singing their hearts out in the aviary by the windows.

When I lunched with him after this visit, he said suddenly, indicating the only picture of a woman in his study – it hung on the wall, a girlish figure in a short-waisted dress standing beside a pedestal on which sat the figure of an owl – "Would you recognize that for the little old lady in a frilled night-cap whom you saw last week?"

I was silent, not knowing what to say, and Jowett continued:

"When she was like that, I asked her to marry me."

Needless to say, I was struck dumb; one had never thought of the Master in human terms, as having had a mother or sisters, for instance, or as dressing like other folk, or having been at any other age or in any circumstance save that at and wherein one knew him.

Jowett spoke again, elliptically – in his small abrupt voice: "It was better so."

When the *Life of Florence Nightingale* was published, a cousin of hers showed me an entry in F. N.'s Diary, which was surely a reference to this episode: –

Benjamin Jowett came to see me. Disastrous!

Nothing more.

Life at Somerville was much as it is to-day. The College was about half its present size. There were only two residential buildings – the Old Hall and West Buildings. I lived in the latter, over which Miss Clara Pater, Classical Tutor, presided. Her brother, Walter Pater, often came to see her, rushing through the garden "for fear of the petticoats", as he explained to Miss Pater, or sneaking in at the Woodstock entrance. When in her room he would sit for an hour at a time without speaking, his head between his hands. A pretty Irish student threatened to break in on this séance to see what would happen. She did, too – making some flippant remark. All Walter Pater said was, "What was that noise!"

The fact that my brother was at Balliol during my Oxford years was delightful for me. We had friends as well as lectures and the river in common. I remember, for instance, one occasion when Richard Burn (later Sir R. Burn, I.C.S.) and my brother, both of Balliol, took some of us from Somerville out on the river, making our chaperones – the Warden and the wife of a Don – tow the boats! They'd had a bet about this, College rules of the time about "River Chaperones" being very strict. The incident was commemorated in *Punch* – "Uses of Chaperones on the River." Our last Summer Vacation my brother and I, and friends of ours, Bonté and Maurice Sheldon Amos – their father was the famous Jurist – went down the river together as far as Richmond in one of Salter's dinghies. The boys had been teaching us to scull, and the experience was supposed to put the varnish on our training. We were three days on the river, rowing from after breakfast to 9 p.m. and sleeping at inns: dividing equally the 28 miles per day (approximately) that we covered. The brothers would not row with us, our training requiring that they should sit together at the steerage ropes, criticizing or chaffing or frightening us – an arrangement which suited Bonté and me admirably.

Is there anywhere in the world a river like the Thames, with its sloping banks and its lovely houses and gardens? Especially, as we savoured it, during the only fine days in a wet summer.

Stantes erant pedes nostri in atriis tuis – Oxonia! [11]

What next? was the question with which I was faced. Lord and Lady Hobhouse, in whose special and beloved care I'd been since my arrival in England, suggested that I ought to try and get some training in the practice of the Law; and during the Long this suggestion moved towards reality. I was staying with the Aberdares, the parents of my College friend, Alice Bruce, at Duffryn in South Wales: and hearing of Lord Hobhouse's advice – "I have a Solicitor son-in-law, and a Barrister son-in-law," said kind Lord Aberdare – "at which end will you begin?" One of the partners of Lee & Pemberton's, the firm of Solicitors to which he had referred, was staying in the neighbourhood and rode over one morning to see me and ask why I wanted to acquire a profession not open to women. I told him.

In due course I heard from the firm offering to take me on as a pupil. I was not allowed to sit for the Solicitors' examination, but should get what apprenticeship offered, and if this would be any use to me, the firm would give me a Certificate at the end of my training. This Lee & Pemberton's nobly did. I had practice galore in draftsmanship and conveyancing; I attended the Courts with the partner in charge of litigation; I learnt how estates were administered: and how clients should be interviewed. As a rule the clients took me without comment. But two old ladies, in before-the-Flood garments, who drove in from the country once a year in an ancient barouche to see their solicitors, regarded me with bated breath. When the "Chief" was not looking, they bent forward – "Are you," they said, "a New Woman?"

My special "Chief" is still in the firm, and I find each time that I run in to 44, Lincoln's Inn Fields, that the memories of long-ago kindnesses, received in that ancient building, are not only as alive as they were in 1893, but are burnished with gold, because I know now how sadly I should have failed many a *Purdahnashin* in India, but for this experience.

When I left Lee & Pemberton's, to my amazement my fees were returned. I had had the stupendous luck to detect a flaw in some title deeds I was examining; any pupil would have done the like, but the partners generously said that I had saved the firm more money than the cost of my training.

Truly, the debt that I owed to the world was growing with every breath I took!

Lord Hobhouse was a Bencher of Lincoln's Inn, and he and Lord Mathew, one of the many legal "great ones" (Lord Macnaghten, Lord Haldane, Lord Selborne, Lord Thring, Sir James Fitzjames Stephen, Sir Edward Fry, Lord Phillimore) whom I had met at 15, Bruton Street, obtained for me the privilege of reading at that august Sanctuary. I worked in the Library, sitting at the Benchers' Table in the luxury of a scholarly and dignified solitude.

In 1922, after the Bar was opened to women and I became a Member of the Inn, special privilege was naturally superseded in all particulars.

But life in England was not all work – anything but! I was taken to Art Galleries, Plays and Concerts: to Ranelagh and Hurlingham: to sittings of the Privy Council, to hear debates in the Houses of Parliament, to tea on the Terrace.

The House of Commons delighted me. Julia Peel was acting hostess for her father at the time. I had met her and her brothers at Oxford; and she was wonderfully kind to me: would apprise me of exceptional debates; and I often lunched and dined at the Speaker's House in the thrilling days of the Irish Home Rule Controversy, "tasting the whole of it", and seeing that rarely-seen final ceremony – "Who goes home with the Speaker?"

I remember asking at one of these House of Commons parties what I should read in order to understand the Irish situation. The answer came from Mr. Balfour.

"The Real Charlotte. [Somerville and Ross] It tells you all that is material about Ireland."

In the course of the years I have heard every Prime Minister speak, since Gladstone: and mostly from the Speaker's Gallery.

Mrs. Gladstone used to sit up at the right-end corner of the Gallery; and on a day when I, being a staunch Unionist, was glowing with pride in a speech of Mr. Balfour's, she came across to me and whispered, "Don't admire that! Wait for my husband's speech." The darling!

It is not in human nature to withhold the story I now tell.

One day at lunch at the Speaker's, Colonel Sanderson, the famous Unionist, who sat next to me, said, "Have you seen a row in the House?" I said I had, and instanced what had seemed to me terribly excited and unseemly behaviour on several occasions.

"Those are not rows. You must see a real one. I'll make it."

"How?"

"Oh, it's easy. You sit on the hat of a Member, or you abuse an Irish Priest."

And that afternoon he kept his word. He called an Irish Priest "a scoundrelly rascal", when referring to some Irish incident being discussed in the House. Instantly there was Bedlam.

"Withdraw! – Draw! – Draw!" shouted one side: and "Hear! Hear!" shouted the other.

Mr. Gladstone and Mr. Balfour both tried to restore quiet, but failed. Then the Speaker, who as a Speaker was perfect – he looked like a Mme. Tussaud waxwork, and seldom spoke except in *extremis* – asked that the expression used should be withdrawn. Colonel Sanderson immediately complied, with the charm in which he was an expert:

"I withdraw the words 'scoundrelly rascal'," said he. "I substitute for them 'excited politician'!"

In a minute the House was rocking with laughter.

I love that, about the House of Commons, more evident perhaps in the eighteen-nineties than now: – its youth and sudden changes, its quick jumps from anger to mirth, from division to unity.

My presentation at Court was a thrill of a different kind. Queen Victoria sent me a gracious message to the effect that "one of my 'pretty colours' (not white) would be permitted": and I wore an azalea *sari* something in colour between pink and yellow. I was given private *entrée*. The Queen said she was "glad to see me there" when she gave me her hand to kiss, and the long sequence of curtseys ended (we did several, in those days, slithering past bunches of Serene Highnesses), I stood beside Lady (Gerald) Fitzgerald, who had presented me, watching others through their ordeal.

The friends made at this time and later in London were manifold. I can name only a few: one of these was Sir James Knowles, Editor of the *Nineteenth Century*, who first encouraged me to try and write. The dinner-parties at Queen Anne's Mansions were stimulating. In the dining-room hung Mr. Watts' famous picture of Lord Tennyson. Sir James said to me one day, when we had been discussing the portrait:

"Odd thing that the sons of great men are always fools. I said that one day to Hallam, and he was furious with me!"...

"I'm a Liberal – ever met a Liberal?" said Herbert Paul one night, taking me down to dinner at the Ritchies'.

I instanced someone. "He's not a Liberal," said Herbert Paul. "He allows you your agreements, but not your differences."

In 1890 *The Times* had a brisk correspondence about "Jessie of Lucknow", and the incident commemorated in the song, "The Campbells are coming". The story was, it will be remembered (everyone believed it to be history), that Jessie, a Scotch girl, had sensed the approach of the relief, by her gift of second sight, and encouraged the besieged garrison to hold on – thus saving the situation. *The Times* correspondents were wrangling over "Jessie" – some saying she was alive and claiming her as a maid: others equally claiming her, but saying she was dead.

I was staying in London at the time with Miss Adelaide Manning (the daughter of Sergeant Manning), who said, "This is very funny – there's only one person who knows who Jessie was: and she has not written to *The Times*. Would you like to see her and hear her story?" I said that I should love to do that. So we made an expedition to a suburb of London, and found a dear old lady sitting by the window in her charming room. She had pink cheeks and wore her snow-white hair in curls under a lace cap. She looked very French, but was English, the widow of one of Talleyrand's secretaries.

Miss Manning said, "Writers to *The Times* are quarrelling over 'Jessie of Lucknow'" – and told her about the correspondence. She flushed with delight. "My Jessie," she said, "still alive?" "Will you tell my Indian friend her story?" She complied at once and with evident pleasure. She said that her sister was married to a Colonel in the Indian Army: that the Colonel and his wife were both with the besieged garrison at Lucknow in 1857. That when the little force was at the very end of its strength, Lucknow was relieved by a Highland Detachment. Mme. X—— was in Paris when her sister's letter arrived, telling her all this. She was thrilled and sent the story (enlarging it, and inventing "Jessie" to make the tale more picturesque), in the form of a letter purporting to have come from India, to a Paris paper. How she chuckled over the true and honourable women who claimed to have pensioned or buried this fictitious person!

"Do write the truth to *The Times*," said Miss Manning. "Never!" said the delicious old lady. "My Jessie is alive – has lived all these years. How can you expect me to say that she was never born!" I believe *The Times* had traced the tale to the French paper in question: but could get no information from the then control about the writer of the letter.

Mary Cholmondeley,* that unique personality, perfect friend, meticulous worker, humorous observer of life, and successful writer of novels, lived in those days with her father and sisters at a flat in Knightsbridge. – "*The* Flat", as her country home was "*The* Cottage" to her friends. We loved her parties. Mary had a gift for the combination of wits and personality which would give the most pleasure, and evoke the most general response. It was really in its way a gift of the *salon*, not then usual in England. It seemed to me that English people let conversation be confined too entirely to *tête-à-tête*; both Margot Asquith and Mary Cholmondeley knew the moment at which to direct the twos into a group movement.

But ideals of conversation vary. I remember Brodrick, the Warden of Merton, saying at a dinner-party, "Some people think that conversation is a gladiatorial exhibition where all must contend. Other people think that that conversation is the highest where everyone is silent and hears one good man speak. And I think so, too!" Mary and her beloved beautiful younger sister Victoria were very popular in London society. Mary's books are not, I suppose, read now because the style of appreciation in novels has changed; but I cannot imagine *Red Pottage, Diana Tempest*, and her short stories failing to give pleasure even to-day, to all but the lovers of "slap-dash". She was a careful writer, spending hours (she said) in the attempt to discover the appropriate word; and her sketches of character were delightful. To find a rather extravagant peg on which to hang her tale, seemed to be a primal necessity – but once found it acted as a magic wand calling her Creatures out of the blue. She once told me that people who fitted on "caps" never meant for them, and who were thereupon "huffy", were a sad trial. "As a matter of fact, I never consciously paint a portrait, though the tricks and gestures of those I know often get into my books, and not always in connection with the types seen."

That, I believe, is the experience of all writers of fiction: but few can have had the experiences which M. C. had with relations over *Red Pottage*!

Una Artevelde Taylor was a daughter of Sir Henry Taylor (Author of *Phillip von Artevelde*), Tennyson's contemporary.

Una lived with her sister in Montpelier Square. Her room was unique; long and simple, the walls hung with tapestries worked by herself, from designs supplied by her friends William Morris and Burne-Jones. She wrote regularly for the *Quarterly Review*, and her poems and mystical tales had a mediæval flavour, as if they could be translated into music suitable to the spinet and the clavichord. Her sense of measured language was due, I gathered, to her upbringing.... When she was three years old her father began reading her Chaucer, Spencer, Shakespeare, accustoming her ear from babyhood to classical English.

But, busy as she was with her needle and her pen, she was always at leisure for her friends: and one knocked upon her green door unashamed, to consult her about the most trivial or the most vital of difficulties. Many an evening did we spend together, she and I, talking far into the night, the only light in the room, in the summer months, that which came in from the Square through the little leaded panes of her uncurtained windows.

She was Irish, and loved to find parallels in custom, superstition and folk-lore between India and Ireland. My deliberate pursuit of these things in India in later years was due to her inspiration.

She gave with both hands, in friendship, alike from her stores of memory (e.g., R. L. Stevenson and the Camerons),[iii] [iii One R. L. S. story was of the writing of *Jekyll and Hyde*. His "critic on the hearth" (Mrs. Stevenson) said it was not convincing as first written, and told him why. He sulked, but sat up all night rewriting in the form we know. Mrs. Cameron's earliest photographs were of Tennyson and Una's father, a very handsome man. "Why do you make me like this and Taylor like that?" said Tennyson. Mrs. Cameron replied, "Ask God for the difference."] as from the contacts of the moment.

Robert Cunninghame Graham and his mother Mrs. Bontine, Graham Robertson the artist, Aubrey de Vere, "Signor" G. F. and Mrs. Watts, the Holman Hunts and Canon Wilberforce, Mr. Arthur and Madeline Elliot, Flora Kirwin, Alice Meynell – are among the links in the chain that I owe to her.

"Shall you paint her or shall I?" said Signor (Watts) to Holman Hunt. They both loved my clothes. It was Holman Hunt who began a portrait of me in my presentation sari: but blindness overtook him and it was never finished. I always loved staying at Limnerslease with Signor and my beloved Mary Watts. She was building her temple to Immortality at the time, with desire to make the idea of death less ugly than it was wont to be in the Victorian age: and he was painting trees for the first time. "They look in at the windows and ask to be painted," he said. The many copies of some of his pictures he explained as "an attempt to get them nearer his ideal". He told me that he always tried to have one old bit of work on hand to this end – which seemed a parable, to me who am apt deliberately to avoid looking at bits of work once done with.

A memory of Canon Wilberforce over which Una and I often laughed was the incident of the Canon and the Aquarium. Una told him of a little French girl made to dive into icy cold water (her contract promised warm water). "She's in your parish!" she hinted. So one day Una conducted him to the Aquarium and sat beside him through the diving turn; after which he marched up to the water and tested it. The interview with the Management which followed was very brief. He marched off with the hand of the little girl tucked into his arm under a street full of eyes!

At Alice Meynell's I met Francis Thompson. The talk and the music at the

Meynells' Sunday suppers are alike an abiding memory.

Of varied interests were the people one met at parties. Irving and Ellen Terry, Sir Squire and Lady Bancroft, Benson, Mrs. Patrick Campbell and Miss Compton, for instance, among actors.

It was at the Baroness Burdett-Coutts' that I first met Irving. He did not like being talked to while he was busy eating: but between courses was quite entertaining.

"The Vikings" had just been put on at the little Theatre in Sloane Square. It had not done well. "Why did you let Ellen Terry play in 'The Vikings'?" asked someone.

"If Gordon Craig dramatized the book of Ecclesiastes, Nellie would play it," said he.

Old Admiral Keppel, the Baroness and Irving made a delightful trio, and put back the clock in an attractive way.

Of her early romance, a subaltern destined for India, the Baroness told me one day when we were alone. Early Victorian discipline forbade an engagement or even correspondence. "Let him come back when he is a Major," said Authority: and her Subaltern sailed away with his Regiment.

There came the day when she was unexpectedly Coutts' Bank, so to speak: and she cabled to her subaltern happily that taboos were at an end. He cabled back that he was already married!

The "addresses" of the years which followed this incident were many, but she "rejected" them all.

Was she not sorry, I asked, about any single one of her suitors?

After thinking a moment: "Yes!" said she, "I was sorry that I could not love Louis Napoleon!"

It was a great moment when I was asked to write an Indian play for George Alexander – Mrs. Patrick Campbell to have the chief rôle. I said that I could not write a play, but would put into suitable form for the English stage a Sanskrit play, reputed as of the second century. (The original took a fortnight to act, and was staged by the roadside, the audience travelling with the players to succeeding scenes, arranged to punctuate the journey!)

In due course this was done, and submitted to George Alexander's critic, who passed it, but said it must be put into blank verse – a fearful essay, but also passed. And then I was asked to stay at Graham Robertson's house at Witley. He would do the illustrations to the play, and I was to read it to Mrs. Patrick Campbell, who was to be of the party.

We read it in the Early English cottage in the garden after dinner – Mrs. Pat lying full-length on the hearthrug. Her comments were characteristic. The play portrays an aged and childless Brahmin wife who urges her husband to marry again, choosing a bride for him herself, a young and lovely girl. Mrs. Pat was to play the young girl. "But this is immoral!" said Mrs. Pat. "I could not bear the old woman to be nice to me. Make it Za-Za, a third-personal situation."

It was no use pointing out that that would be French, not Indian.

Then again:

"But you know I can never play happily unless I am the only important person in the play. Now the Brahmin man is as important as I am. You must change that."

I told our little group that night that I was afraid it was no good. The changes could not be made. The play was not mine, and its value lay in keeping it as close as possible to the original. Mrs. Pat was flatteringly regretful. "Do change it. I long to play in Indian draperies. Do I not remind you of an Indian dream?" I was young and did not know how to frame a polite answer. Evasion she would not allow.

"No."

"Of what do I remind you? You must say. It is something Indian, I am sure." I admitted that it was. "What is it?" Pressed beyond power of extrication, I said, "Of a snake – you move so sinuously, do you not?" To my relief she was delighted.

"I long to be a snake. I always try to imagine myself a snake."

But about the play I was inexorable. Unless she entered into the spirit of it, it was no use. The changes she wanted could not be made.

It was interesting meeting Mrs. Pat. I'd seen her only once before, at an artist's studio on Show Sunday, when she came in rustling – it was in the days of the rustling underskirt – Herr Zwintscher was playing lovely Eighteenth-Century music on a spinet, and Philip Burne-Jones said:

"Who's that hissing with her feet?"

She could say clever and original things – as, for instance, this: "I always tell a woman's age by her throat. First it's all right: then there's a pleat: then there's a gusset!"

After we left Witley a friend sent the play to Bernard Shaw. It came back with the remark that it would be very expensive to stage; but was worth a trial. There was only one addition which he begged me to make. "Introduce," said he, "the incident of the Ninth Lancers and the Durbar!" (Curzon's Durbar, and a contemporaneous Army incident.) I thought that he was laughing at me, even though he sent me a message asking if the change had been made. And I threw the play into a corner of my room. I have since realized that the coupling of the centuries is a Shavian habit: and have always regretted my ignorance and silly touchiness. I might have asked him to do it himself!

Bernard Shaw, in the flesh, I have met only once lately at a House Party in Worcestershire. He greeted me with: "Why are you not in prison?" which helped me to retort that it was clear with what kind of Indian alone he was acquainted.

I did enjoy that meeting. How kindly he is and how gentle, and full of the fun which has no sting in its tail. But – whether deliberately or not (he will forgive me), he makes you feel that he is sitting for his photograph every moment of his life – in public, at any rate.

My brother and I paid a thrilling visit to the Tennysons in September 1892, not long before the Laureate's last illness. After swearing us to secrecy, he read us *Akbbar*, then unpublished. We sat in the garden, he wore the big hat ("the boys in the street say they can see my legs dangling out of it") and cloak with which pictures had familiarized us; and every now and again his son gave him a spoonful of glycerine to moisten his throat. He talked of Gladstone, of Buddhism and of Alfred Lyall. With Lady Tennyson I fell in love at first sight. She looked like an abbess in her lace veil. Her wonderful recovery, after a lifetime on her back, she used in collecting material from her diaries for the Life of Alfred Tennyson.

English country-house visits really need a book to themselves. Life was good to me and I had ample opportunities of realizing what made the Englishmen of the Services what they are, at their best. Through the hospitality of friends I learnt to know many counties in England: I also visited Scotland, Ireland and Wales.

At Easter a beloved friend, Mrs. Augustus Darling, used to take me abroad – to the Riviera, North Italy and Switzerland. She was sister-in-law to our "pretend" Grandmother, Lady Ford, after whom I was named. But Lady Ford was too ailing when I was in England to look after me, and Mrs. Darling did it for her. She gave me the loveliest times, bless her! She was exquisite to look at, and we both loved books and flowers and the countryside; also, the same things made us laugh – perhaps, this last, the closest bond of all. My "English Mother" she called herself, and her wisdom, as I recognized later, lay not in reproof and denial, but in giving in. Monte Carlo was one instance. I had read about Monte Carlo, and when we were at Mentone, I said, "I should like to go to Monte Carlo – to the Tables, I mean." She said, "My dear Child!" – I knew she hated the thought. And, I must have been more odious than even my memory of myself, for I kept saying, "I *do* want to go!"

She said, smiling, "You always get what you want from me." And I grinned back, "That is why I go on telling you that I still want it!"

Next morning she said to me, "We are going to drive in to Monte Carlo this afternoon. You will love the view, Mentone looking like a great amethyst in the distance. And we will go into the Casino. I've arranged for someone to take us round who understands about the play there: and (shyly), "I'd like my Birthday present to you to be some money to throw away."

Was anyone ever like her?

It was I who at the end of the afternoon said, "Let's get out of this, to the fresh air"; the faces of the women who played for gold only, in a room apart, had pricked the bubble of excitement.

I had played myself – and won; but I never want to go to Monte Carlo again.

From Mentone that year, we went to San Remo, driving through Ventimiglia, in a little *fiacre* (no motors in those days); Mrs. Darling's man and maid followed in another with the baggage. At the frontier Customs Office, the maid came to us distraught. "They will not pass Mamselle's clothes. They say they are silks being taken to Italy for sale."

"Explain to them, Rose," said Mrs. Darling. "You've often seen Mademoiselle dress."

"I have done that; they only shrug their shoulders."

"Bring them to me," said my friend, and she explained in French, and in Italian, that what was in my boxes was exactly like what I was wearing.

"Ask us to believe that!" was their reply, emphasized with movements of hands, shoulders, eyebrows.

"You'll have to undress and dress before them," said Mrs. Darling.

I was young – "Nothing would induce me," said I.

"Tell us what to pay," said she to the Officers.

"Impossible!" was the reply. It seemed both French and Italian Customs were involved, and we must wait till nine o'clock next morning, when the goods would be examined by a joint board.

Of course, I could not allow that: and very sulkily, I have no doubt, I said I would demonstrate.

We went into the Customs shed – one pull and my draperies were at my feet. The Officers stood in a circle round us, and how we laughed at their faces! But it was still difficult to drive on, not because they wanted to charge us duty – oh, no! – "everything was free," and they were most apologetic. But they wanted to see how it was done. "Do it again!" they kept saying, as if they were Alice in Wonderland or Peter Pan.

In these days when hundreds of Indian women of all races visit England and the Continent so frequently, a scene like this is hard to visualize. My sisters had preceded me to England, and Miss Adelaide Manning, that generous friend of

Indians, had spoken of the visits of the late Dowager Maharani of Cooch Behar
– but I believe this made the complete tale of us. Indian boys and men had long
been coming in respectable numbers. But their clothes had not the same allure
or suggestion of foreignness. Dear old ladies were always trying to convert me
– for instance – the heathen at their gates. And they would talk to one very loudly
in pidgin-English – "Calcutta Come?" "Bombay Come?" Only once did I try to
undeceive a proselytizing old lady. She regarded me reproachfully, "But you *look*
so very heathen!"

One more tale of "lingerie". "The Widow Green" – as the widow of the
Historian ᵛ [ᵛ Mrs. J. R. Green] was known at Oxford – asked me one day to tea
to meet some "African Chiefs" whom she had picked up somewhere. "I want
them to make their women adopt your dress."

I had my doubts, but I went: and the conversation turned instantly on clothes.
"This," I said, indicating my *sari*, "is six yards long – how many yards of material
go to the dress of an African lady in your part of the country?" The "Chief"
said shortly – "Beads, and – this – " producing a handkerchief!

My only other "African" story is perhaps best told here, though it happened
years later during the Boer War. I was back in England temporarily, and occupied
a flat in Chelsea. I dropped into a near-by Church one Sunday for Service, being
too late for my usual objective. To this accident I attribute what followed.

On Monday afternoon I got home to hear at the door that an English cleric
from this Church had been waiting an hour to see me. I hurried to him, apologetic.
I supposed that it was a parochial visit.

He advanced with both hands outstretched.

"It's so good to see you," he said. "So like Home!"

I'd never seen the man before, and said:

"Do you know India?"

"No."

"Or my People?"

"No! But it's *so* like Home to see you. I've been working among the Coolies
in South Africa!"

In 1894 I returned to India for the first time. The to-and-fro-ings since are
more than I can remember: and there have been many Continental visits – Italy,
France, Belgium, Spain, Austria.

II FEELING AFTER A WAY
1894-1902

MY FIRST CASE, 1894 – THE *PURDAHNASHIN*
IN HER SETTING – THE CROSS-EYED BOY

I sailed back, then, for India, at the end of my English period of training, determined to find a way of helping those whom I claimed as my portion: but as hopelessly without a programme of action as I had been when I left for England.

I had a kind of – was it Faith, or Instinct? – that, if I were destined to help, a way would open, and that all "operations" to that end would be major operations, or should be regarded as such, provided I took every reasonable opportunity that came along, without disappointment and without examination of the label. Everyone who had a right to an opinion had said that the thing was worth doing: no one had pretended to know how it should be done.

"But surely," I said to myself, "that should be enough for an explorer, so long as she keeps an open mind, and an open eye…" "Think of the End, and thou shalt never go amiss," as advised a mediæval maxim.

So when, at Aden, on my way out, I was greeted with a letter from H.H. the Maharajah Gaekwar of Baroda* asking me if I would tour his State and write him a blue-book on Education, I weighed the proposition hopefully. The Gaekwar and his charming Maharani Sahiba were old friends of my parents, and his Highness, even then a leader in things progressive, had lately introduced compulsory education into his State. He wished particularly for a report on the success of his experiment. The investigation would occupy only as long as I chose to spend upon it – said the kind Maharajah, who knew of my real objective.

I felt that, after my absence from India, a tour of a Native State, getting into touch with the *vernacular* in town and village, was exactly what I needed to balance my latest experiences: and I gladly accepted the opportunity.

It was a delightful interlude. My headquarters were at Baroda itself, and I wandered forth in style, with two sets of tents, one to pitch, and one to send forward: and with the impressive etcetera which belongs to the lordly States. I might have been living in the pages of a coloured picture-book of Ancient India.

Incidentally, Jowett, still alive, was delighted that I had found an asylum here, at the beginning of my pilgrimage. Mr. Elliott, an old Balliol man, had been Tutor to the Gaekwar, and the auspices were therefore favourable.

An item not in my official duties was teaching his Highness to row! He had lately made a river through the Park, leading from one Palace to another. But his Staff, with one consent, made excuse when asked to instruct H.H. in the use of the oar. "Suppose H.H. should catch a crab – was it not inviting something equivalent to 'Off-with-his-head' in relation to the coach?"

I had no such scruples. The boat was best Oxford, and the oars and rowlocks were familiar friends.

The Chief Justice, a Moslem gentleman who added wit to great learning, was persuaded to take charge of the steering-ropes: and we got a good deal of fun, first and last, out of the adventure. I will not say that crabs were not caught by Royalty, as by any commoner upon a first essay: but – I kept my head!

Another story of this time, also relating to the Park, concerned his Highness's order that the Park was to be reserved for *Purdahnashins* on one day in the week – surely, an All-India pioneer order, this, in thought taken for the secluded.

One day H.H., forgetful of his own regulation, drove up to the Park: the gates were closed, and the old Subhadar gate-keeper put his head in the dust, but said he could not open. "Why not?" said H.H., and turning to his A.D.C. told him to make a note of the man's name, and of the fact that he was to be removed from his post.

And the A.D.C. himself set wide the gates…. The scattering of saris among the trees brought instant realization, and H.H. not only turned back at once, but reversed forthwith the sentence pronounced in anger – "The gate-keeper was to be promoted."

That story is typical of what enlightened autocracy can accomplish in India.

As to compulsory education – I found a sorry state of things. The experiment was being tried in the cotton-growing districts of the State.

Parents wanted their children to pick cotton, not to learn to read and write. The children were already useful wage-earners.

"Go to the towns, and teach the *Bania's* (money-lender's) children," said they. "Leave us alone."

To my mind, sound advice. But the then Director of Education would have none of it, although he was helpless to coerce. And the schools, well built and well equipped, were empty. What puzzled me was his glowing printed report on the success of the scheme.

I sent for him.

"Had it then succeeded at the outset?"

"No! It has always been as now."

"But – this Report" – (and I did not know how to proceed without hurting his feelings).

"Oh, that is for the Maharajah Bahadur. It would not be respectful to tell his Highness that a scheme, in which the Durbar is so greatly interested, was a mistake!"[12]

Compulsory education in the villages was dropped after a report was made of facts as they were. It was revived very many years later – and is now, I believe, a success in both country and town. Difficult indeed is the path of rulers – in India! But that incident was for myself a flashlight, and often in later years did "the villagers of Baroda" determine personal investigation into circumstances reported with the weight and authority of Durbar officialdom.

On my return to my parents' home – the Baroda Education blue-book completed – I found my foot upon "the next step". My Mother and I had just come in from a drive one evening when a woman appeared from behind the Croton bushes in the garden, and threw herself at my Mother's feet.

"We are in trouble, and they say you have a 'Ballister' daughter. Will she help us?"

(Bazaar and servants' gossip knows nothing of legal distinctions, and the title is not to be taken as sanctioned by anyone in the family.)

She told her story. She was of a woodcutter's family. She and her sister-in-law lived together. Her brother was murdered. The Police said that his wife had killed him: and the Magistrate had committed her for trial.

"But truly she had not done that dreadful thing. Who should know, if not I? We were together all day, and my sister-in-law was cooking her husband's food at the time that they say she was killing him…. Save her!" and she fell to weeping.

"Can you help her?" asked my Mother.

"I do not know. I will discover."

So we told the woman to return later. The trial was to be at the approaching Sessions: and I wrote to Mr. Crowe, the District and Sessions Judge, asking if I might defend the woman, not as having any legal qualification, but as a "person for the defence of the accused" – the Statutory Law of British India, read with the definitions section, allowed an accused any "person" for his defence, and "person" was defined as male or female.

He said he must refer the question to the High Court of Bombay, as it had never before arisen.

The High Court said, I believe, "Have we indeed left women that loophole!" but could not deny that "the Law allowed it".

The week of the trial was, without comparison, the most exciting and the most exhausting of my entire life. I remembered, with a wry face, the story of an English Circuit – later my own:

The Court (to the Prisoner). What have you to plead in your defence?
Prisoner. Nothing, but the youth of my Counsel.

I believed my Client innocent: and I lay awake at night contemplating the rope which my inefficiency would put round her neck: for of course my glooms refused to consider any "lifer" alternative.

The Prosecution was on its mettle. "A woman indeed for the defence!" and though the Hindu male of those days had a profound contempt for any woman straying into male preserves, he nevertheless took precautions. The pick of the Hindu local bar, with leading Counsel from Bombay (a friend of the Public Prosecutor's), confronted a humble "person" as she timidly found her way to Counsel's table on the opening day….

It was the most absurd incident which gave me back my equilibrium.

Hindu Counsel of that period came to Court wearing the turned-up, red-leather Maratha shoe over bare feet. I had passed the shoes, parked outside the door of the Court Room, where the men had kicked them off before entering.

After a glance at me – "Go home and get my patent-leather Europe shoes!" said mine adversary to his clerk. I do not know if I can make anyone understand why that was so helpful! But it was.

In 1894 one could still see little knots of candidates for the witness-box sitting under a *banyan* tree in the Court compound, being instructed in the evidence to be given in pending cases. The scale at the time was, I believe, a rupee (16 annas) per man if he could stand cross-examination, eight annas if he were less skilled in lying.

I felt sure that all those in the box on those opening days had been paid on the higher scale. The story of the Prosecution was indeed well supported. The police had found the body and the various pools of blood the morning after a murder supposed to have been committed at eight o'clock the previous night. Moreover, it was committed with a cutting instrument which was, in fact, my client's (a gadget used in the preparation of vegetables for the pot); and there were not a few villagers who swore to convincing details.

My own story included the fact that the murdered woodcutter lived in perfect harmony with his wife in a hut on the edge of a sloping wood. The murdered man had lent a considerable sum of money to a brother woodcutter with whom he used to go to work in clearings about a mile distant from their several huts.

He had had occasion the week previous to his death to ask the borrower for return of the money. Also, the day before the murder, the debtor had begged the loan of a vegetable cutter from the accused, saying that his wife had broken hers.

The night of the murder there was a terrific monsoon storm, the woodcutter did not return in the cowdust hour,ˠ [ˠ The early twilight, when the cows go home] as he was wont to do, and after waiting for him till far into the night the women ate their own meal and went to bed, thinking he had taken refuge from the storm in the hut of some *brathari* – other woodcutters who lived nearer the clearing.

Early next morning the police rapped on the door, and arrested the accused, showing her the body of her murdered husband lying not far from the hut. The debtor was with the police and had identified the woman.

The only witness I had of my version of the tale was the sister-in-law, not much use, even though cross-examination of the debtor had been helpful.

But that storm gave me an idea. I put in plans of the location, and evidence of the state of the barometer on the night of the murder. We all knew the violence of the Monsoon in the Western Ghats.

The hut was on such a sheer slope that the storm would not only have washed those well-measured pools of blood clean into a drain below, but would also have carried the body a considerable distance towards it.

For the first time, through the trial, I saw a flicker on the immobile faces of the Jurymen... the rope of my bad dreams untightened – a little.

The Judge made (*inter alia*) my point about the storm all right in his summing-up to the Jury. But the twenty minutes of their absence seemed to me as many years.

And how slow they were in answering his questions when they did come back! "Gentlemen of the Jury, have you considered your verdict?"

"Yes! we are unanimous."

Then a long pause.

"What is your verdict?"

"Not Guilty!"

I could have hugged the dear old Foreman!

I turned to my Client and said in her own tongue:

"Those Gentlemen say you have not done this thing."

She looked at me with the reproachful eyes of a trapped gazelle –

"I always knew that I had not done it," said she.

I suppose in every country work brings work. And, after that case, the local Bar – chiefly a Maratha Barrister, Mr. Gadgil – tried to persuade me to settle in Poona, and specialize in the Criminal defence work which needed no professional label in the eyes of the Courts.

But – I knew that would have been a mistake. I was ready to take any specific Criminal work which might come my way, but I wanted to be able to help

Purdahnashins in relation to their property and the disabilities connected with their status. And it seemed imperative that I should try and get some recognizable qualification as a practitioner in the Civil Law Courts.

The Bachelor of Laws degree qualifies for practice as a *Vakil* in every High Court in India.[13] As a Graduate of the Bombay University I was entitled to appear for the LL.B. Examination, and I applied to be allowed to sit for it, straight away, without keeping terms. This was allowed and I passed the Examination, and took my degree.

But – enrolment as a *Vakil* was refused me.

"Could I cite the precedent of a Woman *Vakil*, even one instance would do," was the evasive excuse.

One could not waste time either on resentment or on a fight. Work was beckoning to me in the little network of States known as Kathiawar. Why should I not turn my back on British India, and ask leave to plead successively in the specific Durbar Courts in whose jurisdiction my cases might fall?[14]

An alternative was also at this moment put before me by Framjee & Moos, a firm of Parsee Solicitors in Bombay. Would I work in their office as Consultant for the *Purdahnashin* clients they could not themselves see face to face. I have never forgotten the wonderful kindness of Framjee & Moos in making this proposition. I gave it a trial for a few months: but found that I did not really reach my objective. There was only one strictly purdah Moslem woman who found courage to come into a Solicitor's office, albeit veiled, and albeit to see a woman.

I returned to the wandering idea: and accepted the Kathiawar beckonings. And this plan succeeded.

The Thakur of a State was his own High Court; and, although my case was often brought against the Durbar itself (the Judge being also the Defendant!), I was given a special *Sanad* to appear. Who shall say whether this was due to luck or to curiosity?

Sometimes the case was what was known as "political". The Agent to the Governor-General is the link between the Native States and British Control. He lives at the centres of political authority, is sometimes a Civilian in origin, sometimes a Military officer, but in his office of Agent belongs definitely to the Political Department of the Government of India.

And among his many duties in those days was the maintenance of a roll on which was entered the names of legal practitioners entitled to appear in what were loosely spoken of as the Agency Courts, in order to represent to the Agent, whether by Memorial, or in person, the grievances of Native States' subjects. An appeal to British justice was recognized whoever the appellant might be, even if of the family of the Durbar.

I got myself enrolled in the Agencies at Indore (Central India) and Rajkot (Kathiawar), which controlled my then fields of operation. And there followed a period of delight: work after my own heart – cases dealing with Inheritance, Succession, Maintenance-allowances and *Stridhan* (the Hindu Woman's *peculium*) in an itinerary and setting which were like an adaptation of the Arabian Nights.

I moved from point to point in a variety of ways – by train, riding an elephant, in palanquins, camel carts, in old-fashioned barouches, in a "coach and four" preceded by outriders with drawn swords, in funny little "embroidered" covered carts like the one used by the Thakurani visitor to my Mother who began my story.

Once I was offered a buffalo to ride, but I refused. I preferred my feet. Was not a buffalo the "Carrier" of the God of Death? And where, on his long back, except just above the tail like the children "buff-herds", could one sit? Hotels there were none. I stayed in Raj guest-houses, at Agencies, in tents, or offshoots to the Zenana. And all the time I was learning about manners and customs at close quarters.

The Hindu *Purdahnashin* of those days lived in a Joint Family, more common then than it is to-day. Hinduism is in theory monogamous, but multiplication of wives is allowed in the interest of an heir. And there were from three to four women to a man in most of the *Rajbaris* which I visited.

These lived in one Zenana with the widows or aunts of predecessors. They lived as a rule in wonderful unity. The child of any particular Rani or Thakurani was fondled and petted by the entire bunch of women, as if it were the personal achievement of each one. Occupation, besides their household and religious duties, they had none. Few of these women could read their vernacular: none of them could write, though they could make the mark which represented their signature, the theory being that if women learnt to write they would get themselves into trouble.

Their quarters were apart, with a courtyard attached into which they seldom entered. The outer walls were sometimes spiked like the walls of any gaol: and at the foot of the stairs an armed guard stood, back to the "Inside", facing the door which led to the outer courts. From this sanctuary they went not forth, except on pilgrimage, or (less often than in Bengal) to visit their father's house.

I once asked a Thakur if I might take his Thakuranis out by night in a closed carriage to show them, through the slits of the wooden blinds, the lovely gardens and buildings of the estate.

"It would be nice for them to see the improvements which you have made," I urged.

"Certainly, if they will go."

But with the politeness of firm negation (as I had learnt to interpret the phrase) they said:

"Whatever is the wish of the Miss Sahiba, is our wish."

"But don't you want to see what is outside these walls? No one would see you."

"Did our Grandmothers drive out to see the world?" was their only answer.

"Then come downstairs to your courtyard. I'll send the Guard-man away. Come and run round" (they were young). "We'll play a game."

"Impossible! Would you like to run down the street in your skin? To run round the courtyard would seem to us, even clothed as we are, what running down the street in your skin would seem to you."

These rebellious suggestions of mine were born of an incident. I had spoken to one little Thakurani of the flowers growing in the Palace gardens – "like these," I said, touching the tightly packed, short-stemmed posy, stuck in a vase without water, with which the Palace gardeners supplied the Zenana; "only they grow –" and I described the ways of rambler roses and jasmine.

Her eyes grew very round. "Are these not picked up off the ground like stones?"

Something caught at my heart. She had never seen growing things, never seen a garden. She had been married as a small child, her mother-in-law had been very strict indeed. She had never been in contact with growing life of any kind. They kept no pets, and it was a childless Zenana.

Next day I brought her a rose-plant in a pot. One lovely rose was out, and there were buds. I explained that these would open like the rose, and I called them "the Rose's children".

Next day she met me, all excitement. She had not slept, but sat watching her plant.

"The Rose's child might come full-blown and I not there to see!"

To-day the third generation of this very Zenana visits England: its wives are educated, if still in measure secluded: and once, not so very long ago, a wife accompanied the monogamous Ruler to England.

Things are moving, if slowly.

It is difficult now to imagine H.H. the Maharani Sahiba of Baroda in purdah: but she was so, when first I knew her. Her progressive Maharajah, however, allowed her light and air, and the windows of her Quarters were wide. But, before she walked in her Garden (which she might do), whistles were sounded to shoo away the gardeners; the protection of custom was still believed necessary, even for her.

Except in the case of such as the Maharani of Baroda – whose palace was supplied with English garnishings in addition to lovely oriental things, *kincobs*, etc. – the Zenana of those days was almost bare of furniture. There were carpets and mats; bolsters and cushions; and little carved tables very low, more like stools, sometimes with sloping tops originally meant for writing-desks; and there were stands to hold the sacred book, if anyone in the Zenana had ever been a reader.

On my visits, chairs were brought in from the men's sitting-rooms.

The verandahs were closed in, with blinds of scented grass, which in the time of heat were damped, sending delicately scented breezes through the Zenana. The women slept on *charpais* – four-legged bedsteads of wood and plaited webbing: but the four legs themselves were more often of chased gold or silver than of carved or painted wood, as in poorer houses.

The vessels for water, and the basins (which had just come into use for washing purposes), were of solid silver. The bath was taken standing, water being poured over the body from a large silver vessel (often of exquisite shape as if dug out of Grecian or Roman ruins), with a small silver pot, delicate, and varying in design.

In place of soap was used ground gram-flour, very cleansing.

The bedroom was also a dressing-room; *saris* in use were hung over long pegs attached to the walls; the overflow was kept in chests – rather like the chests of the eighteenth century found in old cottages in Cumberland. The dressing-table was – a portable box! There was a (bad) looking-glass in the lid, and there were compartments for the oils the women used for their hair, and for the red powder (*sindur*) with which they painted the parting down the middle of their heads, and with which they put the red dot on their foreheads after *puja*. The line signifies, I am a wife: the dot, I am dedicated to my Lord (husband). One woman told me it was to her a daily renewal of her vows of service to her Lord when she placed on her forehead the mark first put there upon her wedding-day.... Among the Progressives in these latter days, it has lost all meaning, and is only a cosmetic.

They washed their hair – it was long and black and glossy, with a curl in it – daily, and greased it with coconut and other oils. They dressed it flat against their heads, pulling it tightly ("to make it grow longer still"!), and plaiting it into a coil behind. (In Madras the coil is often to the side over one ear.) They did this hairdressing office for one another sometimes – a very pretty scene.

But the evening dressing, in preparation for bed – just as elaborate and if anything more tightly braided than for the day – had to be done before the Sun dropped, else a demon might peep into the looking glass and bewitch them!

Ornaments of gold and precious stones were worn, differing in fashion and in use, according to the part of the country to which the women belonged –

and this was so whether the ornaments were for hair, forehead, nose, ears, arms or ankles.

The marriage ring was then, as now, for all Hindus alike, an iron bracelet – except in the Madras Presidency, where it is an ornament worn round the neck. On my wanderings in Kathiawar, I have seen the Suttee stone, recognized by the arm bare of a marriage bracelet, which is engraved upon it.[15]

Faithful, according to their lights, were the ancestors of my little *Purdahnashins*, even in death; even as they themselves are to-day, faithful in the lonely compulsion of widowhood.

But, if ancient monuments are to be trusted, marriage was not always in infancy, in Kathiawar at least. There is a disused Temple to Happiness, one of many, which I have visited. It has a charming history. It sits now in the sand of a dry river-bed. In ancient times the newly-wedded walked to it after their first night of wedded bliss to hang on the walls their marigold wedding garlands, symbols of happiness, a thank-offering, and an encouragement to all true lovers – "We've passed this way, it's all right!"

An old priest, who had taken the ruins for his "Cave of meditation", showed me the dead brown petals crumbled to dust lying on the floor. They may never be swept out.

Of first importance in an orthodox Hindu House are the *Puja-Ghar* (House of Worship or Chapel) and the kitchen; each after its kind, serving the ritual of Religion. In a lordly house every woman has her separate *Puja-Ghar*. In this is installed her Patron Deity – most often with women it is the little Baby Krishna. In the days of which I write, he was made of brass or clay. Later, in Bengal, I found he was sometimes a doll made (unknown to the worshipper) in Germany.[16]

It is just – this worship of the Baby Krishna in these houses – the worship of a child by a mother, or by one who yearns to be a mother.

He is washed and fed and worshipped – his food placed appetizingly beside him: and then he is put to bed – in the earliest days on his lotus or sacred *ficus* leaf: later, in an Indian cradle: in Bengal, later still, in a miniature English bedstead with mosquito-nets!

The kitchen has fireplaces plastered with cow-dung, the pots are of brass or copper or silver, and are spick and span, cleaned with Ganges mud.

The meal is eaten off the kitchen floor, patterned with designs of good omen, made in sandalwood or rice-flour paste. Vegetarian food is eaten, differing as to preparation, according to the provinces and districts of the country.

The men may eat fish or mutton. This is apparent in cases where they worship deities who accept blood-offerings. Indian food seems to excel in *hors d'œuvre* – fritters of pulse or edible leaves toned up with chillies: gram-flour savouries (*Sev*,

Ghattia): pickled fruits and chutneys tasting sour and sweet at the same time: curls of curdled milk-of-wheat fried into cakes. Sweets are a favourite item of diet. Wheat milk again being used in the form known as *gelabes*: or balls of sour cream and sugar, flavoured with rose water: or the many kinds of *halva* (a species of Turkish delight), adorned with almonds or pistachio nuts.

There is no family meal, as there is no congregational or family worship among orthodox Hindus. Each eats alone, seated before a brass or silver tray, on which are a mound of rice and the chief curry of the day, or a pile of thin flat cakes (*chuppatis*) made of rice or grain. There are little pots all around the central tray holding vegetables and appetizers of many kinds.

At Caste dinners large dry leaves held together with thorns are used both for plates and cups.

Eating is with the fingers.

The men of the house eat first, and their wives wait upon them. The wife has probably cooked her husband's meal, wearing a silk sari for the ceremony, though her "dress clothes" are of cotton.

The women eat last, after attending to the children, if there are any.

Widows may not eat out of the vessels of those whose husbands are still alive. When living therefore in a Joint Family house, separate pots and pans, and even separate kitchens (for neither may they cook at the fires of the fortunate), are provided for them.

They eat only once a day – a meal often delayed till 2 p.m., as the service of gods and men and "tables" must first be attended to.

The widow also fasts meticulously, and from water as well as food, for twenty-four hours every fortnight. In addition there are the fasts undertaken for a vow, often very onerous. In all cases the fast is "with intention" for her husband – never for herself. All Hindu fasting is rigorous: but I found the fasting in Bengal, as I found the habit of seclusion, stricter than in Bombay.

Raj ladies, then, live in purdah in the way I have tried to describe. But they are not all of a pattern. I call to mind a gay little bride of sixteen, who came out of a fairy-tale.

The estates of her father and her suitor lay side by side: and the Prince had begged the hand of his neighbour's only daughter in marriage.

I expect that it was really the priests of the respective families who carried on negotiations; but the young Prince had heard of the beauty of the lady, and meeting her father out hunting he pressed his suit.

Now the Raja wanted a Ruling Chief for his son-in-law: and the Prince's father was still young, and like to live long. But, not wishing to offend –

"Yes," said he, "if you bring me a white peacock," as who should say, "if you bring me a pink sparrow". That was a Prince who deserved his Bride.

He spoke to an old *shikari* who knew every bird that flew, and was told of the white peacock of Arabia. The Ghost-bird was procured, and taken to the Raja – "who for the sake of his word," says the chronicler, "gave him his daughter in marriage".

At the time I was their guest, the young people lived in a palace of their own, adjoining that of the Prince's father. And the white peacock occupied a perch of honour in the gardens.

I shall never forget Lamp-lighting Time in the Palace.

A long line of torch-bearers ran with dead torches from the Prince's Palace to the main Raj House close by: for two rules were unbreakable – no light must be lit in the son's house till Light had shone in the father's house: and no light must be lighted there at all, except it had come from the paternal home.... So the torch-bearers made the necessary journey: and back they would come, running, looking like bronze statues – their hands holding aloft the great pitch-pine torches which stabbed the early Indian darkness. Outside the gates they paused, to recite in Gregorian chanting the titles and virtues of the Prince: then up the long drive to the house, moving from point to point so rapidly, that I recalled the forests of my youth, suddenly alive with fire-flies.

The Ghost-bird's mistress was a merry little thing and played hide-and-seek on the roof of her quarters with her waiting women, in the hour before the Lighting.

There was a custom of this Raj, which I have seen nowhere else. The Prince, for his protection, slept under an archway of naked swords – the guard being relieved at stated intervals.

We were discussing this one day, and the little lady said suddenly, "My lord is no *Bahadur* (hero)."

I was aghast – never had I heard a Hindu wife speak in such terms.

"No!" said she, "he has no craftiness, he cannot lie: and he has no *Bahaduri*. He would not cut off a man's head if he disobeyed him, or even – if he let one of those naked swords fall on his sleeping body!"

But – it must not be supposed that my Ghost-bird Princess was a rebel. Far from it. Like any other *Purdahnashin* she stood with veiled face in the presence of him who owned her: and she performed her daily *puja* and did her daily household duties as meticulously as the most tradition-bound in the generation of her grandmother. But she had been spoilt as a child in her father's house, and she was spoilt now.

A separate establishment, no aunts- and mothers- and grandmothers-in-law, no critical eyes of other women of any age: and a husband modern enough to express his admiration!

Her criticism was in reality but a characteristic rendering of "common form".

All Hindu women of those days liked men to be autocrats, to command not to beg, to be off-with-his-head-ish, in their relationship to their women and servants alike. And she was Raj-bred; with intrigue had she been familiar since her infancy, not the intrigue of French novels, but the intrigue of power and possession, the intrigue of politicians and diplomats.

And the only armour of which she knew in this game of intrigue was – a lie.

Experience had shown her this as the nearest conceivable approach to cleverness....

I remember when listening one day to the story of a Client, also a Raj *Purdahnashin*, feeling utterly certain that I was hearing a *banawat* (a made-up tale). I took a risk, but said – "Wonderful *gap* (invention), and now tell me the true story. If you do not, I may not know how to help you, when the truth comes out."

She considered a moment, and then told me a story as unlike the first as truth can be to falsehood.

"Why did you tell me that other tale?"

Her answer was pathetic. "We have no one to protect us, we are accursed, everything that happens to us or that we do is cursed. I wanted to tell you something that was not *nagawar* (unlettered)."

"But the *nagawar* story, the truth, as you told it the second time, is far better for you. Now I can help. There is a way out."

I can see her face as I write. She had not lied because she was false, but because she was reaching after – cleverness!

She was in revolt against – ignorance.

Is it not plain that my gay little lady's "he could not tell a lie", and my Client's self-defence, are of the same stock? Is it not here that we find the key to what is crooked in the Zenanas of the ignorant?

Recognition of that fact has been of immense help to me throughout my dealings with Hindu *Purdahnashins*.

It should be said at the outset that my women clients were almost invariably widows. There is no Law of Divorce in Hinduism: and the attempt of the Progressives to legislate on this subject (1932 et *sequitur*) has caused great indignation among both men and women in the orthodox Hindu Community. A woman belongs to her man, even if he predeceases her, till she dies. British-made Law for India permits the remarriage of widows, but no orthodox Hindu widow takes advantage of this: while infidelity in a wife is unthinkable.

About the time of which I write, *Rukhmabai's* Case had stirred the Zenana to its depths all over the Bombay Presidency. Rukhmabai was a young Maratha non-secluded girl married in her childhood, according to Hindu custom. She was brought up in the home of her own parents and educated in her vernacular and (moderately) in English. When her husband claimed her, she refused to consummate the marriage: and being told the consequences, elected to take them.

She went to prison.

"Was the World coming to an end?" said the Zenana. Not a quiver of sympathy from "the Inside" greeted her courage. The newspapers of the day wrangled over her, varying in direct ratio to their Hindu orthodoxy.

Rukhmabai never read the papers, and cared nothing. She had found herself. That was all there was to it – an unusual and fine character, silent and almost stolid. She did not want to marry anyone else, or indeed to marry at all. She wanted to study; to be a doctor: realization of the implications of a marriage in childhood, such as hers, had burst upon her with her husband's demand. She would resist, and maybe resistance would save others.

India was not "news" in the English Press of the day, but Rukhmabai's story aroused great interest in England; and the wife of a well-known Liberal politician, herself a pioneer in the English Women's movement towards emancipation, arranged for Rukhmabai to come over the waters to her, after release from prison, for a training in the profession of her desires.

In due course Rukhmabai returned as a doctor to India, and has served her country with ability and dignity. Throughout her active professional life, she remained unemotional, and untouched by the hysteria of politics or "Women's rights", nor – and this seems to me her greatest achievement – has she suffered for this at the hands of the Progressive hysterical women of later days. "No Patriot" – "Betrayer of your Country" – the jibes thrown at the steady workers who refused to be entangled with the moment's politics – have never been thrown at her.

I have tiptoed off the straight path of my tale, "grass hopping", as a friend calls it, in order to give some idea of the flesh-and-blood India of the time: and of the life of the women, whose difficulties it was my business to try and understand. And now I come back again.

My work fell into three main classes, as I have indicated ... Succession, Maintenance, and difficulties concerning individuals in consequence of their status. The case of the Cross-eyed Boy, as I called it, is perhaps most typical of the first class.

When a man died the multiplicity of widows – especially where there were children by more than one wife, or where the mother-in-law disliked the mother of the heir – made trouble.

In this case, there was only one child, a cross-eyed boy. But his grandmother could not abide her daughter-in-law. And the only way she could think of hurting her was through the heir.

That was odd, because the heir was also her own means of salvation, since it was he who would light her funeral pyre: and he alone now who could pray with most efficacy for the souls of both her husband and her son. But I have learnt in India that women, with a motive good or bad, can see no further than that particular immediate end. Time and again has this been demonstrated.

There was for instance the beautiful old high-caste grandmother, found in a North Country prison many years later – "a lifer" for murdering her grandson.

"I murdered the Child, yes!" – proudly – "I did that with my own hands."

"But you loved him" (she had adored him), "and he was all that was left to you in the name of your 'lord' and your only son."

"Yes! and even so, I did it: and I do not repent. I wanted to make That One suffer" (her daughter-in-law) – "and she is suffering! ..."

In a way it is the absence of a sense of sin, of wrong-doing of any sort. The brutal murder had left her lovely face so untouched in its spirituality that until I heard her story, I had it in mind to recommend her for remission and release, upon the occasion of a Royal visit, when as Prison Visitor, I was asked to make such recommendations....

The Cross-eyed Boy then had been designated for the *gadi* after his Father's death, when his grandmother objected.

"He is not my Son's son. He was bought in the Bazaar!"

This is a favourite opening in a Zenana quarrel.

In modern times, to guard against it, children of consequence are born with all precautions taken. A woman doctor is in attendance, a priest and lawyer and state officials are in the ante-room: entrances and exits to the Palace are strictly guarded – and in the outer Courtyard sits a "firing squad", to wit an ancient retainer on his haunches, ready to put a match to the yet more ancient cannon, which will "speak" twice for a boy, once for a girl – in announcing the news to the world outside the Palace.

"He's a child bought in the Bazaar!"

Here entered the lawyers, or should I say lawyer? For the boy's mother had no access, even through the purdah, to the "Man-of-Business" and the reversioner who, instructed by the old lady, were supporting the charge. Fifteen years they had wrangled, the boy growing up as unkempt as the children of the servant who, taking pity on her mistress, had given him asylum in her *basti* (bazaar) home.

It was then that work brought me to the District: and news of one-who-might-help filtered through to the sad lady.

"And she will come and see you, and it is no cause for care that we cannot pay 'phees' (fees)," said the servant. "Yes – that is a word of truth, So-and-so told me."

It was sufficiently true about the "phees". I could not afford to work entirely un-fee-d: when clients could pay, they paid, and I felt that adequate payment was in trust for my next pauper case. Never did I refuse to enter a Zenana or a Court till demand had been satisfied – a practice of the time: and this is probably what impressed. Again, not being regularly enrolled was not the least of my advantages in a desire to help the needy: for I could take instructions direct, no Solicitor intervening.

When I went into Court, I was usually instructed by a *Vakil* or Pleader.

And so – I found myself inside the Zenana on a day when the Mother-in-law was on pilgrimage, and I heard the little Thakurani's story. But it was only outside the Zenana that I got hold of the Mother-in-law's version, of which my little lady knew and understood nothing, although it had already been presented and convincingly upholstered in the Law Courts.

Difficulties thickened: but we got the decision of the Lower Court reversed, partly upon a technical objection: and the conclusion of the whole matter was satisfactory – the Cross-eyed Boy got his *gadi*.

My own satisfaction, however, was tempered by the thought of those two women *vis-à-vis* in the Zenana. Would the child be killed? Would there be fresh litigation? What actually happened was amazing.

Shortly after the final decree, the child's mother died a mysterious death: and the grandmother took the cross-eyed one to her bosom, cursing all who had doubted (and backed her in doubting!) his legality: giving – in support of the correctness and formality of his birth – evidence for which the defence had sought in vain during that long-drawn-out litigation.

Of that mysterious death, one could get no details. The Hindu dead are burned immediately; nor, even were this not the case, would *post-mortem* examination be allowed in an Orthodox house.

But how often I have wished that I were a research student in toxicology, so unique was my opportunity, and so terribly wasted! During this period, I was myself practised upon. It was "poisoning by smell". My habit of taking my *Chhoti hazri* (little breakfast) in the open air – taming the squirrels which lived in a tree overhanging my bedroom terrace – saved me.

The servants found me one morning in a dead faint after receipt of a packet brought me from the Raj palace. They rushed for the Agency Doctor. When he revived me, he said that the open air had saved me, since out-of-doors the stuff had partly evaporated, and lost its power to kill.

"But what was it?"

"Do you remember that Catherine de Medici's victims smelt a bouquet, and never smelt again?" was his answer.

The case of my "Squirrel-Lady", as I called her, illustrated another variation of this mediæval knowledge.

It is loosely said that Hindu women have no rights to property. This is not correct. Hindu women have absolute rights in the property known as *Stridhan*, i.e. property which descends in the female line, and is secure from the manipulation of males. They have also when childless what is called a "life interest", but is far greater than such an interest as known to the Law of England, in their husbands' property after widowhood. Should there be an heir, the widow enjoys the property till the child attains majority, when she gets a maintenance allowance proportionate to the capacity of the estate and to her social status.

Generally speaking, all widows in a Joint Family have a right to residence and maintenance in the family house.

Till the English Married Women's Property Act, indeed, Hindu women might be said to have had greater rights than English married women. Incidentally, the difficulty was, and still is, in getting into touch with those rights.

THE "SQUIRREL-LADY" – THE ELEPHANT'S
CASE – THE IMPRISONED RANI

My "Squirrel-Lady" was the step-grandmother of a ruling Thakur. She had been greatly beloved of her husband, and dying, he left her her maintenance allowance, charged on certain villages, i.e. safeguarded against the uncertainties of cash payments from Raj coffers.

It was a Zenana in which lived four generations of women, and they had run from three to four at a time in equal status in each generation. It was a populous Zenana. The ladies lived in separate but adjoining quarters, each generation attended by its own waiting women.

Maybe the intrigue which drove the "Squirrel-Lady" from the Palace, was due to quarrels among the servants. I do not know.

When I was taken to see her, my "Squirrel-Lady" was living in great poverty in a house which she had built in the days of her prosperity (and rule – she was Senior Thakurani) for a favourite waiting woman. It was a considerable house, secured by a stout wall and an imposing gateway. She had been driven out of the Palace, carrying with her only her few personal belongings, her clothes and her "*stridhan*" jewels (gifts from her parents upon marriage); what she minded most was that the memorials she had raised to her husband's memory were deliberately desecrated. She had taken personal humiliation without a murmur. They would try insult to her husband; that would get her! She still gave no sign.

The waiting woman, who was married and lived with her husband in the Gate-house not far from the Raj, had kept in touch with her mistress, and, hearing of a plot against her life, had smuggled her out of her then quarters in a palanquin in the wake of one of the palace ladies who was passing through the town on her way to a shrine.

From that moment these selfless ones made the "Squirrel-Lady" their special care. They kept up what pretence of dignity they could. The husband armed with an ancient halberd patrolled the gate. They were simple folk and poor. But a Hindu widow needs little – milk and vegetables sufficed.

To eke out their resources the Faithful Two kept buffaloes, selling the milk in the Bazaar. The "Squirrel-Lady" never knew this. They let her think that she was still living on the proceeds of her jewels – which indeed had long since been exhausted on a pilgrimage made to the Ganges at Hurdwar.

The memory of this pilgrimage was ever with her. She sat on a leopard skin, the sign of a returned pilgrim, and all day she told her beads – the beads acquired of a Holy Man on that pilgrimage – her hand in the "sock" in which the beads rest, her lips moving. She sat cross-legged on the verandah, beside an inlaid sandalwood book-holder on which rested a copy of the *Shastras*.[17] And sometimes she would turn its leaves, memory murmuring familiar words.

The grey squirrels, with the three marks down their backs, where the Great God once stroked them in blessing, came fearlessly from the wild fig-tree in the courtyard to run all over her – head, shoulders, arms.

"Why do the squirrels love you so?" I asked her.

"Because," she said, "they know that I remember the time when I too was a squirrel, and played with them!" This was when she was about seventy years old, on my first visit to her. The Raj had not paid her her allowance, the income of her villages, for close on thirty years. And application to the Durbar was useless.

This was the kind of case which went eventually to the Agency: but the procedure was to do the best first, if you could, with the Durbar.

I was readily granted an interview, and was courteously received. I recounted the facts that I had heard from my client, and asked, "Is this a true story?"

"Perfectly correct."

"But she has a life interest in those villages. Is not the income hers?"

"So my grandfather intended: but father and son, we've found other uses for it. Look early tomorrow morning out of your window" (I was staying at the Agency), "you will see an English Master-of-the-Hounds, taking my hounds for a run – the best pack in Kathiawar. My step-grandmother's money runs that show. How can you expect me to let her waste it on pilgrimages!"

"But, is that justice?"

"Justice! What is justice? To a Ruler – justice is *his will*."

Then, as if to cheer me up:

"That's not the worst thing I've done. Has D—— come to you with her troubles" (he named an old aunt)? " She had lovely jewels; I've taken them all. They are worth more than the villages, and would, unlike the villages, never have been mine in the end. Would you like to see them? They are with me, unsold."

He spoke with the ease and charm of Him-who-must-be-obeyed, the complete Autocrat, sure of the impotence of others.

"Oh! Thakur Sahib, do put this right – " I begged; "I'll have to go to the A.C.G. Sahib if you do not; and I do want to prove that the head of the State can manage his own domestic difficulties."[18]

"You could sue me in my Durbar Court," said he, considering. "I'd like to hear you plead. I'll tell the Court Registrar to issue a *Sanad* at once. You can choose your own day for a hearing, after your departure from the State: and you'll come all the way to appear before me, to find – that the case is postponed by the Durbar – no reason given…. You will be entertained at the Guest House. I'll be delighted to see you, and shall beg you to fix another date…. We can carry on like this, till the old lady dies. Then her income will be mine, even according to your ideas of legality. Yet you will have done your duty by her in coming here so often for the case: so she will be happy, and you will be happy. We shall all be happy and satisfied."

I said a grave good-bye. I was not in a mood for sardonic humour: and I refused to see the "worse-than-that" jewels.

There was no alternative but the Agency – and here the issue was problematical. For though we might get our decree (and we did), it might be years before it was executed. It might indeed never be executed at all. For diplomacy took over after judgment. That is to say, the Agent or the Viceroy himself might recommend right action, but could not, or did not, compel. The only hope lay in waiting for the Thakur to want something which only the Viceroy could give. When he came with his request – "Certainly," he would be told; "but you must first pay the Grandmother Thakurani's dues."

We waited a long time. But at last, when I was away up North, came the Order in due form that my client was to have all her dues.

I was shortly to sail for England on a little holiday. I wrote her the joyful news, saying that I would come and see her *en route* to my boat and conclude the matter, seeing that she received her money.

When I arrived she told me a grisly tale.

Before she had got my letter, she received a communication purporting to come from her step-grandson, the Thakur Sahib.

"Why should we quarrel?" said the letter. "Are you not my grandmother? Wear the garment I send, and come to see me in token that the past is forgiven. Your old quarters in the Palace are ready for you."

The dear old "Squirrel-Lady" was all for forgiveness and peace, all for wearing the garment to please him. But her waiting woman, skilled in the intrigues of Palaces, said, "Don't answer – don't wear it; wait till our Miss Sahiba comes. We'll ask her advice."

So they waited.

Next day had come my letter.

I took charge of the garment, sending it to the Government Chemical Analyst.

Now, it should be stated that a Hindu widow wears only a single garment next her person.

The report of the Chemical Analyst was that the garment sent for examination was poisoned; if worn next the body, the wearer would have been poisoned through the pores of her skin – a "classic" poison, a "classic" death, painful and slow....

Before communicating with the Durbar, I asked her in what form she would like her money.

"Is it much?"

"Yes, a very great deal, arrears are granted." She thought a moment.

"Would it cause damage to the Durbar to pay it?"

"Well! I expect the Treasury would be very empty."

Then: "I am near attainment (death), I want very little now. I should like my waiting-woman placed so as never to want food and clothes, never to need to work, she and her husband, for a living. Can this be done? And then some bars of gold for a last pilgrimage to Hurdwar: and other bars for my waiting-woman to carry my ashes" ("bone-flowers" was the word she used) "to the Ganges, after my death."

The rest: "Could we give back to the Thakur Sahib's little son?" (An heir had lately been born.)

I was touched by her wonderful spirit of forgiveness. I could not forget that but for the waiting woman's caution she might have been murdered over this very matter of payment of the dues, which she was in so large a measure foregoing.

"You are not angry about – the garment, about all that has happened?"

"Why should I waste resentment?" said she. "When others hurt us, God resents it for us."

She told her beads awhile, then spoke again.

"I once had a daughter; she died. While she lived, if any had hurt her, would I have let her feel the hurt? I should have felt it for her. It is thus between us and God."

Her wishes were carried out. Annuities were bought for the waiting-woman and her husband, and money was allotted to her own pilgrimages in life and in death. The rest of the money was returned as a gift to the new little Prince.

I saw my "Squirrel-Lady" once again. It was when I was living in Calcutta. She came out of her way to see me on her return from the Hurdwar pilgrimage.

"And now a pilgrimage," said she, "to my Miss Sahiba."

She seemed to have shrunk to half her size and was bent nearly in two; so light she was, I could have carried her.

The Faithful Two were with her.

She insisted on seeing all over my house, and asked the uses of each room. She was very happy and even gay. "Thus, and thus, lives my Miss Sahiba."

She walked round the garden, looking at the flowers, and finally let an English friend, who was staying with me, take a photograph of her.

It was her last conscious pilgrimage. Six months later, those Faithful ones came to see me after carrying her ashes to the Ganges. She bade them do this to bring me her last messages.

Has she returned to the squirrels? I wonder. I never see the darling grey creatures with their bushy tails, without sending my mind back to the old saint who had learnt – how had she learnt? – that "Love is never irritated, never resentful."

This would seem to be the time, before I leave Kathiawar, Western India, to record an incident which falls into none of the categories of work I have enumerated.

It was when I was immersed in the Cross-eyed Boy's affairs, that a messenger came from the Panch Mahal's several miles distant, riding an ambling pony, and wearing the crooked little Kathiawar sword in his spotted muslin *kamar-band* (waistband), demanding audience.

The servants brought him to me where I sat, outside my tent door in the cool of the evening.

"Will the *Huzur* have an elephant for a client?" asked the man, making the triple sweeping salaam of the district, back bent.

"But of course," said I; "what has the elephant done?"

"It is not what he has done, but what has been done to him," said he. And he told his story.

A Thakur, grandfather to the man on the *gadi*, had a favourite beast, an elephant, to whom he left by deed a large plantation, together with a respectable sum of money for the support during the elephant's life of himself and his *Mahout* (keeper).

Through the reign of the donor's son, the elephant uprooted and consumed the sugar-palm trees of his estate, in lordly ease. But the grandson, then on the *gadi*, said, "A foolish waste. I have need of that valuable plantation for myself. The elephant can go get his food in the jungle."

News had reached the elephant, however, concluded the man, of my presence in the neighbourhood: and he wanted to know if I would accept a "brief" for him! The bearer of the message was the *Mahout*, whose income was of course also involved. I have not cited the actual words he used, but the purport thereof.

He laid a scroll at my feet as he finished speaking. It was a valid document, and duly executed.

I said, yes – we could bring an action on the deed; in the name of the elephant. But it would have to be in the Durbar Court, against the Thakur-Defendant who was also Judge in that Court, and he might not grant me a *Sanad* to appear.

Oh, yes, he would! – he himself had sent the *Mahout* to find me, had offered me hospitality, and had said that I might choose a day convenient to myself for the hearing.

I accepted the last courtesy, but refused the hospitality. I would plead my case, said I, and return to my camp.

In due course arrived a carriage and pair, and outriders with drawn swords. The Thakur had said that as the District afforded no public conveyances save a palanquin, he begged that I would use the Durbar carriage which he had sent, to save myself discomfort on the long journey.

Extraordinarily decent in an adversary! But then the mediæval manners of Raj States are like that; and I was only too glad to escape the palanquin-coffin-on-poles, especially as we were in the middle of the hot weather.

Arrived at the Palace, the Prime Minister and other Durbar officials met me: and there was my client, dressed in green and gold standing in the courtyard. He wore his "dress clothes" – a long emerald green cloth, heavily embroidered in gold; his forehead was painted in ancient devices in the same colours, so were his tusks, which were also fitted at the points with filigree gold metal: the lobes of his ears were tasselled with little ear-rings in gold and precious stones, and long "bobble-d" ear-rings of twisted silk in green and gold were slipped round his ears and hung to his feet. He had "rings on his fingers and bells on his toes" – to wit, heavy gold anklets with pendent tinkling bells.

Even his sturdy tail was adorned with circlets and pompoms of silk at intervals, down its entire length. He stood as tall as a house, and his trunk was upraised in the Raj Elephant's salute.

Never in my wildest fairy-tale dreams had I conceived such a client. He should be served with the best I had to give!

"What is the hour fixed for the hearing?"

"As your honour pleases," said the P.M.

"But when does the Court sit?"

"When your honour pleases. Will your honour first partake of refreshment? It is ready at the Guesthouse."

No. "Her honour" would not – thank you.

Then, when would I like to go into Court?

Immediately.

"I will inform the Raja Sahib" – and he departed, while I talked to my client, and told him to cheer up, his case was four-square, and he should eat sugar palms of his own "slaying" to the end of his days – lordly elephants such as this wind their trunks round the trees and bring them down, insert a tusk, sniff, and if the result is satisfactory, carry off the tree, rolled into their trunks, to the bedding-out place to be savoured at ease.

Presently the P.M. returned.

"The Raja Sahib is in Court. The Durbar Hall where the *Huzur* sits, is up those steps."

Steps and steps, gleaming white in the fierce sun, led from the courtyard, a story high; and on the top step, at the threshold of the Court, sat a thoroughbred English bulldog, looking very fierce and blue-blooded, his mouth open, and his tongue hanging out to cool itself.

I love all dogs, and automatically stooped to pat him as I entered. He licked my hand, and followed me to Counsel's table, curling up on the hem of my garment. The "Court" sat, very lightly clad indeed in a white muslin *achkan* (like a long shirt), on a roomy swing, hung with strong iron chains from the ceiling. This was apparently the Bench. Under the seat of the swing and attached to it was a musical box. As the Court swung to and fro the musical box played. "Champagne Charlie is my name" was the tune that greeted me: and the Court beamed upon me.

"That which you have asked is already granted."

Any Lawyer will realize my disgust at a win of that kind.

"But do you not wish to hear me plead my case?"

"Without doubt. Did my messengers not beg you to choose your own day and hour so that the hearing might be convenient? But – your demand is already granted – "

In the half-hearted way in which one would plead a cause, compliance already thrown at one, I proceeded to justify my plea. The elephant must not be disturbed in his tenure. The terms of the deed must be observed.

"They shall be," said the Court, without calling upon Counsel for himself! And then, to the official, who in that Court wrote the orders of the Court:

"Write," said he, "whoever interferes with the grant of the plantation to the elephant 'Heart's-Emerald' under his deed, shall be trampled to death by wild elephants."

The musical box still played, another tune now.

The Court turned to me. "Are you satisfied?"

I said, "Quite!" and bowing to the Bench left the Court, the dog conducting me to the exit.

Down the steps again, the P.M. following, obsequious, smiling and massaging his hands.

"That was very clever, Miss Sahiba."

"What was clever?" I said sulkily. "The Court gave me no chance to be clever. Success was thrown at me, even as I entered."

"Oh! but it *was* clever to make friends with the dog."

"Now, whatever do you mean?"

"Did your honour not know that the *Dog* decides the cases in this Court? When the Thakur-Sahib became Raja and Judge in the Durbar Court, he made this plan. He knew no law, and cases were long and tiresome. He devised a remedy. This favourite dog of his should sit at the door of the Court and decide all questions brought before the Durbar. Whomever the dog likes, to him the *Huzur* gives whatever he desires, even, as you saw, against himself and his own desires."

About this time my Brother had returned to India from his long sojourn in the West – Public School, Oxford, London. He was a Barrister and had decided to practise at the Allahabad High Court, United Provinces.

I went up North to help him settle into his house: and a thought which had for long been with me arrived at maturity. The work I was doing as a roving and privileged Practitioner of the Law was without doubt interesting: but it did not amount to beating out a path which other women could follow. It was too personal; privilege might be withheld from my successors, curiosity sated: and to what practical purpose was the beginning of work so well worth doing, if provision were not made for others to carry on?

In the interest of professional posterity, then, a recognized title to practise at the Bar seemed a necessity: and to obtain this in British India would mean the best recommendation to confidence. Work in Native States could still be continued from any British-Indian centre as headquarters.

Allahabad differed from Bombay, Bengal and Madras, in that here there were no Solicitors. Barristers took instructions direct. As I have already said, I had in practice found direct contact with clients useful. This was another point in favour of Allahabad.

Practitioners in the United Provinces included Barristers, *Vakils* (i.e. Graduates of Law, of the Universities of any Presidency), High Court Pleaders (qualified by a Special Examination, held by the High Court), and in the Districts, *Mukhtars*, etc. (less well qualified). Barristers had pre-audience: and the High Court had just instituted the distinction of Advocate, i.e. eminent *Vakils* of long standing, who were, in consequence of being termed "Advocate", admitted by grace of the

Court to the status and courtesies of Barristers in the Allahabad High Court. Tej Bahadur Sapru and Motilal Nehru were the *Vakils* so honoured.

As a Bachelor of Laws of the Bombay University I was entitled to be enrolled as a *Vakil*, and I made an application to this effect in 1897.

After consideration by the entire Bench – Sir J. Edge, C.J., presiding in what I believe was called "English Meeting", i.e. the Controlling and Administrative Department of the Court – I was told that as the University door was not their own special High Court door, the Court hesitated to make an innovation on the ground that I had cited. But if I would do the High Court Pleader's examination (their own creation) they would have power to act.

By this time I was sick to death of examinations, and this new one included proficiency in *Shikasta*. Now *Shikasta* (lit. "broken" writing, or writing "in ruins") is the running-hand of the Persian character, and a nightmare to decipher. Dots and strokes, both so essential to the distinguishing of letter from letter, with other characterizations, are omitted: and letters are joined which are only recognizable apart.

Shikasta is used in Court documents, though the language of the Courts is now Urdu: and its inclusion in the tests for this special High Court Examination was obvious.

Yes – I was thoroughly sick of examinations; but there could be no question of my not complying with the new condition – "one more river to cross" – and I buckled to the re-study of Hindu and Mahommedan Law, of the rubbish-heap of codified British-Indian Law, and the acquisition of *Shikasta*.

The bright spot of the adventure was my dear old Moslem Munshi who taught me Persian, Urdu and the reading of Court documents.

He was a character, and deserves a monograph. In due course I passed my Examination: but the High Court said, almost shamefacedly, that "on reconsideration" they felt it would be impertinent of an Indian High Court to admit women to the Rolls before England had given the lead.

It was a bad jar, and I could have said much in protest. After all, in matters of this kind, the advantage of India lay in the very newness to which I suppose the Court referred; in having, that is to say, unlike England, no traditions to outrage. She was therefore herself in the position of Leader; and it would have been fun if that particular Court had recognized this!

But protest would have been of no use. I was a single individual. At that time I could not produce even one other woman student of the Law: and I had no assurance that other women would want to follow my Profession.

There was nothing for it but to continue being a "rover", working from the end of a need to be met, not from that of an equal title with men to the reward of legal work.

And with this intention I set myself to collecting the opinions of experienced judges, lawyers, and administrators all over India.

I wrote first to such as I knew personally. I had found, said I, this or that – not stating my worst cases – instances where although the most efficient of men lawyers were indeed available, *Purdahnashins* had no possible means of access to or contact with them, the result being needless hardship and injustice.

I kept the lights as low as possible.

The answers were most gratifying:

"Oh, but we know worse...." They also added instances where the seclusion of women had prevented important evidence from being put before the Court, e.g. in property cases where the rights of women were in question.

Purdahnashins of the highest status, in strictest seclusion, are excused attendance as witnesses in Court. Their evidence is taken at their homes by a Commission. Judges and Lawyers both expressed a doubt on occasions as to the identity of the witness thus examined. The men might not see her for themselves. Again, how did they know that the witness spoke freely? They could not tell who were shut in with her behind the purdah: or what fears and coercions assailed her.

They might not even hear her voice – a third person being the medium of both question and answer.

When the witness attended Court, there was the like difficulty; she came in a palanquin accompanied by a male (claiming to be a relation) who acted as "carrier" during her examination, speaking to her through a slit in the doors of the palanquin and broadcasting her answers to the Court.

One of my correspondents, a Parsee Judge from Bombay (the least secluded of Provinces), told me an amusing story in this connection.

He had his suspicions during the progress of a certain case about the witness in a palanquin, and ordered the palanquin to be taken to his chambers for examination of the occupant by the matron of a hospital.

"You are quite safe," said the Matron, the palanquin duly deposited in the Judge's Chambers, behind closed doors. "Come out now."

She pushed back the palanquin shutters, and drew the curtain – a bearded old man stumbled to his feet and confronted her!

An experience of my own in later years was equally illuminating. The High Court of Calcutta appointed me Commissioner to take at her house the evidence of a *Purdahnashin* in the matter of an important reference then before the Court.

The requisite address had been supplied by the litigants and was on my commission.

I drove down to the house indicated, and it was evidently a surprise to the men who received me that I was a woman.

"Oh, well!" I said. "It's better still, is it not? I can go into the Zenana and examine the lady face to face."

"Oh, no! You would not like that. Zenanas are very shut-up places. You will get ill. Sit here, outside the purdah, on that red-plush chair we have put ready for the Commissioner."

I said I knew what Zenanas were like, and must go in, thank you.

But they were very reluctant to let me pass that purdah. So I said, "I'll return my Commission to the High Court, stating the reason why it has not been executed" – and I walked towards the door.

"Wait a moment," begged the men; and I waited while they talked together in a corner.

They came back to me. "Are you determined to see the lady?"

"Yes! I have told you that I must see her and be satisfied of her identity – or I go away, my work not done."

"Then," said the spokesman dejectedly, "she is not here. I will take you to her."

We drove twenty minutes before we arrived at the right house. I had been received by the representatives whose interest was in opposition to hers! Whom I would have interviewed behind that purdah, in the wrong house, I never discovered.

The "spotlight" case of this bit of the road was that of my "Imprisoned Rani"; and it came to me in a curious way.

An old priest appeared at my brother's house one morning. He said he had been tracing us from town to town. He did not know our name: but he was looking for "The Brother and Sister Ballisters".

His search finally narrowed to Allahabad, and he was directed to our yellow bungalow with the orange honeysuckle climbing over the porch.

The story he told was pathetic.

He was Chief Priest in a north-country Raj, which his ancestors had served before him, being rewarded with a grant of lands. His patron, the Raja, was sonless. He had two daughters, and consoled himself by educating the elder "as if she were a man", which meant, in their vernacular, the Hindi tongue. Her aptitude was so great that she even edited a Hindi newspaper from the Zenana, and her father desiring to keep her beside him, deferred her marriage.

She was sixteen when her mother felt that marriage could be delayed no longer, and the Confidential Priest, complete with horoscope, was sent on a tour to find a suitable husband. At Benares, he met another priest on a like errand, looking for a suitable wife for the adopted son of the Dowager Rani of Amarpur.

"The lady must have brains and be educated," said he of Amarpur.

"The very thing," said the other. "My lady is cleverer and more learned than a man."

They compared their respective horoscopes, and found them to agree in essentials. The stars of each were favourable to the other, and marriage arrangements went forward.

Now the Amarpur priest had omitted some vital items of information. The prospective bridegroom was "wanting" – "God had made him a Fool" – as said his royal bride, later on – had said it in no accusation or bitterness, indeed as if speaking of one sanctified by the notice of God – even to his detriment.

And, his natural father and uncle were Ministers of the Amarpur Raj. These men had plans other than the Dowager-Rani Adoptive Mother's.

They had in fact already bespoken a non-Royal bride, meaning to control the Raj upon the death of the Dowager. She was *Purdahnashin*, and they were all-powerful: so that on the marriage day two wedding processions made gay the streets of the town. First came the royal lady's. And, looking on her, her mother-in-law, the Dowager, so loved her that the *Runumai*, or "seeing-of-the-face money", which she gave her, was greater than was ever known in the history of the Family: and is spoken of to this day. The second procession, which the Dowager did not see, took place after an interval of a few hours; the Raja being married secondly to the non-Royal choice of his Ministers.

That his lady was however Pat (Chief) Rani was some consolation to the Confidential Priest who saw both *tamashas* (shows): but he felt terribly deceived, and did not know how to face his patron.

Custom in Amarpur shut the door on all connection with the Royal Bride's people instantly the marriage ceremonies were concluded. The Pat Rani was not allowed even the ministrations in her new "Chapel" of the Confidential Priest.

And her father in his northern hills had perforce to be content with custom. One comfort was that his daughter could write: and there was great rejoicing over the birth of her first son – rejoicing turned to mourning at report of his instant demise.

The letters of the Pat Rani were restrained: no details were given, and her mother might not visit her. It is contrary to general custom for an orthodox Hindu mother to go to the house of her son-in-law, even when her daughter is in trouble.

According to Raj custom elsewhere, the child might have been born in its maternal grandmother's house. But the Amarpur priests said that their own custom forbade that.

Soon letters stopped coming altogether, and the Pat Rani's parents were miserable. They could find no way of getting past that misfortune: and her father fretted at his helplessness. In about five years from the date of his daughter's marriage, he died.

But the Pat Rani about this time did write a letter, though not to her home. She wrote to the nearest British official, saying that she was again about to be a mother, and that she claimed British protection for the birth of her child. She said that two children had already been killed after birth: the first being stifled in tobacco fumes, the second strangled.

Her children were sons, the second lady's all daughters, and the Raj officials said that the Pat Rani had bewitched her co-wife. The Dowager had been very kind to her, but she had died within a year of the marriage, so that the poor little lady had been alone in her trouble, and was still defenceless within the Raj.

"I claim protection from the British Government for the birth of the Raja's heir," said the Pat Rani in her letter; and it was then she added, "The murders are not his fault: God has made him a Fool." She begged the British official to make his own investigations as to the truth of her story. He did so: and apparently found it correct, for he arranged for the removal of the Pat Rani to Sihur, a fortress five miles distant from Amarpur.

It was a fort in good repair, had a reliable wall loopholed for defence, a relic of early wars, and a very strong gateway. There were indeed two gateways with an inner and an outer moat. The British official put a guard on the Outer Gate, Indians from a British Tehsil.[19] That was wise, but he made one mistake – he allowed the Amarpur State to pay the wages of the guard.

The lady was to receive a maintenance allowance as long as she remained in the fort. Had he known more about conditions in Raj estates, he would have made the guards' wages pass either through the hands of the Tehsildar at the nearest British outpost, or of the lady herself.

It was understood that there was no quarrel between the Raja and the Pat Rani; and that the Raja would visit her whenever he pleased. Apparently (as I heard later from the Pat Rani) he had "pleased" only once, when, while out hunting, he "lost his way" into the fortress through the guards' private wicket; and then after sitting looking at her for a while, said, "Let me go, lest I be moved to compassion and help you!"

The Pat Rani's third son was born in the fortress and stayed alive....

The story thus far had filtered to the Pat Rani's people through the British Official: and had greatly reassured her old mother. But that was ten years previously. A new Administrator was now in charge of the District who knew nothing of the lady in the fortress, and said he could not interfere in the affairs of an estate not under his control.

The Confidential Priest had tried several times to get access to the fortress; but found unfriendly guards on the gate who threatened to shoot at sight any messenger from the "prisoner's" relations.

It was at this stage that the Confidential Priest – remorse for his part in arranging this marriage ever gnawing at him – heard of me, and came seeking.

"Would I go and see the Pat Rani, and at least bring news of her to her mother, taking whatever steps I might find necessary, according to her situation, thereafter."

The story of this adventure as it unfolded itself, I told at the time, August 1899, in letters to a friend in England, at whose instance the Letters were published.[vi] [[vi] 'Concerning an Imprisoned Rani', *Nineteenth Century and After*, October 1901.]

Here, I will only say, briefly, that I went by train and palanquin – a tortuous journey not without its excitements; that using a mixture of bluff and authority, I made my way into the fortress past the guard, and found the lady with her son, a boy of nine years of age; that they were in abject poverty, living on the terrace of the topmost story of the fort; their furniture two string beds and a chair; their provisions a little rice, and pulse and grain; no milk, no vegetables. The villagers just outside the fortress had been forbidden to supply her with anything. She never, of course, left the fortress, but a half-witted Brahmin brought her monthly, from a distant village, her meagre stores, and drew water for her from the well in the courtyard. To eke out the stores, the Pat Rani herself ate only one slight meal a day. She cooked and kept the little terrace as clean as she could, sewed garments for the boy made out of her *saris*, and read over and over again all old newspapers which she could find at the fort.

("I should have gone mad if I let myself think," she said.)

One little thing which annoyed was a religious taboo; neither she nor the half-wit might use a broom (that would have been against caste rules). But she thought of a way out. The boy not having yet been tonsured, or given the sacred thread of initiation, was outside caste for the moment, and he was set to do the sweeping.

Every room in that fortress was the home of malodorous bats. The terrace, in reality a flat roof verandahed off where they slept, was at least airy, and the Pat Rani showed her intelligence in retiring to it when deprived of the servants whom the British official had seen accompanying her into her retreat.

The next deprivation was that of her maintenance allowance. For two and a half years she had had not a penny, and only the dry stores which the half-wit brought her.

Her supreme anxiety was for her son. He was still the only son – though girls came thick and fast in the Junior Rani's Zenana at the Capital.

And the nights were her terror. She decided not to sleep at all, and kept her vow, walking up and down armed with an old sword, while the child slept. Luckily the door which gave on to the staircase was iron-studded. She kept this barred and bolted always: and in the afternoons, the boy fed, her household work done, she repaired the sleepless night, while the child played beside her, and as it were guarded himself. For he knew he must wake her if a soul – whosoever – approached.

She was wonderful in her fearlessness.

Having got my facts and cheered her up, I returned to Allahabad, and arranged through British intervention for servants and food to be sent her. Later, after discovering how I could rightly serve her interests, I went back again with two empty palanquins to bring her and the boy to the guardianship of her mother in British India. Permission to take this course was given in response to an application put in by the mother, it having been proved that the Pat Rani was virtually imprisoned in circumstances originally designed for her protection.

The second journey was thrilling. I was warned that the Amarpur people had got wind of my programme and had planned to dacoit us on the homeward journey and carry off the boy.

Two armed Tehsil peons had been provided by the British Administration for our protection, but we lost them, diverted by some trick of the Amarpur folk.

I determined to try and outwit the dacoits. I had my own servants with me, and sent my headman on by the regular route, telling him to sit by the village watch-fires at night and listen to the *gap* (gossip); though travelling quickly, so as to reach the fortress, in any case by the afternoon of the second day, when we were due to leave for Allahabad. I myself, with the other servants, the extra palanquin and a rabble of thirty bearers, went a short cut across country, arriving at the fortress only eight hours before we must again take the road. Would that space of time be long enough to dig the lady and her son out of their prison?

It all depended on how the great excitement of an escape affected my little lady.

It was indeed a ghastly day. She broke down, and was hysterical, presenting difficulty after difficulty. She could not travel except under the Gold Umbrella of Royalty in a heavy ancient Raj palanquin found in a go-down near the Guard-house. The poles of this relic were rotten, and the bearers refused to carry it.

Again, she could not travel apart from her son: he and she must be in one palanquin.

I conceded that.

And in the same palanquin must be put her *huqqa*, all her personal belongings, the food cooked for the journey, and her pots and pans and cooking vessels! I knew that cooking and eating vessels she must take, for not being a widow she might not use those found in her mother's house. But it would have been no use suggesting that *all* the luggage might go together in one of our spare palanquins. She was too upset to be reasonable.

So I contented myself, since time was racing, with persuading her to do without the Gold Umbrella, but (*baksheesh* making the bearers willing) I packed her and the son and the luggage into the Raj "relic".

"At least let me have the embroidered-*kincob* cover," she begged. And we threw it over the palanquin.

Quick then, past both moats, through the outer gateway.

Here my headman met us, breathless, and took me aside to give his news. We were to be dacoited at seven o'clock that evening on the regular route, the way he had come. I had to make an instant decision. We must take the cross-country road in the opposite direction and start at once, for any moment our change of plan might be discovered.

It was extra important now not to risk the heavy worm-eaten "relic". So since hysterics could avail my Pat Rani nothing outside the gates, I turned the entire guard inside the fortress and shut the gates on them. We then put one of our light spare palanquins close beside the relic, covering both with the betraying *kincob* (it was useful now), set the doors between wide, and made the Rani and her son creep from the relic to the other, transferring also their impedimenta.

The *kincob*, having served its use as a purdah, I firmly folded up: my *ayah* (maid) I put into the second spare palanquin: and we started off in a long "line of march" – I first, and the Rani's palanquin between mine and the *ayah's*. The men-servants and "relief" palanquin-bearers brought up the rear.

Every nerve was a-stretch throughout that devious journey: the fields of tall corn, on a pitch-dark night, which might conceal anything, a squad of dacoits for all we knew; the open spaces, where we ourselves were only too visible; rough ground where the bearers had to be encouraged every five minutes – and then the early dawn when things look gloomiest, and the long hot day that followed, though this was happily in safer territory.

But the journey had its humours in the songs made by the palanquin-bearers about the Rani and myself – personal descriptions, and conjectures (for instance) as to how much we ate! I was slim in those days. Also, my not being in purdah, had evidently greatly intrigued country folk unaccustomed to women of my race – Who could I be?

"She spoke like the *Burra Lat Sahib* (Viceroy) to the guard, turning the men in, shutting the gates on them. *And they obeyed.* Who can she be!" sang the leader. And the Chorus chaunted – "Who *can* she be?

"She wears garments of silk, but" (contemptuously) eats only one bread a day."

The Chorus – "Half-a-bread!…"

We travelled from 5 p.m., when we had left the fort, all that night, and all the next day, with only one break for food for the Rani and the bearers – getting to railhead at 10 p.m. on the second night. Here a reserved railway carriage, next to my own compartment, was secured for my charges, and in due time she was delivered safely to her mother.

The end of the story was happy. A Lunacy Commission made suitable arrangements for the care of the poor Raja: the boy was put under British protection and his estate administered till his majority should give him the *gadi* of his inheritance.

III A GLIMMERING OF
HOW TO HELP

GOVERNMENT RECOGNITION – THE COURT OF WARDS, 1904: AN EXPERIMENT – "SITTING DHARNA" – "FLESH AND BLOOD" INDIA

About this time my health broke down, and I was ordered by the Doctors out of India. Arrived in England, I soon got rested, and it seemed to me that this was a good time for stock-taking, in reference to the mission which I believed to be mine.

I had learnt certain facts, and had learnt them not only from my own experience, but out of the mouth of expert male authority. I had, in short, learnt that the work which I had prescribed for myself met a real need: that it was worth-while and satisfying, and should be carried on after my time.

But I had also learnt that, if I would make such work possible for other women, I must find primarily the *right type of woman* – with the equipment, or at least some of the equipment, in the vernacular and legal training, which to myself had been indispensable. While the ability to live hard days, to face rough travelling, and to forego (at this stage at any rate) professional ambition and the rewards of a profession, was also essential.

I knew of no European or Indian woman, at that time, whom I could ask to adopt the life which I was living. Nor would it be fair to ask them to test their vocation for it, unless their imagination had been fired as mine had been, by accident or circumstance; because there was, then, no recognizable goal in sight.

What we needed as an alternative was an official post, which would serve both the needs of my *Purdahnashins*, and the necessity (for the worker) of earning a livelihood.

Now in the course of my study of conditions and possibilities in India, I had found that the Provincial Governments had themselves become aware of the problems which were "my meat day and night", and had prescribed a way of help for the secluded widows and minor children of deceased landed proprietors. They had passed the Court of Wards Act, which enabled the Government to take under management and administration the estate of a minor heir pending majority. If the widow were childless, she might apply for administration in her own behalf.[20]

The Act also included provision for arrangements as to the health and education of women and children and for the general care of dependents of deceased proprietors.

Here was an opportunity which might afford exactly what I wanted for my Professional posterity!

The Act was excellent; but the Secluded Woman was still behind her barriers, still outside direct contact with her "rights", or with the officials – all men – who would act as her Administrators and men of business.

Moreover, no provision whatever seemed to have been made for the effective implementing of the sections as to health and education. Under the Act all intervention in the household was to be with the consent of the women themselves. It was ridiculous to suppose that men could get the requisite access for persuasion to what was necessary, could understand or help to adjust customs and conditions behind the purdah. The very passing of a Court of Wards Act implied that the Government was aware of the handicaps to be faced. Was it not possible to plead that the Government had in fact bound itself thereby to make available the help of a woman in the administration of the Act?

In the language of the Secretariat, was not a woman Zenana official "*indicated*"?

I talked the matter over with my friends in London, and was advised that a scheme should be drafted, well buttressed with cases, for submission to the India Office; and that, while it was before the Secretary of State, a question should be asked in the House.

I set to work upon the scheme, outlining the duties of an Adviser to the Court of Wards, i.e. to *Purdahnashins* and Minors belonging to the Estates administered by the Court.

I proposed that such an officer should be attached to headquarters in every Province where the Act was in force, and that her sphere should include help as to Health and Education, as well as in the Legal or business difficulties of the women: that she should in fact be the *liaison* officer between the Zenana and the Government, as she would in effect be the *liaison* officer between the Zenana and the outside world. I explained that it would be necessary to clothe her with authority, because her position would not be easy, since the appointment, in its protection of women and children, would virtually mean interference with the intrigue which is the breath of all Raj Estates.

The then Secretary of State was Lord Midleton, members of whose family I had known as long ago as my undergraduate days. He was so kind as to give me ample opportunity to explain the situation, in regard both to the interests of the women and children under Government protection, and to the duties of the Government towards its wards.

Neither Lord Midleton, nor, later, Lord Morley,* had realized in the slightest degree (why should they?) the position of these women and children, and the scope of the Court of Wards Acts. Lord Morley indeed thought that the Court of Wards was a regular Court of Law.

In due course arrived the moment when a Question would help. The Hon. Arthur Elliot and his charming wife (née Madeline Shaw Lefevre) were amongst the beloved friends of these days. And I was advised that the presentation of the subject – the position of Secluded Women in India – could be in no better hands than Mr. Arthur Elliot's, acceptable as he was to both sides of the House – if he would consent to sponsor it.

He generously did consent, and I turned my papers over to him. His questions were favourably received and the House was told that "the matter was under the consideration of the Secretary of State".

This would of course take time, as the Governments of India had to be consulted. And a gracious friend, H.H. Princess Marie Louise,* invited me to accompany her on a visit to Ceylon during the tiresome period of waiting for the result of the reference. So in the winter of 1903, we set sail for Colombo on a Pacific liner. Ceylon was an experience unlike anything that has happened to me before or since, except when in the same beloved company I went to Burma in 1906.

Things now moved more quickly than our rosiest expectations. While I was in Ceylon the Government of Bengal asked me if I would work my own scheme, as presented to the Secretary of State, in connection with the Province of Bengal.

I can recall every detail of the day on which this communication reached me. I took it out with me to the beautiful Lake at Kandy, and I sat down to meditate. Somehow I had never foreseen this possibility. I had thought that if the Government did approve my scheme I might be commissioned to hunt for a likely candidate and that her post would be created while she was in training and then offered to her like a pat of butter on a lordly dish, the frog sitting atop, patterned to every detail.

Of myself I had thought as returning to my Native States and my roving *Sanad*: but with a joyful heart, because now "posterity" was provided for.

Nor had I thought of Bengal as the theatre of the scheme. In those days Bengal seemed to me the uttermost part of the Earth. It would mean learning new languages, new customs, new everything.

But I was thrilled to the core – at the amazing luck of being asked to stage my own dream; and there never was any doubt of my answer.

Had I been less thrilled about eventual possibilities, the conditions attached to "the experiment" might have given me pause, especially at that moment; for the salary was to be only a retaining fee, with liberty to take professional work outside the Court of Wards, as and if Court of Wards duties permitted – until the Government was assured of the success and advisability of the Scheme, when whole-time service would be considered. I was in fact to prove at my own expense the faith that was in me.

It was to be a day of thrills. From the lake-side at Kandy I proceeded to the Bank, to hear that one result of the Japanese War was to smash Watson's, in which Bank I had put a great part of the little legacy which had made my holiday possible!

But the wind was tempered to the shorn. To my amazement I discovered that this unexpected obstacle was more of an exhilaration than a depression.

And had not Jowett said to me years ago:

"When obstacles exhilarate you, thank God, for you are at last beginning to grow." So I lifted up my heart and re-tackled the morning's puzzle; for the "next step" must now be groped for in this new rubbish-heap of worthless securities. I had meant to go back to England and conclude there with the Secretary of State the arrangements about the Court of Wards post. I could not do that now; I must leave details to the Government of Bengal and accept forthwith the opportunity to launch my scheme. A consequence I had not foreseen faced me later on – in 1916 – when the conditions and salary attaching to a permanent post were determined: and I discovered that the accident of my initial acceptance in India had condemned me to the lower status, i.e. to the status and "equations" of officers not educated in and appointed from England. But by that time Life had given me every excuse for learning how to measure things otherwise than "with thumb and finger", and the urge to continue working after retirement – which is one consequence of that mistake as to the *venue* of my negotiations with Bengal – is perhaps the happiest ending which I could have asked to a story packed with delight, whatever the circumstances.

But to go back to 1904 – I accepted the then vague offer of the Government and arrived in Calcutta to join my appointment on May 15th, 1904.

I found that I would be attached to the Board of Revenue and would work under the direction of the then two Members of the Board. That instructions to give me they had none: that they would simply notify the cases of difficulty, give me assistance as to how to get to the requisite localities, put me in touch with local Government Officers – and leave the rest to myself.

That I would serve what are now known as the Provinces of Bengal, Bihar and Orissa, and Assam; that my retaining fee would only just about cover the rent of an unfurnished flat; and that I must provide my own office accommodation, since liberty to continue my professional life implied the necessity of Chambers, which the Government would allow me to treat as my office.

There did not seem much prospect of my earlier type of work in these new circumstances. But at any rate I had a chance of making my experiment – it was up to me to make it a success, in spite of or just because of these further difficulties. And it was a very joyous Pilgrim who took the new and untried road.

I want to say here how glad I was that my dear old friends Lord and Lady Hobhouse were still alive to hear of the Court of Wards experiment. Lord Hobhouse had been Law Member during the Vice-royalty of Lord Ripon, and they were both tremendously interested in hearing about old landmarks and the changes in the face of modern Calcutta: while the fact that the Government had acknowledged a need, which I had been hunting in the dark, made them very happy.

Lord Hobhouse was, alas! on his deathbed when my Calcutta letters reached them; but he said, "The rough bit of the road is over for Cornelia" – which I took as both prophecy and blessing when Lady Hobhouse reported it to me.

It is difficult to write about those two beloved friends in words which will be printed. They were unlike anyone else in the world. Lord Hobhouse represented for me "Rectitude" and "Unafraidness".

He combined clarity of vision, sound judgment, and an immediate taking of the road which seemed to him right, with what for want of a better word might almost be called contempt of the adverse opinion of whomsoever, except that he showed also a seemingly irreconcilable and touching courtesy towards the opinion of others in relation to the so-different road which they themselves had elected to take, and a gentleness and loving compassion towards all created things which I have never seen equalled.

The Hindu saint cultivates the slaying of all personal feeling in order that he might obtain detached vision. Lord Hobhouse seemed to have both the detached vision which is the Hindu ascetic's ideal and the warm human lovingness of the man who lives among his fellows with his heart stirred to the core.

There was no assumption of greatness about him, no advertisement of the things he had done in implementing the great public reforms for which he was responsible; alike when he took me to Privy Council or on walks in his dear Somerset countryside (where I stayed with them in the autumn), he treated me as if our eyes were on the same level…. There was one rule which all his young companions learnt to remember. On these country walks he loved best to talk of the country. And much lore of mushrooms and toadstools (we often went mushroom gathering), of tree and meadow and farmyard, have I learnt from him.

They both loved young people – and filled the house with them all holidays. Their house, whether in town or country, was one of my "English homes": and I loved my visits.

Lady Hobhouse was also unique in her way, with a real wit and an understandingness which both stimulated and soothed. I adored her. On my holidays I would find a programme of delights which each had compiled for the days ahead. I loved it best when we carried these out all three together, I sitting bodkin between them. How often in the years since they have slipped out of sight have I not paused to ask myself what they would advise?

"Never be active in your own defence – be ceaseless in the defence of others," was one of his maxims.

Sir Frederick* and Lady Pollock were among the beloved friends of Oxford days who also rejoiced about the Court of Wards appointment: and who remain in intimate connection with my life, unto this last.

The "Dean of Jurists", Dr. Murray of Columbia University happily described Sir Fred when honouring him on behalf of America upon the English lawyers' visit to that country in the autumn of 1929. How glad I was to be at the ceremony in New York, and to see the enthusiasm which America knows so well how to express for those whom she delights to honour.

But Sir Frederick must be a "Dean" in other departments of thought as well. There would seem to be no subject about which he cannot enrich one's knowledge, and with a beauty of language too rare in these days. So at least I have found, who have gone to him as to my *guru* in a thousand difficulties. While at their home dear Lady Pollock, the most selfless of beautiful hostesses, has made for me many memories and many contacts in the legal, social and literary world.

My first Bengal case related to a Raj lately deprived of its head, compelling the Widow to come under the Court of Wards during the minority of her son. It involved extricating the *Dewan* from a charge of forgery. I remember a rapid journey taken to and from Darjeeling (Government Summer Headquarters) in the extreme heat to obtain withdrawal of a prosecution upon the accidental discovery that the forgery had been committed by a late member of the family, and that the *Dewan* had shouldered the blame to save the honour of the Raj. This faithful old man never knew what ended an ordeal which he was prepared to face, without the remotest chance of escape: but he did connect his freedom with my arrival, and was touchingly grateful, and for ever observant of all directions I had to give concerning the estate. He was a rigid Hindu, and worshipped the Goddess *Kali*, who is believed to thirst for human blood.[21] I had realized from the beginning that I could never understand my Wards, unless I understood their attitude of mind towards Religion: and I had not before met the Goddess Kali. So I said to him one day, when he was late over some official duty, because he had been lying prostrate before the Goddess:

"Beni Babu, you are kind enough to call me your 'Father and Mother', tell me what you would do if the Goddess Kali thirsted for my blood?"

He went ashen, and raised joined hands in reverence at mention of her name.

"God forbid, Madam," said he, "for I should have to give it!"

The heir was just married to a lovely little girl. It was the first year of marriage, and throughout that year her head must be bowed, and her mouth shut in the presence of anyone older than herself. This seemed to me pathetic, and I used to tickle her under her chin to make her look up at me. Her great eyes, and her charming expression, were aspects of beauty which I felt I could not miss. And the kind Zenana would go into fits of laughter at this evasion of ritual; for we had already begun to love one another: and when, after arranging for the heir's education, and for the health of various members of the family, I said that my little Boho-Rani (the bride) must also be educated – no objection was raised. Indeed, after a while others in the Zenana begged to share the lessons which a carefully selected governess was giving according to a time-table drafted by myself.

It was a Joint Family, that is, the heir's mother and sisters, the married sisters older than himself, with their husbands, as also other and collateral relations, lived in the Raj House. And questions about the maintenance allowances of the women, chiefly of the Raja's widow, made a good deal of work. The women were always getting into debt, vicariously, through their men relations about the place – and had to be disentangled ... while the gentle little Rani widow, herself spending long hours in prayer and meditation, was at the mercy of a diversity in intrigue which took one's breath away.

One compensation in the crowded Zenana lay in the presence of the grandchildren – and personally I was glad that they were under a roof within my jurisdiction, for the application of Infant Welfare principles was badly needed.

"How do you know how much food to give your baby?" I asked of one of the young mothers.

"I tie a string round his waist, and when the string breaks," said she anxiously, "has he not had enough?"

If you were regarded as a friend, the dear women came to you about everything, trustingly: and what was more amazing, followed your advice.

I had to "vet" the prospective bridegroom of the unmarried daughter of the house: and it says a good deal for the readiness with which the women opened their tradition-crusted hearts and minds to new ideas, that the Rani should have said to me, "I want you to tell me if he looks sickly" (herself she could only peep at him through a hole in the purdah), "and if he looks good and kind." She was evidently learning something: her test was not only, as formerly – the right caste, the right conjunction of horoscopes, the advisable income or prospect of income.

I had the experience of budgeting for marriage ceremonies, and of mastering a hundred new things about the scale of values of the orthodox Hindu.

There came a day too, alas! when I had to make the "saving-of-the-soul" budget for my dear widowed Rani Sahiba friend: and to see it carried out.

Her death was a mystery, which even I, privileged though I was, could not investigate.

She had for some time been suffering from a disease which needed careful watching: she had submitted at my request to the attendance of a woman doctor, and among the doctor's directions was a caution that a certain article of diet would prove fatal.

I'd seen the Rani on my way to office about 10 a.m. and she was worried about a quarrel with a male relative over a sum of money the replacement of which had become imperative, being excused by the Rani's death alone.

I comforted her, saying I would come in again on my way back from office, and see what could be done.

That afternoon I was sent for in haste – the Rani Sahiba was in the coma which precedes death. Later enquiries revealed that the male in question had discovered the doctor's injunction, and had bribed a servant to admit him to the Rani (who did not observe purdah in regard to him).

He came bearing a dish which he said he had prepared with his own hands in order to express penitence for the quarrel; he was so terribly sad at heart, would she show her forgiveness by eating his offering instead of her midday meal? The forgiving creature ate: with the result reported.

I stayed with her all that night. She never regained consciousness, not even though the priests rang bells and burnt melted butter under her nose. They were trying to revive her that she might dedicate her private property to the priesthood. A final demand was to take her down three flights of stairs that she might breathe her last on Mother Earth. I gathered that this would mean bumping her on each step, a desperate last clutch at that gift-making return to consciousness.

But this I forbade, the heir and the old *Dewan* supporting me. Only when the doctor said it could make no difference, that her body was past feeling outrage

– did I let them carry her out; and it was on the landing of the Zenana floor that the breath left her body.

There was one pretty custom connected with that; for a month thereafter, every night at the hour of the "second twilight", the union of light and darkness, little Boho-Rani would light a "death lamp" – a wick floating in a flat earthen pot of oil – and set it down at the place where the dear Mother-in-Law Rani's own lamp of life had flickered out.

It was meant to tell her that she was not forgotten.

The "Saving-of-the-Soul" budget was a great business. I found that at the expenditure of Rs.20,000 (£1,500) we could buy sinlessness for my Rani through one thousand rebirths. They had claimed three times that amount, but examination of precedents, etc., showed that Rs.20,000 would suffice: and it was all that the estate could afford and which I could advise the authorities to sanction. With this amount we fed Brahmins; we made gifts in kind and money to the priesthood; we hired priests to sit in the courtyard and pray for days together – beside a capacious mirror placed where it would catch the Rani's spirit passing by – if she deigned thus to express her approbation of the prayers.

The Legal Adviser not only found this of intense interest, but was able to prevent catastrophe.

Thus at the feasting she says to the Prime Minister, "For how many Brahmins have you made provision?"

"For three thousand."

The gates were wide, and they were coming and coming and had already exceeded that number.

This I pointed out.

"But it is unlucky to shut the gates," said he, worried, but facing the inevitable.

"But if I had them shut?"

"Oh, that would not matter. Luck and ill-luck concern the Believer alone."

In the courtyard great cauldrons of food were steaming. Here was one stirring the rice, and ever boiling more and yet more. On the verandahs sat Brahmin cooks cutting up red pumpkins and brown-green *brinjals* in their shiny skins: skinning potatoes, grinding curry stuffs, dancing red-yellow grains of pulse in the winnowing pan. Other Brahmins ran to and fro, serving the food as it was made ready. All was orderly confusion at which the women peeped from the third-floor balcony. They were the disciples of priests at the expense of whose appetites we were buying merit: and they sat in rows, hungry and clamorous, before plates and cups of great dry leaves held together with thorns. Scarce could they be served fast enough.

"But how long will they sit here?" I asked of the old P.M.

"Till they are fulfilled" – was his delightful answer. And it gave me courage to shut the gates!

The administration of the Rani's private estate was a very big undertaking: her affairs were terribly entangled. And, in answer to the usual advertisement in the *Gazette*, crowds besieged my office, bringing with them bonds for more money in the aggregate than we could pay.

I found that, since recovery was doubtful, the custom was to set down on paper three times (at least) what was legally due. So I announced that I would pay the amounts actually due, immediately: that if the Creditors did not care to accept such amounts, they could sue in the Courts of Law for the sums named in the Bonds.

The actual amounts were in all cases accepted – and I was feeling light-hearted, when a shrivelled-up old Brahmin dressed in a loin-cloth, his caste marks, and the zouave of bones of his anatomy, appeared before me to make a claim for a sum which would have bought us a second millennium of sinlessness.

Why had he not sent in his claim within the period advertised for presentation of claims?

He was an old man and did not understand rules.

Well! Where was his bond, or proof of any sort which might support his demand?

He had none.

It appeared upon cross-examination that there was really no debt; that there was nothing due on any ground whatsoever.

"But I want Rs.20,000," said the desiccated one, "and if I am not paid that amount, I will *sit dharna*," i.e. he would fast on the doorstep and die, and his blood would be upon the head of the person from whom he claimed the "debt": and upon her descendants to the hundredth generation.

I said, "The 'debt' must be claimed from me." And I invited him to *sit dharna* on my doorstep.

I looked forward to this illustration of a custom which I believed had died with Abbé Dubois; and I was determined what to do – I would make him comfortable in my spacious garden, under competent observation, removing him in an ambulance to a Hospital the moment that inanition was like to prove fatal.

But the wily old man outwitted me!

Next morning I found him sitting under the *pipal* tree at the foot of an image of *Ganesh*, the god of Wisdom, in the Raj compound.[22] We all realized the added intimidation of the position he had chosen. "Ganesh was backing him!" was what he wished to suggest.

The Zenana was a-twitter with alarm. The women sat awaiting me, their conjoint jewels spilt upon a table, a dazzling scintillation, the motes in a sunbeam petrified.

"Could these be sold to pay him, and avert a curse?"

I said, "Nonsense, leave him alone; put beside him daily, within reach, water and the savoury food which he might be likely to love." But I added that, as soon as he showed signs of weakness, it would be necessary for them to keep me informed of his condition from hour to hour. Meanwhile, I visited him, myself, daily. He would not break his fast. Food was placed beside him, even as I had advised: and he would turn painfully on to his side – he lay all day now, too weak to sit – and sniff, and sniff: and then turn over and shut his eyes, lest even the sniffs should prove sustaining. We had a doctor now in attendance: suicide could not be permitted.

Then, suddenly, a summons – "he was dying – would the Miss Sahiba come at once."

The women had poured their jewels at his feet, but he was unconscious, and beyond realization.

It was no use hoping to persuade the women past their belief in that curse. In my official capacity I certainly could not pay the claim: I must (reluctantly) let the women pay something at any rate: and I must see how cheaply we could buy release.

The priests, the doctors, the heir had yelled at him.

No voice of man reached him.

I ordered rupees to be chinked on a stone – the way *banias* test money: his eyelids fluttered. A Brahmin lifted his head and got some water down his throat. When he was sufficiently revived for comprehension, I said, did he know who I was?

He blinked "Yes".

Well! I promised (I knew that he would believe me) that if he would help himself alive again I would see that he was given a sum of money – not his demand; but the amount which I should allow: and he was a rogue – an old *budmaash*!

The rogue smiled – whatever the amount, he had won: and he set himself to live and eventually walked away with his bag of a hundred rupees (£7 10s.), seemingly content.

There is a story about one of the older members of this family which cannot be omitted since it relates to the correct attitude of a Hindu woman towards her husband.

Upon the death of her mother, one of the daughters of this household had gone to live in a separate house with her husband and her son.

The husband took to drink, on good Scotch whisky: and when in his cups would beat and ill-use his wife indescribably. She never complained, and I learnt only vaguely and obliquely of her condition. Till one evening about eleven o'clock, the heir, now head of his family, and no longer a Ward, appeared at my house with his uncles and other senior male relations.

The wife of the drunkard had run away from home – taking her little son with her. A servant said that she had gone to Sheraphuli, several miles outside Calcutta. It was an unheard-of proceeding. A wife belonged to her husband to kill or to keep alive. She had by her action disgraced both the family and her religion.

None of the family could, however, intervene, because that would be to suggest that she was right in acting independently. Would I compel her to go back to her husband? She would listen to me.

I said that I would go and bring her back, if that were their wish; but that I would not force her to return to her husband. I could only help if the Raj Zenana, i.e. the Joint-Family Zenana, to which as a daughter she still had right of entry, would receive her as "a guest in my name", and take care of her for me. That after she was safely inside her old home, they might send the husband to me. I would deal with him. I knew that I was asking a great deal; but, such was their beloved kindness to and trust in me, that they promised to do as I asked, and to receive her into the Raj-Zenana. And I knew that their good manners would secure comfort, and an absence of all nagging and dispeace, reproach or righteous indignation, in the treatment of the "Guest in my name".

There were no more trains to Sheraphuli that night – it was then past twelve o'clock – but I took the dawn-hour train and found my rebellious wife sitting in a swamp by a drain, outside a disused hut, her son hugged to her – both of them chilled to the bone, and running Heaven knew what risks of malaria.

She had no intention in her flight, except to get away: the money which she had with her sufficed, as she found on enquiry, for a railway ticket to Sheraphuli; so to Sheraphuli she went; and, finding the empty hut, had sat down with her back against the wall, waiting for she knew not what – able only to realize that her broken body and shattered spirit were getting a moment's respite.

Later on, I heard that one of her women servants had followed her afar off, had heard the conversation at the ticket office, and seen her poor tortured mistress hurry to a train just about to leave for Sheraphuli. That was how we knew where to look for her.

I sat down beside the poor lady, and told her that I had come to take her back to her parents' home.

"Oh, but neither my brother nor the Zenana would let me go there! I've run away!"

I explained that they would, and that all would be well.

She was trembling with terror.

"*He* will find me and take me home again" (an orthodox Hindu woman may not say her husband's name).

"No, he won't. You'll stay in the Zenana and be loved and cared for."

She came with me, and the Zenana was perfect in courtesy: the women let their tender hearts do all that I could desire for the poor little lady, healing the wounds of body and of soul.

The husband was rather shamefaced when he came to see me – and tried bluster, but not for long.

He said that his honour was outraged in that his wife had left him: he would be a laughing-stock, etc., etc. Our interview ended by a suggestion from me that he should go far away on a three months' tour, and that I advised his taking the pledge before setting out. I would trust him to keep it. That upon his return, if he felt that he was cured of a habit which after all was outside the habits of his race – and if his wife were well enough to go back to him and consented to do so – I would help her to return. He accepted this programme, and after three months we took stock of the situation, he and I, and he consented to a further probation of three months. He had kept his word all these months, had interested himself in work, and was, according to the report of the family, new-made in every sense....

The reconciliation was to be at my house. The lady would come in a palanquin accompanied by her brother: husband and wife would meet in a private room, when he would have an opportunity of pleading his cause. Naturally, neither the brother nor I would be present at the interview; but the lady begged that we would stay close by, for "he may murder me!", said she, "and if I cry out, you will come in and save me, won't you?" We promised that indeed we should.

No sound came through the shut door; and in about an hour, a beaming husband and a very shy little wife emerged: and, after receiving our congratulations, made their way to their own home – the husband humbly walking beside her palanquin.

There was never any more trouble in that household.

In the Raj house, however, as the days went by, there was sadness, for the beautiful little Boho-Rani was childless. She was now eighteen years old, and she said to me, "I must ask the Raja Sahib to take another wife, for I have failed him."

I said, "Tut! tut!" and got the Raja to consent to the ministrations of a woman doctor.

In due time my little Boho-Rani, all smiles and happiness, had a secret to tell me.

One day she asked me what my English friends did in like case in preparation for "the honourable guest of the Mother heart".

I told her.

But she could not sew, because it is forbidden to close anything during this period: and sewing a seam would mean holding together and "closing up things".

This is an inexorable rule: doors must not be shut by her, nor cooking-pots covered, nor the lids of boxes let down – the idea being "the reclosing of the womb" by such action.

When, however, I spoke of the thoughts my friends think to their babies she was greatly excited. "*That* I could do." And the next time I saw her, she told me that she had sent for all the books that she could get about – Akhbar and Napoleon; and she was reading them, as she wanted the influence of these two personalities for her baby!

I was aghast at what I had done. What thing of blood and thunder and imperialism might not result!

When the message of the child's arrival reached me, I hurried to my Boho-Rani, to find – the darlingest little baby girl, such a wonder of beauty and tranquillity, that when asked to name it, "Peace Queen" seemed imperative: and a Peace Queen indeed she remains to this day.

Sons followed, and we could rejoice together that the pessimism of her eighteenth year had been saved from the drastic measures of ignorance.

THE "DOG-GIRL" – TWENTY PRIESTS LEARNED IN MAGIC – THE VICTIM OF A HOROSCOPE – ENGLISH FRIENDS IN INDIA – MISSIONS

It will be recognized that I have gone on telling stories of my first Wards' Zenana, although the stories do not all relate to my initial connection with it. I propose to adopt a like method in other stories.

My first Bihar case related to a quarrel in three generations. "Successive Commissioners and Collectors," said the Hon. Member of the Board, "have tried to compose it, but to no purpose. Take authority to do everything feasible to secure peace."

The Raj was an ancient one dating back to the days when there were Hindu Overlords in that region. The Overlord asked the service in battle of the owner of the estate: but he, afraid, went and hid himself. And "*Na-mard*" (Coward: "not-man") said his wife in humiliation; and buried herself alive.

An old sour-plum tree, still prolific, was shown me as having been planted over her living grave. The Overlord left his vassal to be dealt with by remorse. All he said was – "The women of this State shall be called Ranis, but their men shall never be Rajas."

It is interesting to record here that I was able to secure from the British Government confirmation of the title of Rani as a personal distinction for one of the Ladies of this estate in recognition of her public benefactions.

The circumstances from which I had to squeeze out peace were these.

The last owner of the estate had died, leaving a widow, a daughter and his aged mother him surviving. But his widow the Rani, in possession of the estate till a son of her daughter attained majority, would have nothing to do with the other two. The little daughter lived in the quarters of her grandmother – quarters complete with courtyard and a personal staff, separated securely from her own mother.

The atmosphere of hate in the palace could be felt as a physical depletion. Impassable deserts might have lain between the women: no contact was there, even between their servants.

But one living thing did dare to walk superciliously from courtyard to courtyard on his tall stilts. It was a red-throated grey *Sarus* (crane), and he looked to me like an embodiment of the hate pulsing in the very air he breathed.

The Guest-house was ready for me, and I settled in with my servants, prepared to stay till I had effected something. As a preliminary I wanted to discover more about the quarrel than the Authorities could tell me.

The countryside had never seen an official like me, and I soon learnt that curiosity would help me as much in my official life as it had done in private practice. The very first day of my visit, the collateral representatives of the Raj and other leading men turned up to ask for interviews.

I granted every request, listening and learning.

From the Rani herself came a messenger, hot-foot. It was her bad fortune that she was ill and could not receive me immediately. She sent the then customary offering of *dalis* – trays of fruit and vegetables – carried by a long procession of Raj servants who were dressed in loin-cloths, but waited outside the gates to don their dazzling red-gold uniforms before making the presentation.

I saw them from my windows, and rejoiced in the symbolism of the little scene.

None of my visitors could discover why I had come; but apparently all were afraid that Government had discovered something to their discredit: and each man abused his neighbour, confidentially, finger-on-lip.

What was significant was that all of them alike kept the italics of abuse for the Rani's priest, a Brahmin under whose complete domination they said she was: that he robbed her right and left, and that it was he who caused and fomented a quarrel between mother and daughter because he could not expect like leniency from any heir to the Rani.

His salary was fifteen rupees a month (about £1), but he was gradually acquiring land all over the district. How did he do it?

I felt that it was time to see the mother-in-law faction, and sent a message to this effect.

Before it could be answered a post-haste messenger came from the Palace – "Such was the beneficent influence of my presence in her Raj," said the Rani's letter, "that her serious illness had suddenly disappeared. Would I honour her with a visit at my early convenience, and in any case before I saw her mother-in-law."

It was almost guileless in its transparency. She had gone to bed "ill" upon my arrival only because she did not know what I was after, and wanted time to discover. The quick recovery was due to the fact that she wanted to get in her story first, before the mother-in-law's.

I went straightway to see her, treating the visit as "for observation only". I had opportunity, for the priest was present, suave and insincere. The Rani was without doubt hypnotized by him.

On then to the mother-in-law. She was very old, and had a gentle face, her appearance marred by a goitre and the beginnings of *leuco-derma*.

Her granddaughter was thirteen years old – just a child, devoted to dogs – I called her my "dog-girl". A pack of pariahs, mangy and dangerous, lived in a room on the ground floor, and fought all day. She knew they were "outcast" dogs: but said that the priest-dog had probably made their mothers quarrel with them and turn them out on to the street, where they had to remain, changed by the offal they ate into outcasts, because they had no kind grandmother dogs to take them in!

The chance of suggesting peace soon came in both Zenanas. But in the Rani's Zenana, I had to get rid of the priest before unfurling my flag.

Odd, how in my profession the remotest things help… Lord Curzon was just about going on leave before his extension of service, and mindful of the necessity to contradict Congress rumours that the Viceroy was being recalled because of the Partition of Bengal,[24] I said conversationally:

"See how our Maharaja-Bahadur (the King) rewards the Officers whom he delights to honour. They are given a holiday to go to their *bastis* (village huts) and refresh themselves." Suddenly "the way" flashed upon me, and I added, "Would you not like to honour, thus, the priest who directs all your business?"

And she said, "True talk. He is indeed worthy of honour" – and sent him away to his *basti*.

I had to "keep my body under" (together with my tongue), and "bring it into subjection", lest I spoil all by being too precipitate. But there came a day when I could safely say – "Let there be a Peace Making to show how Peace Makings are conducted in this part of India."

What made her consent (and it is discomforting to my vanity), I discovered later through my *ayah* (maid). I had not known that every action of mine was spied upon through the skylights in the roof of the Guest-house, the Rani's women being stationed there for the purpose. (I now have all skylights painted when I stay on business in Raj *baris*!)

One day they saw me using a bit of pumice-stone. The next day the Rani professed herself agreeable to the Peace Making; her waiting-women had told my *ayah* that the Rani had said she would do anything that I wished, because I was a worker of magic!

"Whatever did she mean?" I asked.

"Oh! the *Ji-s* (waiting-women) told the Rani Sahiba what happened when the Miss Sahiba stroked a stone!"

The Peace Making was a great ceremony.

The Rani sat behind the purdah, and her daughter came into the chief Raj apartments for the first time since she was a child of five. The appropriate salutations had to be made, my "dog-girl" a little scornful.

And then the Rani made presents – strings of pearls, of emeralds and rubies, of turquoise and topaz, with ornaments to match for nose and forehead, ear and ankle: for toes and fingers, circlets of gold and precious stones, connecting by showers of pearls and stones with toe and finger rings.

Silver palanquins: vessels of gold and silver: gold and silver "four-legs" … what not!

The list, with the value of each article, was read out by the Officer of the Treasury. "Is it there? Is it there?" And from behind the purdah, "It is here! It is here!" said the waiting-women. And every now and again the "dog-girl" would take up an ornament and look at it critically. "A pearl is missing in this nose ring," is what she said!

It was an amazing scene – waiting-women lined the long room, each waving a huge glittering fan of peacocks' feathers, planted like a standard in front of her. *Flap! Flap!* went the fans like an elephant's ears: and the serving-women's ornaments shone like stars on arm and forehead. The darkness deepened; we finished the inventory by the light of tall brass lamps, cotton wicks floating in pans of oil. The hand-maidens still lined the walls, still waved their jewelled fans….

When the priest returned from his holiday he was, quite naturally, furious. But the Rani and the entire entourage were, I knew, uplifted in heart; they had made the first breach with a tyranny they feared, and had made it without responsibility. That was mine.

My next move was to arrange for the "dog-girl" and her husband to come to Calcutta, for they went in fear of their lives at the Raj Estate.

The "dog-girl" was soon to be a mother, and the priest had sworn that nor child nor mother should live – seeing that the death of these two would make the Rani his pawn to the end of her life.

So we took a house for them, and put an armed guard on the gate: and my "dog-girl" promised me that she would eat nothing, and would heed no messages sent from the Raj.

The priest, finding his way to his purpose barred, tried cursing *me*. If only I were out of the way, he would regain his ancient power. So, after a recent visit to the Raj, I received a letter in Hindi, saying, "Twenty priests, learned in magic, are sending a devil into you." They had made an image of me from "the dust of my feet" (I had walked in the garden opposite the Guest-house: there was much "dust of my feet" to help the magic), and were sitting round it throwing incantations. The State Superintendent wrote to tell me these details. I was much intrigued. Would the devil take visible form? How I longed to see and photograph the scene! It would fill my English friends with envy, I felt sure!

So I wrote back urgently –

"To the Chief Priest of the Twenty Priests most learned in Magic sitting in the Garden of X—— in the District of Y——

"Keep the devil till I come."

I heard nothing in response: but a week later, as I was driving out of my gate, I saw the dearest old priest in the world, sitting against the gate-post: and when he saw me, he chanted ominously, to a wonderful Gregorian setting.

"Who are you?"

"I am one of the twenty priests learned in magic who sat in the Temple Garden at X—— sending a devil into the Miss Sahiba. But the Miss Sahiba laughed at the devil. It is talk of wonder, and of danger. Does the Miss Sahiba know no fear of ill-luck? So I am sent to curse, as she goes in and out, and presently she will dwindle, and her days will end."

"How long will it take?"

"I cannot tell."

"Oh! but be comfortable while you curse. See, my *Mali* (gardener) who lives in the gate-house is a high-Caste *Ooriya*. I will tell him to let you share his house: and he will cook for you, and care for you. And, inside the gates, you will see me more often, and can curse more often: and maybe your work will be the sooner done."

He came and lived in the *Mali's* house; and that good Hindu was delighted to be able to serve a priest. And the priest sat in the sun, and cursed me many times a day. I loved to see the picturesque old man, who truly had the dearest face, tattooed with sandalwood paste; and he wore becoming rosaries of brown seedlings, punctuated with red beads.

And, day after day, I went to see my "dog-girl" and wide-eyed she would gaze at the defier of the most powerful curses. And I thanked God that day after day, as she saw that I prospered exceedingly – I and "Vanity Fair", my beloved brown horse, and "Wanglo", my high-caste chow dog – the power of priest-craft was loosening its hold upon her.

"I do not believe in curses: I believe in blessings," I had said. And she had answered – "I, too, will learn to bless, and to believe in blessings."

The dear old priest gave it up, after a fortnight. He had made his report to the priests learned in magic sitting in the Garden, and was told to return. But the night before he left, he made one last effort which the servants found next morning. On the steps which led to the lawn lay a black kid with its throat cut....

"The Curse of Kali!" said the servants, terrified.

"Now we shall all die!"

"Nonsense – remove the kid and wash the steps." But the sweeper said he "dare not", and I had to bribe a *dôm* (a carrier of the dead) from without my gates, to clear up the mess.

In the summer of 1907, while I was on a short three-months holiday in England, my "dog-girl" died. Just before her baby was born, her mother (or so they said) had sent her a basket of fruit with a loving message. She felt at peace, dear child, with all the world: fear, which had theretofore ruled every moment of her days, was dead: she would believe that her mother loved her at last. What a small thing to do for your mother! – to eat a little of her gift and tell her so. It would mean "I love you now: I trust you now." ...

She died in agonies of cholera. The fruit had been poisoned and had come not from her mother, but from the priest.

The Rani's grief for the death of her daughter and the possible heir was genuine. She attributed the double tragedy to the right cause. But the Government could take no action: a *post mortem*, as has already been indicated in this record, would have been sacrilege to an orthodox Hindu.

The Rani lived on in her solitude, though often now there were meetings between her and her mother-in law, and the door between the courtyards was on the latch. An odd thing was the disappearance of the red-throated Sarus. The servants said he had flown away on the Peace-Making day. Gradually the Rani's eyes had been opened to see the priest as he really was: she loosened his hold upon herself, finger by finger....

His retaliation was awful. I got a telegram one day telling me that the Rani was very ill, and begging me to come at once. I went, taking with me a woman doctor... There was nothing to be done. She was dying of arsenical poisoning. She knew: the cook, also a Brahmin, had confessed to using the white powder supplied by the priest, though the cook did not know its nature.

I told her that the Government would undertake to deal with the priest, who was apparently responsible for the end of both herself and her daughter. But she begged that nothing should be done.

"I have but one wish left now," said she, "to die in Benares." And we were only just in time to give her her wish.[23]

As to the priest, he disappeared, and was never found. But had we found and prosecuted, what single person would have been brave enough to witness against him?

The pathetic old mother-in-law succeeded to the Raj, and spent the end of her days in prayer and fasting, and in works of Charity. These last included a wonderful Pilgrims' Way over the Ganges – which was also of great use in the economic development of the countryside. While the bridge was building, she camped beside the river, "praying blessings into every stone": and fasting in apology to Mother Ganga for the modern machinery which must overshadow her.

Curses play a determining part in the life of many an Indian woman. There is not only the curse used by others upon yourself: but the curse which you must use, however reluctantly, in self-defence.

Take the case of my Victim-of-her-Horoscope, a Maharani upon whom, eventually, we were compelled to hold a Commission in Lunacy. She was a Buhiyar Brahmin, a high sect of Brahmin of which few representatives exist.

She must have been a lovely child. When she was added to my Wardship she was about twenty-five, and still most attractive to the eye. In her horoscope it was written that whoever married her would die within a month of marriage. Many requests had her parents received for her hand: but the horoscope inspected, they were withdrawn. No bridegroom wished to be cremated during his honeymoon.

So, the child remained unmarried, cursed daily by her parents themselves, as "a luckless one".

"What would you? She was long past the last limit for marriage: for her parents remained nothing but a hell of re-births: but still must opportunity be felt after, lest worse still befall."

There came a day when hope stirred… A great Maharajah, a Buhiyar Brahmin himself, wanted a third wife: he and his two wives were old and childless, the new bride must be young: and as she must be a Buhiyar Brahmin, and Buhiyar Brahmins were few, "the shastric limit of age", said the priests, "might be overlooked".

"We must fake a horoscope," said the parents' priest. "We cannot risk losing this chance."

So, she was married, and great were the rejoicings, and entirely satisfied were Maharajah and priests alike.

The Maharajah died within a month of marriage. Not by intrigue in support of the infallibility of horoscopes. No! he died from natural causes. His foot slipped as he was alighting from his Royal Saloon carriage, on a special train which took him to his capital; he fell between platform and train. His leg had to be amputated:

he died under the operation.

The poor little bride felt now that she was doubly accursed.

The years ahead included subjection to the two aged co-widows. She served them faithfully, and performed their death ceremonies with rectitude when they "passed out", severally, not so very long after their common husband.

My Bearer of Curses was thus in entire possession of a very large property in one of the most fertile tracts of India. The Court of Wards managed it: and was now able to make the best of it for the benefit of the Ward.

The little lady was, however, difficult. She was not without shrewdness: she could read her own language very well indeed: she could write only her signature. She was spellbound by her priest (how can they avoid this hazard, these poor orthodox widows who are claimed for the religious life?), a distinctly undesirable personality: and, despite the fact that she was a Ward of the Court, she was still in control of very large sums of money – a dangerous combination, especially as she had no friend at hand to help her.

The authorities she saw, before my time, through the purdah only, that is to say, they interviewed her about her affairs – a thick curtain between.

From the earliest days she used to fly into uncontrollable rages. Her servants (there were about a hundred of them) lived in terror of her: she trusted no single one of them, not even about the giving of a message; and employed two page-boys of about eight and nine to run her errands. These also she bullied, and threatened to kill: but the imps laughed at her and ran fearlessly in and out of the Zenana.

It was, of course, their fearlessness which she liked.

Upon this state of things I entered.

She had a very real sense of fun, and would give me priceless imitations of the scuttling maids-in-waiting. She even imitated the authorities and was particularly successful over a Scotchman whom she called "Hey! noo!" because she said he was always using those words.

And once she went further still, in confidence about this man.

"He should grow a beard, to give him sense," said she

"How do you know that he has not got a beard?"

Then she laughed, and told me this tale.

"Of course, I am in purdah, and no man may see my face. But 'Hey! noo!' made me very angry one day, and I could not scold him sufficiently because of that curtain which hid him from me. You try to scold a person whom you cannot see, Miss Sahiba, and learn how it makes your anger hotter still! So I said to him, 'Is any one there?'

"'No,' said he.

"'Not even a boy?'

"'Not even a very little boy.'

"Then, I pulled aside the curtain, and *spoke* –

"'This is what I think of you,' I said.

"It eased my heart. And that is how I saw the beardless one."

The official in question confirmed this tale. He said the scolding was terrible! She was famous in the Division.

Another official told me that, when refusing her how-many-th petition for release of her estate (in order that she might manage it herself), he had explained the difficulties of management for a secluded woman, she had retorted, "In my opinion I could not do worse with bandaged eyes, and hobbled feet, than you do with your eyes open and your limbs unfettered!"

When she and I got acquainted, she was at first on her guard: but there came a day when she "passed" me.

"I've been making enquiries about you," said she. (As I discovered afterwards, this she had indeed done. She herself boasted about it, laughing at my unconsciousness. No detective could have shadowed me more closely: her messengers had kept watch all night, and followed me about all day; they had interrogated my servants, and the servants of my friends, and had even tracked me to the Cathedral on Sundays and kept watch from the door!)

"You are either mad or a *puja-in* (a religious), or why should you live like a man or a tiger, eating out of the hand of none: eating only what you kill! But the Member Sahib, now, he is not mad, and certainly he is not a 'religious'. I've made enquiries about him also. Yet he would not take a bribe. I should know where I stood if he would take a bribe. He's getting more than a bribe out of me, that's what it is! Now, *what* is he getting out of me?"

I persuaded her to come and live in Calcutta, where I could see her more often than when hundreds of miles lay between us. And I looked her up, as often as I could, making her tell me stories, folk tales and else, getting her to read to me from her vernacular books and papers: teaching her how to play games.

She was quick at learning, but the games "Halma", "Hoop-La", card games, had to be "pretend" appearances in Court.

"You may win, Miss Sahiba, before the idiot in the District Cour-ut, but this time we play before the High Cour-ut. It is I must win."

Later still, "I'll let you win before the High Cour-ut. It knows nothing, sitting two and three together – '*Phull* Bench', to try and reach wisdom. But I win in Ph-ri-vi Consil (Privy Council). *Khabar dar*, take very good care."

This acquaintance with the law grew out of her own case, which was a never-ending diversion.

She was, as I have said, without an heir, and every Buhiyar Brahmin State within range hoped to succeed her, manufacturing reasons why, and fighting her even to the Privy Council.

I was compelled to tell her every detail of the fight – on what the claimants based their case, how we kept them at bay, etc. And I thoroughly enjoyed her comments, and was often helped by the information which she gave.

The claimants were not deterred by the fact that till the *gadi* was vacant, the Privy Council could make no declaration: and a great deal of good money was wasted on both sides over these experiments.

One of these claimants was her particular aversion. But seeing a painting of him in her bedroom, I chaffed her.

"We keep our best-beloved in our private rooms," said I. "I don't believe you hate him all that much. You want your eyes to fall upon his face when you awake."

"That, certainly," said she. "That is why I had his portrait painted, and hung there where I can see him from my bed, and begin to curse him in the moment of waking."

This opponent, most amusingly, gave me a chance of learning the weakness of his case. He asked to consult me as a private practitioner. I refused to see him, saying that in my official capacity I was already pledged to the Maharani's cause. He then applied to the Government for my services. The Maharani wished terribly much that I should hear what he had to say; and the Government thought it would not be a bad way out of the situation, if I could – subject to anything new which he had to show me – persuade him of the facts, viz. that as the late Maharajah's property was obtained through an ancestor, who had received that property in reward for allegiance to the British during the Mutiny, it would escheat to the Government upon failure of heirs: and that indeed the Privy Council had, *obiter dicta*, said as much in a case lately before it.[vii] [vii I trust that, after the death of the Maharani, the Government will claim the escheat. A Training Ground in Estate Management and Practical Agriculture is badly needed. No tract of country could better serve this purpose than the estate in question; officered by experts it would provide exactly what young Zemindars need all over India.]

So in due time I made a most interesting journey to the citadel of the enemy. I was royally received, and was taken by boat to the Zenana Water Gate, past the Ladies' Bath – a magnificent house-boat without a bottom. Then, through narrow tunnels, guarded by armed sentries, up stair after stair – into the daylight of a gorgeous portrait gallery. Here I sat for some few minutes, during which time I have no doubt that I was being inspected by many eyes.

Finally, his Highness appeared accompanied by an imposing body of officers. I told him our position immediately and frankly.

He explained that he wanted me to see his own documentary evidence, evidence not yet disclosed to anyone. Maybe when the Government knew of this, it would at once declare him heir, and so prevent further fighting.

There followed a scene which was wasted on an audience of one. A jewelled casket was produced, and, in silence, the officer in charge of the key stepped forward and opened it. But the document was not inside; there was only a smaller casket, opened by yet another officer … and so on through a nest of six caskets, a separate man in charge of each, and each man, producing his key with a flourish, added his own interpretation of secrecy. It was a symphony in secrecy: bold ("What d'you think of that!"); obstinate ("Death would not drag it out of me!"); tight and misleading ("There isn't really a secret"); arch, sly, even coy…. Last of all his Highness, the key on his chain – "Victory! now you'll see!" – as from the inmost and most jewel-bespattered box he produced a document. The Maharajah handed it to me, and the entire company sat back on its haunches watching me read, letting me feel the while that there was plenty of time, I need not hurry.

So I read – not without an expectant thrill. But when I had finished I could have laughed aloud. The document was the will of a lady in no way entitled to deal with the contested property. It was she who had left it to his Highness! As I folded up the paper, they sprang at me.

"Well? " said his Highness.

"It is of as little use to your Highness as would be a like bequest in my own will," was what I said.

They took it very well. I was questioned about the Law, and the power of will making which had come into the country with the British, about its scope and ability to give a title, etc. They were inscrutable as they questioned, now H.H., now an officer. Whether they accepted my statements or my opinion, I could not tell. But their courtesy did not fail, and I was as magnificently conducted out of my strange experience as I had been ushered into it.

To my Maharani the tale gave great delight. Over and over again, I had to describe each key-holder, and she would let her imagination loose.

"The fifth should have taken snuff."

"The sixth been a dwarf with a goat's beard, his shoulders wrapped in a green Kashmur shawl …."

It was about this time that she established a code between us. If she wanted me urgently, she would send an orderly on a *white* horse. If not so urgently, he would ride a chestnut. This she invented, because she was afraid to put her messages into words, lest the orderlies (who were faithful enough, poor souls, only terribly afraid of her) should maliciously pervert them.

The messages were sent at any moment that took her fancy. The men had orders to sit in my compound till I spoke to them. She was very whimsical over this. She knew that when working at Headquarters I left the house about 10 a.m. for the Secretariat, and rarely got back till after five o'clock. Yet, she often sent the men to the house "*Khabar dar*, if they dared to go anywhere else," at eleven o'clock to await me! And coming home tired, in the late afternoon I would see a much tired-er orderly still bestriding white or brown horse, silhouetted against the pink antigonum which covered the porch.

I'd say, "Bother! she may be dying – " (for of course I could not question the men except to ask when they had arrived), and would drive straight on, only to find some trivial nothing. Yet, I could never bank on its always being nothing, and always did go instantly, as she knew I would do, if the white horse stood in my garden. One day when the "Come-this-minute" man, as I called the rider on the white horse, had thus fetched me to her, I could hear that she was in a rage. From outside the gate I could hear bare feet thudding up and down her shut-in verandahs, her heavy anklets jingling.

"What's the matter, Maharani Sahiba? I'm glad that you're not ill!"

"Ill? Would you have me ill?"

"No! no! but – "

"It's worse than illness: it's *badnam* (an insult) damage to my caste. One of *those people*" (she named a Theistic lady of Hindu origin) dared to drive up to my door, and ask to see me."

I did my best to soothe her. I explained that as the lady had not approached her waterpots, no harm had been done: that no insult had been intended. Since this was the new way, the way the Theists had of showing honour, etc. etc.

She would not be appeased.

"What was the Government going to do about it? She would beg release of her estate if we did not punish That One." I tried distraction. "Tell me about 'That One's family'" I said – "there must be a story to it."

She yielded immediately. "A story certainly." And I not to know it! I must know then that the Great God, Shiva, bored with virtue, said he would go down to see what pretty girls could be found on the earth. His search ended on the property of her caller.

"Come now!" I interrupted. "If you are going to tell me you are jealous of pretty women, I do not sympathize with you. You have no grievance."

"Wait a bit!" said she. "He went as a beggar, because it is only to give to a beggar that a woman goes to the door: his search ended in X—— and at the door of a sweeper. He married the sweeper's pretty daughter and founded the estate to which *That One* belongs."

"But then she has the Great God for an ancestor. Could you ask more?"

"We're sure of the mother," said my Maharani, with a sniff. But her good-humour was restored. She loved telling a tale.

Another "Come-this-minute" occasion related to the announcement in the papers that we were to have an Indian member of the Executive Council.

"What's this, and where are Minting (Lord Minto), Edward Maharajah (King Edward) and Maulvi Jan (John Morley, then Secretary of State)?"

"They're there, Maharani, all right. What's the matter?"

"Look at this!" and she thrust her paper upon me.

"I won't have other Hindustanis managing my property. I want the Burra Lat Sahib, and the Chota Lat Sahib" (the Viceroy and the Lieut.-Governor), "and I want Edward Maharajah and Maulvi Jan. Tell the Member Sahib, now, at once ."

That took some explaining. But later, when I was in England, I told Lord Morley the story, and he loved his new name: and would use it to me.

Now, under our Act we were compelled to give to a proprietor, yearly, the surplus which remained after payment of debts, and administration of the estate in all its branches, including public works, education and social service.

There was one particular year wherein the surplus announced was three lakhs of Rupees (£22,500). And I asked the Maharani what she would like done with this, telling her about investments, etc.

"I want the entire amount paid me in Rupees," said she.

I doubted whether the Bank had so much silver available, and "where would she put it, if we could get it?"

"In my strong-room, here, in this house."

I put my foot down, on that. I could not be responsible for her life with a thousandth of the amount in cash under her roof, said I. "But what can you possibly do with any money at all? Every want of yours is met – clothes, food, servants, ceremonies, *pujas* – what is there to do with money if you can't go shopping? I've often wondered how you spend your monthly allowance of Rs.5,000 (£375)."

"Lots to do with money," said she.

"You need not tell me. It's no business of ours how you spend your money. But what is there to spend it on?"

"Curses!"

"*What!*"

"Yes – curses. My priest taught me that – putting curses on people who hurt you. When the two Maharanis died, and the Raj was mine alone, managed by the Government, my priest said to me – 'Many people hate you and will put evil on you!'

"'Oh But,' said I, 'what have I done to anyone? Why should they hate me?'

"'They do,' said the priest. 'Are you not cursed enough? You must set-far this new hatred.'

"'But how?' And truly, Miss Sahiba, big dread had hold of me.

"He said, 'Put curses on people. Say "May your eye fall out!" "May you be lame of a leg." "May your back be hunched." …

"'Begin with the English Manager Sahib' (I was to see him shortly), 'say "May you be lame of a leg": and if you pay me Rs.10,000 (£750) when you say those words,' said my priest, 'he will be lame: and any harm he does you will come to naught.' What could I do? I paid him Rs.10,000 – and next day, when the Manager came to see me, truly he was lame, *he was lame of a leg*."

And I said, "Silly, Maharani Sahiba, he was lamed in a polo accident, ten years before you saw him."

I gathered that she had said similarly, "May you be a leper," and other gruesome things in relation to other persons indicated by the priest, paying him large sums of money with each solemn aspiration. But she had seen only that first one of her victims.

"Yet, my curse came true with the Manager Sahib: it must have come true with those others also. And, at any rate, I am safe and well, the fruit of my cursing!"

Amazing! especially with this particular lady, shrewder than most, than any I had known, careful about business, suspicious, even miserly in relation to all money transactions. The Court of Wards accounts, for instance, were translated to her, and she pored over them for days together, her private Secretary (*amla*) sitting the other side of the purdah, to answer questions: while, with her household, she was almost mean, flying into a rage if twopence worth of melted butter were wasted. Yet tens of thousands, and more, she paid out obediently to her priest, testing him but that once.

I tried to interest her in works of charity –

"The Government maintains my schools and hospitals," said she. And did I not once give money when "Prinseps Mary" (so they called our Queen upon her visit to us as Princess, confusing "Princess" with the familiar Prinseps Ghat, beside their sacred river) "came to Calcutta, money to build a hospital for *Purdahnashins* to keep the Prinseps' name among us? Tell me when the Prinseps comes again. I'll make a bigger hospital." And I could get her no further.[viii] [[viii] I can never forget a wonderful drive with my younger *Purdahnashins* through the streets of Calcutta during the visit of the Prince and Princess of Wales. I obtained the consent of grandmothers and male relations to take them in purdah-ed carriages to see the illuminations. They talked of the adventure for years. A joke which they could not share was the pair of scales which lit up the High Court. One pan very much heavier than the other! It reminded me of the *Pushtu* translation of a familiar Biblical injunction – "Do no justice, lest justice be done unto you".]

Eventually we agreed to give her her three lakhs gradually in very small instalments, and she consented to take the money in largish notes. The guard on the gate was doubled, and the strong-room next her bedroom made really secure.

I had to go on tour to District Wards. And, alas! on my return, I heard that the "Come-this-minute" Man, sent on this occasion by a terrified staff with a spoken message, had found an empty house. But my wise head-servant directed him to the Secretariat, and to the doctor lady whom I had before taken to the Maharani.

The Maharani had gone suddenly crazy, and had rushed into the garden unveiled.

It was a violent type of madness: no one dared approach her. She shouted at the top of her voice for "Sorabji", as she then began to call me, and said her servants were keeping me from her.

The anxiety of those days does not bear talking about, enhanced as it was by the difficulty of protecting her customs and her prejudices; and protecting also those who served her – the Minto Nurses, who were invaluable – against her attempts at murder. Finally, however, the violence passed, but we were compelled, upon doctors' certificates, to hold a Commission in Lunacy at her house.

A Judge of the High Court came to conduct this, sitting the other side of the purdah.

I had explained the situation to her beforehand. She was pleased. She looked forward to tackling the Judge, who could speak her language.

"So," said she, "you have brought the High Cour-ut to my house – where is my Barrister. The Member Sahib has taken Sorabji." (I was representing the Court of Wards.) He said he'd brought a man, in case she needed him.

"*Your* man, you expect me to take that!"

The Judge said that he would postpone the sitting, to enable her to engage Counsel. But she refused this offer. She conducted her case herself!
Then, "What notice have you given me of this Cour-ut?"

"It's posted on your gate."

"And you are a Judge of the High Cour-ut! Of what use is a notice on the gate to a *Purdahnashin*?"

("Who says this woman is mad!" said the Judge in an aside to me. It really was very funny.)

I knew that as long as she kept her mind on a case she would be sane enough;

but soon, alas! she lost her hold, and there was evidence and to spare of her sad condition.

In course of time we moved her to a place near her childhood's home, putting her under the guardianship of her father, and allowing her more liberty than in sanity, for the grounds were purdah-ed with tent walls, and she could wander at will all over house and garden.

She still lives. The priest has disappeared, and is believed to be dead. Her servants alleged that he had administered the concoction of Dhatura which caused her madness. The strong-room was empty of all but Rs.16 (£1 4s.).

Myself, I have never got over a feeling that whatever the immediate cause of her madness, the lack of love in her early years contributed to it. "How can you know," she had said to me one day, in sanity, "what my life is like – going from one room to another, alone, no child to care for, no husband to worship, no one – and I, cursed from my birth!"

That she realized before her mind failed that I, at least, did care, and that we had many happy days together, is my only comforting reflection about the poor little lady victimized by her horoscope.

One delight of my life in Calcutta was that I was able to entertain my many friends. While the Government of India had its headquarters there, every tourist of note spent part of the cold weather in the capital. And among the tourists were personal friends who stayed with me and came with me to visit my wards – sometimes even accompanying me on tour. My *Purdahnashins* loved these Western visitors and would take them by the hand and walk up and down the roof terrace with them to show the friendliness which could not be expressed otherwise for lack of a common tongue.

On one occasion a child in one of the Rajbaris was greatly excited because she was to see a woman from the country of our Maharajah Bahadur.

"What will she look like?"

"You'll soon see," and she would count the days which lay between on her fingers, dancing with joy as they narrowed to "to-morrow". But on the morrow she was too excited to come into the room where the English visitor sat. She peeped at her through the "*jhilmils*" – the Venetian shutters of the doorway.

When she had gone –

"Well! I saw you peeping – you saw – what did you think of her? What was she like?" she was asked.

"Why," said the child, "she was so very like – a woman!"

This story has always appealed to me as a parable on international relationships. We have travelled a good bit of the road when we discover that men, women and children are, the world over, very like men, women and children!

On another occasion, when I took a tall and lovely creature to the children's *puja* at the house of my orthodox holy woman friend, the "Wisest-of-the-Wise", a little Hindu girl of four years of age slipped out of her place when the *puja* was over and fell at her feet – "I did not know," said she, "that goddesses came down to the earth!"

As a compliment, can that be beaten?

Among touring friends who stayed with me were Gertrude Hadenfeldt, the artist who illustrated one of my books about children, and whose paintings of Kashmir are so well known; Elena Rathbone, whom I greatly coveted for a colleague; Victoria Cholmondeley, Winifred Gould and Stella Benson.* Stella I had known since she was nine years old, when I was immensely impressed by a short story she had written, French in beauty and construction. It was the tale of how everything in a room fell in love with a lamp alight, standing on a table. The lamp accepted the love of the flimsy curtains blown by a wind towards it. And there was a conflagration! I used to chaff Stella's aunt, Mary Cholmondeley, then at the height of her fame, and prophesy that some day she would be known only as "the aunt of Stella Benson". My dear Stella came to stay with me in the post-War years after the world had learnt to look for her books – and spent almost an entire winter with me. She was unique in her type of genius, her humour, her unselfconsciousness and the utter fragility of a body that dared the most shattering adventures. About her writing, I felt in the earlier years that she had not decided whether to be an Algernon Blackwood or a Mary Cholmondeley. She was part fairy and part a shrewd observer and portrayer of human foibles. In *Tobit Transplanted*, however, the pendulum had swung steady – and all her friends delighted in the success which that book achieved. It is hard to realize that the pages of the book of her own brilliant life on earth are closed for ever.

Society, in the India that I knew, was stimulating. Till about fifteen years ago, we had to do without pictures, music and the theatre, and relied the more upon conversation and friendship one with another. We lived among men who were doing things and who were making history in unhackneyed parts of the world – men tremendously interested in their jobs.

At the formal governmental and official parties one talked with Kitchener* or the Viceroy: or one recaptured friendship as with Lady Maud Warrender, who would come with the Admiral from their Eastern Station to make glad our hearts with wit and song. There was Sir John Cowans, drawing his inimitable caricatures of famous persons on the back of the menu at every dinner-party at which one sat beside him; or there were Civilians, Engineers, Scientists, Archæologists,

Agriculturalists, not unwilling to talk about their work, or to swop clever nonsense across the table. On more intimate occasions one met one's special friends, played games with them, drove or walked with them. And how often the homes of these friendly ones have been "green isles" of peace, in the "deep wide seas" of arduous touring in times of unrest. The names of Sir Charles and Lady Bayley, Sir Robert and Lady Carlyle, Sir Havilland and Lady Le Mesurier, Mr. and Mrs. E. H. Walsh, the H. C. Streatfields, the Percy Lyons, Sir Archdale and Lady Earle recall much that must always travel the heartward way of memory; while the hospitality and good-fellowship of the planters of Bihar and Assam introduced a new element into one's life. And when the wives of my friends came to stay with me in Calcutta, we bound fresh faggots into our bundle of experiences.

Among special friends on the High Court Bench were Sir Harry and Lady Stephen, Sir Charles and Lady Chitty, and Sir Richard and Lady Harrington. It meant a great deal to me to have the Stephens as near neighbours in Calcutta; I knew the Judge's people, and Lady Stephen was rare among the "Judgesses" of the time. She was a Girtonian and keen on the interests which that fact represents. It was to her that, in the fullness of time, we owed the Indian branch of the Federation of University Women.

Since the War most English women have made jobs for themselves in India – Social Service or social bridging of inter-racial gaps. Rudyard Kipling's classics of early Indian society are now superseded, I should say, in every particular. We want another Kipling now to write about modern India – especially since Progressive Indian women have begun to share the social life of the English.

In 1904 and the years which followed, I was, for instance, the only Indian woman at English dinner parties in Calcutta. Now there is scarcely a large party, whether in Delhi or Calcutta, at which you do not see the most attractive of Indian women of all races – able to take their part in any interchange of conversation – grave or gay. It was at first the nonsense which nonplussed them. They were apt to be too serious, as their menfolk (politicians) were apt to be too serious. But I lived to see this change, as I was fortunate in seeing the political atmosphere change at Council meetings and Assemblies, where Gokhale* first (sparring with Sir Edward Baker and the present Lord Meston), and many who followed him, gave as good as they got in all good-humour.

I have often been asked in England about Missions in India, and have been forced to listen to much argument on the subject. All I can say of the Mission which I know best – the Oxford Mission to Calcutta – is that India would be a far poorer place without the men and women who represent it in Bengal. "They give to work the time they can spare from prayer" – as the Metropolitan once said of them. And this alone means something to all of us, apt to be engrossed too much in our work, in doing things. It is also what appeals tremendously to the religious-minded Indian. The educational work done by this Mission – almost all University men and women – has been appraised by those qualified to judge; and the hostel system, so invaluable to us with our examining (non-residential) Universities and so increasingly important in present circumstances – e.g. youth movements and political unrest – has had its greatest impetus from the Oxford Brethren.

There is more still not easy to put into words. But for myself I know how often, harassed with insoluble problems and out-of-gear generally, I have driven out the six miles to the Mission Station at Behala, and without a word said, have gone back, the focus of life readjusted. Again, not the least part of the attraction of Behala is the centre it makes for contacts between Indians and the business and official, Naval and Military English community, and the version of India, unobtainable elsewhere, which it affords. To see Father Douglass (infectiously happy as the Brethren are wont to be) giving waggon-loads of Tommies a swim in his tank, or making them sample the milk of the coconut, drinking it from the shell (after they have watched, open mouthed, the feats of the Indian climbers swarming up the pole of the palm trees to dislodge the fruit), is a sight never forgotten. The visitors tour the grounds, seeing how Indians live; they tea with the Sisters, and often insist on staying to evensong in the most beautiful thatched chapel in the world, the men sitting cross-legged on the floor among the boys, and shouting the hymns in their own language during the Bengali service.

You must have lived in Cantonments in India to realize the value of all that. And it leaves you disinclined to argue about Missions. You just know.

IV SUCCESS: PROBLEMS
OF THE WAY

STATUS AND POSITION OF LEGAL ADVISER – THE BURNING GHAT – CEREMONIES – OATHS AND CURSES

The first idea had been that my work was to be considered an experiment for a year – an experiment made practically (and I was quite willing that it should be so) at my own expense. And so generous was Government, and so genuine in the wish to serve an acknowledged need for the good of the country, that long before the year had run out, all the officials with whom I was concerned were converted to the scheme. I was particularly happy at the conversion of Mr. (afterwards Sir Launcelot) Hare, the then second member of the Board. He had, I believe, been dead against even an experiment. Later on, as Governor of Assam, he was one of my chief allies – if one may use such a term of a Chief in high places.

It was soon found that private practice was impossible – the Estates for which I worked having grown from three in May 1904 to thirty-three in 1907 (by 1919 the number was one hundred and twenty-six). But, though I was thus a whole-time officer from the date of my appointment, being able to leave Headquarters only on rare occasions for special work, I was still in 1907 serving Government on a retaining-fee basis – the purely legal work connected with Estates being separately paid for. In all other respects I was under Civil Service Regulations, getting travelling allowance, for instance, on the scale allotted to Commissioners of Divisions: and bound by Civil Service leave rules. Precedence was a difficult matter: and, although I was willing to accept what Government could offer as to emoluments, I made my own terms from the beginning as to other incidents of whole-time service.

This needs explanation. Since I was attached to the Secretariat at Headquarters, as members of the regular Civil Service were, but without the privileges of a Graded Service, and compelled to face all the hazards of a new appointment, I asked that I should be free of "Graded" restrictions and etiquette in respect of access to superior officers. The way the Court of Wards worked was this – the Collector, i.e. the District Officer within whose jurisdiction an Estate happened to be situated, was practically in charge of the Estate. All matters relating to the

Estate would initiate with him, go on appeal to the Divisional Commissioner and thence to the Member of the Board at Headquarters, who would refer to the Governor what he deemed necessary.

I was attached to the Board, but was expected to be at the disposal of all officers from the Collector to the Member, as well as of the Wards themselves. Any one of these individuals could demand my services. Inter-official etiquette was very strict. If, in any particular instance, I were dealing with the lowest officer in the scale, it might terribly handicap urgent work, if I had to wait for his opinion on a case to be submitted to the Commissioner and then to the Board before I could utter.

Also, then as now, the Court of Wards is only one item in a busy officer's programme; and the habit of leaving Court of Wards affairs to head clerks (men naturally exposed to local influence and to Raj intrigue) was, I soon discovered, at the bottom of a great deal of the trouble with which we had to deal.

When I could get into personal touch with officials, a way out was easy. I can never be grateful enough to the many officials of all grades who so generously helped me throughout my career. But officials were always changing and officials were of various temperaments – some regarding my appointment itself as a personal affront ("who was this person pitch-forked on to a great service, and attached not to the bottom, but to the top step of the ladder?"); hide-bound as to procedure, disinclined to co-operate except through the file which would eventually reach me only through the Board's Office.[ix] [ix One official even started a file—"Is she of the rank of a Collector? If so, she has no business to approach the Board direct, or to approach the Commissioner except through the Collector." On another occasion, when someone said to the most able and lovable of Provincial Governors, "Is she a Licensed Accountant? What does L.A. Court of Wards mean?" (L.A. = Legal Adviser), he replied with the laugh which his officers loved to hear, "*Light-'arted* Court of Wards"!] I did so understand and sympathize with them and yet – the essential thing was the individual Ward and her need; and one must work to that end, and that alone. It was clear that once again I must claim no label, in order that I might "rove".

A way suggested itself to me. I would gladly treat every official, even a sub-divisional officer (i.e. the "Griffin" just recruited), as a "Chief", and run to do his bidding; but as compensation, for not being of a graded service, I must have direct access to whatever official the exigencies of the case required, even – saving my Member's presence – to the Governor himself. And the Member of the moment, Mr. F. A. Slacke, bless him! with a grim smile consented.

My second demand was that my post must be made permanent – that is, it should endure after my time. And to this end I asked for an Assistant who could, from the beginning, be trained to carry on. This also was granted.

And in 1907, after Bengal was partitioned under Lord Curzon,[24] I was formally gazetted as a full-time Government officer, with an office in the Secretariat, Board of Revenue Department – an office complete with Government clerks and all necessary equipment. My salary was temporarily revised; but the matter of pension and status was somehow overlooked, and I was too busy to worry about it. So that it was not till 1916, in the middle of the War, when I did not feel it right to fight a personal case, that proposals (less beneficial than the offer already made and accepted at the time when Government negotiated the matter) finally crystallized, I was paid arrears to date – and pushed the whole silly matter aside.

Nothing could mar the joy one had in the work itself; the opportunity of studying the real people of India in their setting; the opportunities of travelling off the beaten track;[x] [In 1919, 26,313 miles] of learning legend, folklore and custom; best of all, the delight of contact with the Indian Purdahnashin. My official family numbered over 600,[xi] [Government Report, 1919-1920] and varied in age from a hundred (it was actually so – a dear old Thakurani great-grandmother bent in two and living on the pickled sour-plums which alone could tickle her jaded palate) to the "littlest one" of a few days old, born in some *Rajbari*.

I can never repay what I owe to the British Government for releasing these opportunities of contact. What they taught me needs must be at the service of the Government and of India, to the end of my days. Even though the latter-day official, with his ignorance of the needs of the Country, may not always appreciate the necessity for expert knowledge of the indigenous.

In 1905 Bengal was "partitioned", i.e. re-distributed into the three Provinces of Bengal, Bihar and Orissa, and Assam. I continued to serve all three Provinces (an inclusive area of 218,459 square miles), and the necessity of finding an assistant was more pressing than ever. I could find no possible candidate in India, not even a Parsee girl, whose training I was willing to finance myself. I spent my rare holidays – accumulations of privilege leave – in England, visiting the Universities and pursuing every chance. My search ended with a Scotch girl, Josephine Stuart, who combined all the qualifications I desired. It seemed to me that since we could not immediately get an Indian girl, and since personality and not nationality was of primary importance, we should recruit the Britisher and let her run in double harness with the Indian (myself).

By the time that she was ready for an assistant another Indian might have materialized….

The Chiefs of all my three Provinces agreed to this, so that I was within sight of my assurance of continuity, when a newly-appointed Chief in one of the

Provinces objected to the appointment of a non-Indian. The matter was shelved: I carried on alone, and upon retirement was told (as if it could be any consolation) that I was to be paid the compliment of having no successor, because I had been right, no Indian was available; and since I was leaving, no one at all could be put in sole charge of a specialized job. I have written the word "Success" across this section, for the experiment had succeeded; but my heart is still sore with disappointment for my frustrated official progeny. I cannot bear that other women should have missed this joyous adventure. My one consolation is that, the Bar being now open to women, the situation in regard to available advice for the help of secluded Indian women generally, is not as hopeless as when I set out on my crusade.[25]

And now to return to my story —

As confidence grew my area of work grew also. Being a Government official, I naturally did not interfere with Religion. But the strangest requests were made to me.

"Who is the proper person to have charge of our Temple of the God of Wisdom?"

"How should I know?"

"But of course the Miss Sahiba knows."

"And would you accept my advice?"

"But without doubt."

Well! here was a chance of protecting the little questioner. I took my puzzle to my "Wisest-of-the-Wise", an orthodox Hindu friend. She knew, individually, the priests of the District in question, and told me whom to avoid. Black Lists kept in a certain Department of Government could also be appealed to: and I was able to say, "I think these" (specific) "persons might not be acceptable to a God of Wisdom" – and so helped my *Purdahnashin* patron of a benefice to the necessary elimination.

Or again, in regard to practices believed to be sanctioned by religion. The women knew that I admired all that was picturesque among their ancient customs, and this knowledge, combined with the wonderful love they gave me, helped me to beg the intermission of customs which were against decency. Gradually all the Zenanas with which I was associated intermitted such customs. When the women began to see for themselves the reason for my disapproval, I knew that the future was in good hands.

The strangest confidences also were made by a people whose very appearance of frankness conceals depths of reserve undreamt of by the Westerner. Often there were tears in my heart as I listened. There was, for instance, the case of the Hindu lady whose husband had acquired a Mohammedan mistress who lived just outside the Raj Fortress, and whose lusty sons would swagger inside the Palace Gates, boasting of their paternity, and sneering at "the blind mouse", as they called the little Hindu heir. After the Raja's death, these men had to be given into Police custody for attempted murder. But, the little widow said, "My husband loved them. Make them and their mother special allowances." When I had to refuse this, she asked that her own, none-too-large allowance (the Estate was heavily encumbered) might be halved in their interest!

Or, there was the Rani whose husband was ruining the Estate with his cocaine-taking, and his multiple households. In order to save the Estate for their son, she bought out her husband's share (it was a Joint Hindu Family Estate) with her private monies, and gave him a house and a monthly allowance, so that he need not be personally incommoded in regard to his extra-marital and other dissipations!

We put through the business transactions for her, and, at her request, took the Estate under management. The tragedy was that her son, poor lad, was *non-compos*. Mercifully, however, he died of cholera before he attained majority. But the end was pitiful. She refused to leave the corpse. "Rub his feet," said she to her waiting-women. "Don't you see he is cold—"

When she fainted, they were able to take the lad away. But when she came to, and realized the truth, she climbed to the roof of the palace in order to throw herself down. I came to her, of course.

"Why give – to take away!" she said.

And one felt that she was speaking the language of the bereaved the world over. My eye caught the little child-bride, sitting by, humbly disconsolate.

"Listen, Mother," I said, "is it worse for you who have had, and lost, or for her who can now never have?"

"Oh, for her!" said she. And I knew that I need fear no more for that selfless one.

There was in one of my Estates a widow who had awaited death for fifty years and more.

"Look at my finger," said she, showing me the shrivelled-up little finger of her right hand.

"Ever since I was three years old I was taught to be *Suttee*. We stirred boiling rice with a bare finger, to learn how to bear fire when our time should come. But, when my Lord died, there was a law which said that I must not be *Suttee*. So I have waited…."[26]

Her son, a ne'er-do-well, made no secret of desiring her death; and at the smallest sign of illness he would telegraph to the Local Authority for a grant of money for his mother's funeral ceremonies. The Local Authority would telegraph me, and I would hasten out across the river to my dear old Rani, and joyfully wire back, "Alive and Kicking!" or words to that effect.

There came an awful day, however, when, hearing that I was out of town, the son actually carried his mother down to the Burning Ghat, although she was alive. I got home from tour, just after a faithful Brahmin clerk had telephoned the fact, and I drove straight to the Ghat.

The Priests, four deep, were round her, and she lay very still with her feet in the Ganges, yet was obviously breathing.

"I assure you, Madam, she is dead," said her son. But they made room for me; she was alive, I could not contaminate her. I took her hand and said, "Mother, why do you lie in this strange place?"

She smiled at me, and said:

"To have one's feet in the Ganges is good." But I knew that she knew of her son's intent, and that so far from resenting it, there was in her heart a gladness that after all she might still be *Suttee*....

The terrible thing is that once brought to the Ghat as dead, or in expectation of death, you may not be taken home again.

But there was shelter, a corpse dressing-station on the near-by bank, which we could reserve, and where she might lie in comparative comfort. I had her carried there and a watch kept by a woman doctor to certify to her aliveness. Whether she really did die the second day, we shall never know. A Hindu doctor brought to her by her son, testified to her death about 2 a.m., and though I was getting telephone messages of her condition every hour, she was on the funeral pyre at "the Ghat of the Soul's Departing" when I arrived, already anointed for the burning and looking so happy wrapped in her prayer shawl of gold and crimson.

The woman doctor, not being an orthodox Hindu, had not been allowed to touch the patient after her superimposed colleague had pronounced his verdict. There was nothing to be done, except – and I have no doubt I did that irritably – to request an "American-returned" priest, in his Western clothes, to remove himself, if he wished to continue smoking cigarettes (as he was doing nonchalantly) beside that quiet sleeper.

I saw her grandson put the coal to her feet and to her lips, and then turned away from the grisly procedure.

In a country where death certificates are not usual among the orthodox, and where the dead must be immediately disposed of, one cannot be sure that the cremated are not alive.

I remember an awful experience my first week in Calcutta, when driving through the City, I looked up from the book I was reading at the sound of the death chant.

"*Ram bolo, Ram!*"

"That, at least," I said to myself, "is the same as in the West Country." And then my heart stopped beating, for the wind had blown the cloth off the face of the dead, as the bier passed me, moving in the opposite direction, and – the corpse opened her eyes and looked at me!

"Follow that!" I said to my driver.

He was an old Mohammedan, slow in obedience, and whether he did not deem it lucky to follow the Hindu dead, or whether his excuse that he had lost the procession was valid – I could not tell.

Of Burning Ghats there are many – and finally I had to give up the chase, sick at heart.

I sent for an orthodox Hindu friend. "Tell me that I could not have seen what I saw," I begged.

"Why not?" said he. " My own grandmother was taken down for dead to the Burning Ghat, to be burnt. But being a lively old lady, she refused to be burnt, and leapt off the pyre. When I was a little boy, and went to my father's burning, there was an old woman bent in two, wandering about the Ghat, eating the offerings to the dead.

"'That is our grandmother,' said my eldest brother; and he told me the story. Of course, we could not take her home again, or have anything to do with her; she was defiled." …

The utmost we could do as a Court of Wards was to secure valid death certificates. But as none but the orthodox may touch the orthodox dead, and as our jurisdiction was very wide, and death certificates inexorable as to time – I have never felt happy about even our strict vigilance….

Once I took the risk of interference with religious custom.

A Bihari widow with an only son, aged about five, was very ill, and came to Calcutta to die, so that she might be near me. I visited her daily, and she told me her hopes about her son. "I leave him to you. He is so clever that he will become '*chalaki*' (difficult to translate: a sharper) "unless he is under strict care and discipline. Do with him what you will." He was both clever and sensitive, a dear child of deep feeling; but even at five, one saw in him, as his mother did, the tendency to over-reach, to out-wit. It was his sensitiveness that just then, however, needed protection.

When his mother died, he put the coin on her lips, as the priests commanded. I did not object, her body was still warm. But when they said that the child must accompany her to the Burning Ghat, must light her pyre and stand by to collect in his little palm the ashes of her eyelashes and her nails, I put my foot down. I said, "No" – he would come away with me to my house, and that the brother of the lady or some other male relation must complete the ceremonies. I pointed out that I was acting in my personal and not in my official capacity, and that they were at liberty to take what action they pleased against me. The child stayed with me till all rites were over. And that was that! And I drove off with him. His thread ceremony had not been performed, and he had no Caste to lose. I had no shadow of doubt that his mother would have wished me to protect him, at any cost, against a shock from which his system would never have recovered.

The relations were very nice about it. "He is your son now," they said, and I not only had no trouble about this incident, but later when I arranged for the child to be a resident pupil at a College for Raj boys conducted on English Public School lines, though with due protection for Caste, I had their entire co-operation.

I expect the orthodox know too little of Child Psychology to realize the damage done to children by some of their ceremonies.

In a Western Indian case (1932) where the Court of Wards had no officer like myself, who could have intervened, a boy only eight years old was compelled to follow his father's body on its "farewell tour", across fields and through villages on his Estate, till finally the corpse was set up against a wall in a sitting posture, while all the Chiefs and Sirdars, led by the boy, did obeisance to it – a grim ceremony, concluding near midnight.

This matter of contamination in death came vividly before us in the North of India in a case which eventually got to the Law Courts.

There was an estate represented by five brothers who all died amazingly quickly one after the other, none of the brothers occupying the *gadi* more than a few years. Last of all, the fifth brother died also, and the five widows, all childless, asked for Court of Wards management. Luckily the fifth widow had been given power to adopt a son (adoption is not valid without such authority), and we took charge of her estate, and persuaded her to exercise her power.

Not long after the little heir was on the *gadi*, a strange thing happened. Rumours were current that the second Kumar (Prince) was alive; this was a revival of tales whispered in the Zenana itself, twelve years back. And as *ryots* were beginning to be restive about paying revenue – "for if the second Kumar were alive, he was ruler; and it was to him they should make payment, and not to the adopted son through the Government" – I was instructed to do what I could to discover the truth.

Now the story that I got from many sources, including the Zenana, was this. The second Kumar had ailed in the plains during the hot weather, and his doctor sent him to the Hills. "Your blood wants cooling," said he. He did not, however, get better; he died quickly and inexplicably, and was in due course taken down to the Burning Ghat to be cremated. A storm broke just as the rites began, broke fiercely with hailstones, and the "firing-party" ran to take shelter, leaving the body unguarded.

But the man was not dead, and the rain and hail beating on his face revived him. He sat up in horror. "I'm a corpse," said he; "once a corpse, always a corpse." And from behind him echoed a cheerful voice. "You're a corpse; once a corpse, always a corpse!"

It was a Bhutan Lama, who, passing that way, had come upon him. And the kindly man, realizing what was in store for an orthodox Hindu who had neglected to be validly deceased, urged him to accompany him. "We do not believe you to be contaminated, come with me, and be initiated into Buddhism. You can become a Lama and live amongst us. Don't trouble your heart about what the Watchers may think when they return. Come! the rain may stop any moment." And he went. But after twelve years it is allowable for a Holy Man to return to his own place and see how it is with those to whom he belonged; to see, without disclosing himself. And, at the appointed time, the resurrected one returned, and made (possibly indiscreet) enquiries. The last thing he had wanted was discovery; but he was recognized by his *shikari* (huntsman) and by his own sister among other people. Maybe there were those who thought to make profit out of a refusal to pay revenue. At any rate, the story blazed forth, and before the man could escape an official declaration was made locally to the effect that he was an impostor. That was a surprise to some of us, since it put upon the Government the burden of proof. We had thought that arrangements would have been made for payment of revenue into the Treasury pending reference to a Court of Law, since the Law alone could decide how far the facts had resulted in Civil death or a disclaimer of rights, leaving the Adopted One still in possession of the Estate. Local tactics, however, succeeded for the moment; the "second Kumar" disappeared, and recalcitrant tenants paid their dues. My investigations had elicited among other interesting tales the story of an insurance policy paid upon an alleged death certificate ("If an Insurance Company wants a death certificate, it must be produced"!) and an amazing statement from the widow. I had begged her to peep from behind a purdah at the man. "You will be able to say, better than anyone, if it is really he," I begged.

"I will not look at him," said she. "What am I to do now with a Lord who is not dead? A Lord alive I serve and worship; for twelve years I have served and worshipped faithfully my dead Lord. Twelve years of prayers and fasting – where have they gone? The *Shastras* do not tell us what to do with one who comes back from the dead. What can anyone do with such a one? We may not eat with him;

he is outcast; the Burning Ghat is his home! No, I will not look. I serve my Lord who is dead."[27]

And I could get no further. It was intensely interesting, for she was a good and faithful wife: she had not desired release, and she would continue to live a dead life herself, poor soul! with the doubt now at her heart that she was not even buying merit for her Lord after all.

But "the District" had closed the matter. My investigations remained incomplete upon my files.[xii] [[xii] In 1933-4, the matter came into the Courts of Law after all.

I have said that I was interested in all old ceremonies; and my Zenanas were kind enough to secure that the auspicious days for these should coincide with my ability to attend.

The Adoption Ceremony is one of the most interesting. Adoption covers a large body of Hindu Law, and the fiction of a son is carried so far that the son adopted to a man by his widow, must be the son of someone whom he could legitimately himself have married. Thus, his own sister's son, for instance, could not be adopted. There are other inexorable rules in practice, as to caste, etc. The vetting of these was my business. But, rules complied with, the actual rites covered a time of genuine "joy-making", differing according to the locality.

The Adoption I enjoyed most was connected with a Kashmiri Brahmin's Estate – the initial ceremonies including the dance of the wild peacocks by moonlight in a clearing in the foothills of Orissa, and the last act being the release of the Raj bodyguard of peacocks – awesome birds who guarded the Zenana stairs by flying at the eyes of anyone who looked like a man!

The ancient custom of a boy's initiation into Hinduism is still maintained among the Orthodox. The Hindu of the Vedas divided a man's life into periods, the first of which covered apprenticeship to a spiritual guide (who was also a tutor, in the ordinary sense), with whom he retired to the forest to meditate. It was not till after he had attained majority that he married, and lived the life of a householder, returning to meditation and the making of his soul for the final period of his life (often entered upon while he was still lusty and full of years).

The only one of these "stages of man" which is retained to-day, and that in the form of a symbolic ceremony alone, is the first.

Between the ages of nine and twelve the orthodox Hindu boy has his head shaved, leaving the small strand of hair or top-knot peculiar to the twice-born; he is invested with the sacred thread and is thus formally admitted to the practice of Hinduism.[28] The observance of caste is now *de rigueur*. And, as his forbears upon admission to their spiritual heritage renounced the world, he symbolizes the act. Dressed as a priestly mendicant, in an azalea-coloured garment, and carrying (for staff) the branch of a sacred tree, and a beggar's bowl, he travels the round of the guests invited to the ceremony, asking alms…. Then he goes back to the priests, to be conducted with prayers and *mantras* to a "pretend" hut in a "pretend" forest, staged in the men's courtyard, where he sits a while in meditation, a pretend meditation also, releasing him to great feastings in the Zenana and to lavish gifts of ornaments, clothes and other vanities. The "joy-making" lasts far into the night, including theatres and cinema-shows. Up to the forest scene, I always enjoyed this imitation ceremony; the solemnity and dignity of the children, who looked adorable as ascetics in their pilgrim robes, never failed to attract; and I kept wishing that they could indeed retire to the forest for tuition and meditation. I have a sneaking conviction that the ancients understood the Oriental temperament as modern educationists cannot do, and that India will not enter upon her inheritance till she returns to her Second-Century ways.

But this is, of course, rank heresy….

The dignity of Indian children over things ceremonial is due, in part, to the fact that they are actors in traditional robes, almost from the day of their birth. There are the "naming" and the "rice-taking" ceremonies to start with. Then there is the "chalk-in-the-hand" ceremony, so suggestive I wish that it could be adopted in Christian countries.[29]

I met it first in the case of a very special Baby Ward. His father and grandfather had both died under thirty years of age, and when for the third time the estate came begging for management as a Widow's Estate, the heir was only a few months old and there was nothing but that frail little life between us and an undesirable line of collaterals.

With the consent of his mother and grandmother we gave him an English nurse, and the child grew into a sturdy little boy, speaking English and two vernaculars, riding a pony, learning English Nursery games, and hearing English Nursery stories. There is no parallel to these latter in Hindu Zenanas, and he would recount them to the women, and indeed reproduce his entire Nursery life upstairs, putting his grandmother in the corner, to her great delight. "Already he is ripe," the women would say, " a Maharajah Bahadur. He will be a Lat Sahib; truly a Lat Sahib will he be!"

One day, when he was about three years old, I got a telegram which greatly alarmed me – "Would I come at once, the disaster was too great to be told by wire." I went post-haste, and found my Mother and grandmother Ranis awaiting me in the dawn hour.

"Kamala Ranjan has drawn a horse!" said they, a-twitter with excitement and fear.

I knew what they meant; no orthodox Hindu child might use his hand for any recognizable purpose till it has been blessed. Kamala Ranjan had been playing with a box of crayons which Nurse had given him. I looked at the paper – "it's all right," I said, "no one could call that a horse." And I advised them to choose a day for the "blessing-of-the-hand" ceremony and present a petition to the Collector for sanction. I promised to see the thing through at my end, as soon as possible. It was my duty to prepare a Note on the ceremony, and to examine precedents as to what ought to be spent upon it by Raj Estates of Kamala Ranjan's rent-roll. The ceremony being not only harmless but picturesque and desirable, as well as compulsory to orthodox Hindus, and, the Estate being in funds, there seemed nothing to prevent the Ranis recapturing ease of mind. But there were nevertheless alarums and excursions; and sheaves of telegrams were rained upon me, the gentle little ladies saying their religion was attacked, and that a judgment would overtake their beloved Kamala Ranjan. The Collector, the Local Officer, had refused sanction.

The Collector was the only officer of Hindu extraction in the series of officials who had to deal with the case. He was Hindu by race, but an "England returned" (as they called him) progressive.

He wrote on the Ranis' Petition –

"Gross superstition. Disallow." This alone was communicated to the Ranis.

The Commissioner, an Englishman to whom the petition went, in ordinary course – wrote –

"What is this Ceremony? Refer to Legal Adviser" (myself). The Secretary Board of Revenue wrote "To L.A.", and sent me the file.

The necessary information being given, sanction was accorded by the Board, and the ceremony went forward. But the Ranis did not quickly get over that refusal, and the inability to understand their point of view, on the part of one of their own race. And truly the incident does provoke thought about the future relationship between orthodox and progressive India. In the near future it will be the English-educated progressive who will almost entirely rule the orthodox masses.

The ceremony itself I found charming.

My three-year-old was admitted inside a circle of priests, and prayers were offered. Kamala Ranjan was blessed in all his ways, in all learning, and in all that he might do with his hands and see with his eyes. Then the oldest priest among them put a piece of chalk between the baby fingers and together the old man and the child traced a letter or two of the Bengali alphabet….

After which Kamala Ranjan was free to commit what mischief he pleased –

all curses averted!

The English-educated of the "gross superstition" school do not realize how much there may be that is admirable in these old customs, or how the possibilities of the indigenous might be made to serve moral teaching or the very latest methods and discoveries in education. Take the child's "Worship of the Cow" – even that. What is it? A baby girl led up to a cow, in the women's courtyard, rather frightened, but encouraged to recognize that the kindly creature gives her the draught of milk which she so loves. Will she not do something for the Mother-Cow, in return? Pour the holy Ganges water on its hoofs, garland it, put the sacred red sandalwood mark on its forehead to secure for it the protection of the gods? …. And baby hands lift the vessel of water, and a trembling baby finger makes the red smear, and slips on the garland of marigolds – learning thus early perhaps, some heartward way, that man and beast can be friends.

But – the modern Educationist could surely build upon this incident, lessons as to the care of the cow (and of other animals); and through the younger generations, and through ancient custom itself, eliminate that perversion of the worship of the cow which ends in the *pinjrapol* [xiii] [xiii *Pinjrapols* are hospitals where the sacred cow is maintained by the religious.] maintenance of diseased animals preying upon the resources of a poverty-stricken people.

Or take the ceremony in times of drought to invoke the Rain-God, when little girls walk into the shallow washings of the river bank, and pour out their libations from the jars held over their shoulders (they look adorable!) to the Rain-God, and sing the invocations, which will move him to send the needed rain. One sees a whole series of lessons built upon that – including teaching about how to lessen the hardships of drought, by the deep trenching adopted at American agricultural centres.

The "Worship" ceremonies include the worship of the Aged by little girls (what fun if we could get that adopted in England!), the worship of little ones by the Aged (is that the real ancestor of the Youth Movement?), the worship of brothers by sisters (I would scrap that! they are domineering enough as it is), and the worship of Friendship – a delightful ritual, when two little girls exchange bracelets of red cotton, binding themselves in eternal loyalty.

Of Moslem ceremonies I found the Baby Fête-days captivating. You should see a baby Moslem dressed as a Persian Princess, and carried on a pink cushion by her mother to be shown the world for the first time; the Koran and crossed swords are held over her, to remind her that religion comes first in a Moslem life; but that it has always been a fighting religion.

Yes, I found these and others, with the Betrothal and Marriage ceremonies, most interesting.

One curious thing about an orthodox Moslem marriage ceremony is that husband and wife may see each other for the first time only as reflected in a mirror during the ceremony – an awful moment, as girls have confided to me! What if he should have the sort of face she could not abide! As orthodox Moslems, photography is denied to them and may not lessen shocks, either way.

From Ceremonies to Oaths and Curses, which also play a vital part in the life of the orthodox, as has been indicated in this narrative. I discovered this fact, early in my wanderings, and eagerly collected the specimens belonging to the districts through which I travelled.

It is my conviction that truth could less infrequently be obtained from a witness in Courts of Law, if the Oath which alone in his conception binds an individual, were administered to him. Affirmations as requisitioned in Law Courts make no appeal whatever, because they carry no inherent retribution.

Should Counsel ask his orthodox Hindu witness, before he goes into Court, if he is prepared to repeat the statement contained in his "proof", after, e.g., "touching the five sacred things", or using the formula "I sitting in this room, all washed white state…" (i.e. "May I be a leper if I lie"), the man would draw back in horror; and the conclusion that he has lied already, is irresistible.

Oaths are very important things indeed. And, as for Curses – they are not only useful to a Legal Practitioner in the elucidation of mysteries; but are in brisk action among modern Indian Politicians – a fact too little realized by the West.

My most picturesque case in this connection related to "the bone under the bed".

We had just taken charge of an Estate in Bihar, upon the death of a Zemindar whose son, aged about five, we had put on the *gadi*. The Estate was represented by the widow and her mother-in-law. The mother-in-law hated her son's widow and upon his death had instantly begun a serious quarrel. "The boy was not her son's son, he was bought in the Bazaar. She claimed the *gadi* for the son of her second son (deceased, with his wife), a child of three years of age."

He certainly was an adorable "Pretender", with a head of black curls, and the most roguish of faces; and I fell in love with him straight away, seen beside our sleek dull little heir.

But we looked into the question, and having confirmed the heir's undoubted legality, entered his name on the roll, and assumed charge of the Estate, pending his majority.

The mother-in-law would not leave it at that. She and her daughter-in-law, the Rani, fought without restraint, although they were somewhat hampered by the fact that they lived in separate apartments divided by a stout wall, the door in which, leading from courtyard to courtyard, was their only point of contact.

As is usual in Raj quarrels, the servants of each lady made her cause their own. There were only two officials in the district, both English, a Collector and a policeman. The quarrel soon passed from personal abuse to riot; the policeman was compelled to go down to the *Rajbari*, and thought to end dispeace by the simple expedient of bricking-up that connecting doorway.

You must not be too hard on him. He was a bachelor, and had little experience of women.

Then, indeed, did hell break loose! The women climbed on to their respective roofs and laved one another in curses.

In one thing only were they united – hatred of the policeman who had prevented more personal approach, and they made the stock accusation, they said he had broken their purdah. He had, of course, done nothing of the kind, had seen neither of them.

But, he had had enough of women, and refused to go near the place again. So when, on a day a retainer of one of the ladies was found dead by a drain, the collector wired to me, and asked me to deal with the ladies.

I left at once for the District – the dead man incident having been duly disposed of by the police and local authorities – and, on arrival, made straight for the "Superior" Zenana, i.e. the Zenana of the Mother-Rani. I had long since learnt the obligation to observe strict etiquette in these matters. We talked throughout a day about peace being better than strife; and about the absurdity of fear for her son, when he was our child, protected by the Government. Finally, the Rani said she would forgive everything, and make friends, were it not for *the bone under the bed!*

I thanked Heaven that that curse was in my collection. I said solemnly, "If the boy has been cursed, that also is our business, not yours alone." But knowing that there were very special elements requisite and necessary to this curse, I added, "If we find that it is not 'the Cursing bone' of which you and I know, that in fact it is not a curse at all – will you make friends?"

She said she would, and I knew she would keep her word.

But I now required a priest to pronounce on the bone. "Was her priest at hand?" Yes, only just returned from a priestly tour. Good, thought I, he has had no time to get involved in this intrigue.

"Send for him." And he came with his chief disciple.

Oh, how I did grudge not having an English friend with me to enjoy what followed! That has been my one big miss through every thrilling Zenana experience; no one with whom to share a wink!

We sat in the chief room of the palace – it was a long room, bare of furniture except for the boy's bed at the extreme end. The bed was a low *takht-posh* covered with a lovely counterpane of purple and gold *Kincob* which reached to the floor. The only other article of furniture in the room was a carrying chair of ancient design, enamelled in green and gold. I sat on this, the cursed boy on my knee. To my right, by the open windows and balcony, sat the priest and his disciple. To my left, the Rani and her waiting-women. They sat on their haunches; all alike were dressed in dull white *saris* drawn securely over head and face, revealing no single feature even in the case of the Rani, who was smoking a *huqqa*. She smoked her favourite mixture, treacle and tobacco. There was no sound save the gurgle of the *huqqa*.

I opened proceedings in the vernacular of the District. "They say," said I to the priest, "that there is a bone under that bed. The Rani says it is a curse."

"Yes, a very bad curse. None worse."

"Has every bone power to curse; or is the cursing bone a particular bone?"

"To constitute a curse, the bone must be a human thigh-bone."

"And if the bone under the bed should not be a human thigh-bone?"

"Then, there is no curse."

This was, of course, the thrilling moment. I had to say, " *Bring out the bone.*"

But the bed was so low that it was the child alone who could slip a hand under it. The cursed one secured his bone, and laid it at my feet.

It was a darling little leg-of-mutton bone!

"Phew!" said the priest, picking it up and tossing it into the yard to the pariah-dog, who no doubt was responsible for it.

After that, the way to peace was easy. We un-bricked the door between the courtyards and went through to the mother-in-law lady and her little Pretender with offers of friendship, which were accepted because it pleased the old lady that the Rani should sue.

I was now free to go forth on my lawful occasions, but, knowing the danger of leaving the newly-reconciled women without supervision, I had one last duty to perform.

Rameshwaram is the most distant and most expensive pilgrimage in India, for the dweller in the North. When saying farewell to the mother-in-law, I broached the subject of pilgrimages.

"All my life I have wanted to go to Rameshwaram," said she, "but where's the money! And now that the Government is in charge, there is less money than ever to spend on Pilgrimages."

"I'll see that you have the necessary money," said I; a promise which an understanding Collector helped me to keep. And I left for Headquarters happy in the remembrance that it was a long way to Rameshwaram. It would be several months before the Pilgrim could return to her courtyard. The gods had granted joy without dissimulation, peace without stagnation.

But in my note-book the incident is represented by a single maxim in rubric –

"When you have forced two quarrelling women to make friends, separate them immediately."

THE BLUE-GREEN PARROT – THE BLIND RANI'S
DAUGHTER – THE YOUNG RULER'S TRAINING

Our dull little boy was given a tutor and grew up soberly in his distant Raj, his life punctuated by the religious rites belonging to his Caste and his locality.

The chief ceremony was his marriage, which, according to the custom of his family and the practice of his religion, had to be solemnized before he was ten. It was in emergencies such as this that the Government was in need of more than human wisdom. To refuse to acknowledge or allow the claims of custom and religion would have been madness. It would have been sheer waste. It would not have convinced the women of the cruelty of infant marriage; it would not have prevented it, in even this instance. They would have outwitted us. Even we could not police the Zenana – coercion would have been useless as well as foolish. And coercion was against the principles and promises of the British.

We did what was best in the circumstances – allowed the ceremony, but secured delay about the bride's transfer to her husband's home. And I knew that, by patient teaching, I could convert the women to right doctrine, and maybe delay things till the boy had attained majority. We had done this in almost all cases of which I had personal experience.

The "dowry" paid with the bride was our business interest in the matter. Since the bride's father owned valuable coal-mines, we instructed the negotiator to concentrate upon a village in the mining district.

But the Raja's Prime Minister tricked us. The marriage treaty contained a long list of movables; jewels and *kincobs*, furniture and utensils, camels and elephants and palanquins, but not a square inch of real property. Our own "keeper of the rules" was not himself, however, without shrewdness.

"There is one chance," said he; "during the ceremony, the bridegroom may ask what he will – and it will be given, since it is ill-luck to refuse a request made at that time."

So he instructed the boy to say at the crucial moment, "Give me a village with a coal-mine."

He looked a most desirable little bridegroom riding to the tryst, and he behaved perfectly through the religious ceremony. The great coal-owner felt he had indeed done well to bestow his daughter on this neighbouring Princeling.

The important request has to be made just before the move to the ceremonial meal. Everyone was in great spirits. The men sat in the Durbar Hall, the Raja already fingering the emeralds and rubies for which he felt sure the boy would ask. A servant came to the door. "The dinner is served," said he.

In the hush that followed, the bridegroom remembered his duty, the last item in a long day's ritual. He looked up –

"I want," he said, "a village with a coal-mine." Thud! went the Raja's baubles on the floor; and consternation was on the faces of his staff. The Prime Minister alone kept his head – a wad of betel-nut in his cheek, he strolled forward. "That stone-headed one has erred," said he, "the meal is not yet ready."

The Raja's sigh of relief was audible. He had every confidence in his Prime Minister; and watched that oily and astute one, as he turned to the boy.

"Have you seen the Raja Sahib's birds?" said he. They were indeed a marvellous collection. Parrots and cockatoos of many colours – blue and green, crimson and yellow, and little paroquets with red-ringed throats. The poor little bridegroom had seen nothing but sparrows and brown mynahs hopping in the dust of his arid estate. He was unconscious that a duty still remained to him (as indeed, in honesty, it did not); he was a child once more; he turned to the Raja Sahib.

"Give me," he said, "this blue-green parrot!"

"The dinner is served!" said the Prime Minister from the doorway.

And the feast over, the bridegroom rode home with – a parrot in a cage!

We had lost our last chance of improving his revenues.

It would seem appropriate to tell here by contrast the official dealings with a marriage in another Raj State, not under the Court of Wards. It is interesting as an example of the latter-day attitude towards the control of a parent over a minor girl in relation to her marriage.

Somewhere in India, there is a Hill State, set in rather primitive surroundings, both as regards man and beast. The beast indeed has often been shot from a motor-car on an evening drive; and man has risen against his rulers (not so very long ago), with the orgies of the tribal savage.

The Ruler of the State died, leaving him surviving, his widow and little daughter. The Rani was, alas! blind, and as she adored the child she declared her intention of relinquishing the *gadi* to the little girl. The child could not, however, be installed till she had attained majority. The Rani occupied the position of

Mother Regent while the Estate was under management connected with the Political Department of Government – an Australian being appointed manager. The Rani was an intelligent woman and had brought up the child admirably. She was given an American governess, learnt to read English as well as Hindi, her vernacular, to ride, to play games, all with due protection of "purdah"; she had even under safe escort gone shikar-ing, and killed a "spotted-one". She was a darling child, the chief attraction to myself, about her, being that she retained all the gentle graces of the secluded, while getting the best for mind and body which has always been available to those who live in an unsecluded world.

The devotion of the Rani was touching, for the child was the daughter of the Raja's first wife; but no one remembered this, since the Rani had taken the child to her heart as a baby, upon her own mother's death, and no bond of nature could have bound these two closer together. The family was, by tradition, deeply religious. The child's grandfather had indeed been almost a priest, sitting more often in *puja* and meditation, his body smeared with the "god-marks", than wearing his robes and jewels, sitting on the *gadi*. In the palace grounds was a gem of a little private chapel, and the Ruler of the State was bound to worship there every day, night and morning, going as a Ruler, accompanied by his staff. From the earliest days of her abdication the blind woman had insisted on the little girl's carrying out this duty of Queendom. And I loved seeing her slip through the private way from the Palace, a leafy shrubbery, to the door of the *puja ghar*, her waiting-women following her.

Best of all I loved watching her at the *Arati*, or lamplighting ceremony – a simple office when she passed the little lamps (open vessels with floating wicks) in symbolic movements of invocation, before an invisible idol, standing slim and graceful, while the priest sat cross-legged, mumbling Sanskrit. I used to steal to the open door, and look in, my heart caught with my own prayers for the future of that child trained in new ways, but inescapably bound to face conditions and prejudices as old as Time.

When I first knew her she was twelve years old, and her mother had come to ask my help in circumstances which she found devastating. A marriage had been proposed for her daughter, by the Political Authorities, with a penniless and landless collateral connection of a State in a neighbouring Province. She objected to the proposal because, first, the present practice of this State was not orthodox Hindu; and, secondly, she did not wish her daughter to marry so young. "Let her wait," she begged, "and marry in the fullness of time some orthodox Hindu, heir to a Hindu State." When pressed, she suggested the names of some such applicants for her daughter's hand who were known to the Governors of the Provinces in whose jurisdiction they lived, to be without reproach, of ancient lineage, and of rent-rolls, not unworthy of candidates for the hand of a Rani. When his own proposals were found unacceptable the Manager had refused the mother access to her daughter, or indeed to her own Palace; and appeal to the Political Authorities was of no avail. All we could get was postponement of the marriage upon which the Authorities had set their hearts, till the girl was fourteen. A prayer that there should meantime be no communication between the boy and girl or through emissaries on behalf of either, was also refused. Indeed, contrary to Hindu etiquette, the people in charge of the girl encouraged a correspondence between her and the boy, and an exchange of photographs, and of gifts – all under the rose, the worst type of clandestine courtship.

The mother's allowances were stopped, wholly unjustifiably, and this I managed to get put right; but a prayer that the child might spend at least one year with her mother before marriage was thrust upon her, in a Hill Station under the eye of the officials, and upon undertaking given that not one word would be said by the mother about the proposed undesirable marriage or any marriage – although, poor soul, her own wish had been to postpone marriage till the child's accession to the *gadi* – was absolutely refused, even upon appeal to the highest Political Authority. The only reasons given were that –

(a) The mother was really a stepmother, her wishes need not be considered.

(b) The local authorities had made a promise to the Raj relation of the proposed bridegroom that they would see this thing through, and the said Raja had in reliance on that promise made a donation to a public institution then in need of funds.

(c) The girl herself (aged thirteen) was now terribly in love and wished the marriage.

Shortly after receiving this final decision the mother died, of a broken heart. I tell this story without comment.

Little boys are a great responsibility. We realized this over the children aged three and five who came into our charge upon the sudden death of their father, together with another Bihar Estate in the Hill Country. The history of this estate was interesting. The founder was a stalwart priest, who had obtained the land from a Raja as a reward for slaying a man-eating tiger who harassed the District.

"Whoever brings the beast in dead, may ask what he will."

"I ask," said the priest – following the carcase of a gigantic beast hanging by his feet from the pole on which the beaters carried him – "I ask a grant of as much ground as I can cover travelling from sundown to sunrise. The ground to be measured to include so many cubits to right and left of my passing."

"Take it," said the Raja, "but you travel on foot, and my men go with you to demark the route." The priest most certainly was a sprinter, and I have since thought that he must also have been a mineral diviner (if that is possible), for he chose the richest tract of land in all that countryside, honeycombed with valuable minerals. He was the great-grandfather of our little boys, and, as nothing had been done by their forbears about the minerals, it was left to us to survey the possibilities, and to find that through a long minority we had the chance of developing a very rich estate indeed for our small wards.

But that was not the problem which gave us trouble. As usual it was the situation in the Zenana, where (a Zenana habit) the late Raja's mother hated her daughter-in-law, and thought to hurt her through the children. We were faced with the horrifying evidence of an attempt to poison our wards.

After a consultation with all the Authorities, a suggestion to "kidnap" them was approved. The maternal grandfather, also a Zemindar, who lived in an adjoining district, and who with his brother, the children's uncle, could drive a car, obtained leave to remove his daughter and the children to a place of safety under British protection.

The children needed a change and the palace needed rebuilding. Everything could be accounted for without making any charge against the grandmother or against the Advisers who had probably inspired and were responsible for the menace: although, of course, the utmost circumspection was peremptory for the protection of the children and their mother in the carrying-out of our plans.

So, on a day, there was a great gathering of officials at the end of the palace most distant from the grandmother's quarters, and at a time when she was shut away in her *puja ghar*. The Commissioner, the Collector, the Civil Surgeon and I were all present in the Raj office room, examining Estate papers. A responsible police officer was not far off, and the maternal grandfather and uncle, with their cars, were within hail, albeit invisible to the Palace entourage. Some inkling of what was afoot there must have been, inside the Rajbari, however, for I saw the corridors leading to the Zenana lined with guards, armed with guns. I told this to the Commissioner, and, while I played with the children who had been brought to me at once, he strolled down to examine the weapons, returning with the reassuring news that they were "relics", and would probably hurt those who used them more than anyone else. We had the children safely, then; but the next move was difficult – the conduct of their mother, with due protection of her purdah, through the lines of guards to her father's car. She knew our programme, which, indeed, had been made in response to her own prayer for help. As soon as she and the children were in the purdah-ed cars, we were to get away across the hills to safety. I myself would be in a separate "bodyguard", close-up car.

The first hitch occurred at the Zenana quarters. Her priest had insisted upon the Rani's going into her *puja ghar* whither I could not follow her. But she had seen me come, and I used the interval in arranging a "walking purdah" for her – placing her waiting-women in two lines *vis-à-vis* holding long lengths of *saris* as if they were tent-walls. Having made her obeisance to the idol, the Rani slipped out into this shelter, where I awaited her, and I hustled her along past the guards between the moving purdah walls, and straight into her father's car, which was then under the porch. We were nearly outwitted, however, because the children had yelled and refused to move. I rushed up the stairs to the office, and, with one in my arms and one clinging to my hand, got them down, and also safely bestowed.

I was without anxiety about what we had left behind. The most competent of the officers of District and Division were there to deal with it. But the long and lonely route across the hills had far greater thrills than the leopards which ran scuttling in the car lights on the many occasions when I had previously made that journey. We halted once to give our charges a meal; but for the rest ran on top speed, till we got by nightfall to safety.

The grandmother raged, and vowed vengeance; but vengeance is difficult of execution under British protection, and she chose the better part. She renounced the world to live as a hermit at a place of pilgrimage.

As year succeeded year the impression grew that in the Court of Wards the Government had an opportunity unequalled in any direction – an opportunity of training the future self-ruler, as well as of helping him to be a model Zemindar, developing his resources and teaching the conservative illiterate villager how to get into touch with modern progress.

Again, Raj Estates could be made to punctuate with construction and peace the chaos of Revolutionary movements. The "Youth" which stood for stability and a stake in the soil would be the counter-attraction to the "Youth" captured for disruption. An indigenous "Youth" movement of this kind is obviously what is needed to oppose the imported youth movement which has its headquarters at Moscow.

Being within the political area of British India, these small estates are, from the angle at which we are now considering them, of far greater value than the lordly independent Native States. And after release from Government administration, if chances of personal contact and friendship are wisely used, the boy Zemindar could be shepherded and helped through the difficult initial stages of independence. That is the rock on which most of them split. They are held too tightly and meagrely during their wardship, and enter upon the administration of money and property without any training in handling either commodity. During my time, helped by friendly Collectors, I tried to minimize the danger by getting allowances for our boys when they were seventeen years old, and encouraging them to keep accounts as to the spending of the first sums of money they had ever handled. For, always and always, we had to remember that the Zenana in its (loving) ignorance was pulling against restraint, pulling the wrong way, buying for them what we had denied, at cost to themselves, when possible: when not possible, at cost to the Estate through a *bania*. Of the ethics of spending they had no conception. To help the boy here was clearly our opportunity.

The great difficulties in the way of rural economic development in India include –

(a) Fragmentation, i.e. the impossibility of dealing with estates parcelled out among co-sharers in absurdly small allotments;

(b) Ignorance as to modern methods of agriculture and the reluctance of the peasant to forsake the ways of his *bap-dada* (father-grandfather).

I have in mind one estate at least in Bihar where I met with immediate co-operation from the Zenana when the "small parcels" situation was explained. The estate was represented by the two widows of the owner and the minor son of the younger widow. The women were friends. The boy was treated as their joint property, and the elder widow meant to leave her " little parcels" to him when she died. But it was likely that she would live many years, and management of her share apart from that of the minor was complicated by the fact that the shares overlapped hopelessly – two acres here, three elsewhere, and so on…. After getting the stepmother to agree to have her share computed and measured out over adjoining and contiguous fields, I got the minority administration to accept a like proposal. And the difference which this made, not only in cultivation but in cost of management, was a great victory.

Meanwhile we had won another victory in inducing the boy and his mothers to consent to his being given an agricultural training in England, instead of taking a B.A. degree and reading the law. And when he came back to Bihar, he appreciated to the full the fact that he was owner of a consolidated estate. He had been trained as a practical farmer. One of his first discoveries was that the Indian plough did not bite deep enough; but that a plough on the English pattern would be too heavy for our slender cattle. He devised a more effective plough of the Indian type, got it made locally, and induced his tenants to use it. His stepmother was still alive and her property was managed separately. The readjustment of shares saved riots and quarrels between the tenants of the two Zemindaries, and prevented the lad from being (excusably) autocratic across his stepmother-neighbour's landmarks – as must needs have happened had the shares been entangled.

It was never easy to persuade to an agricultural education – and oddly enough the official was less persuadable than the Zenana in the days before the Agricultural Commission directed the policy of Government at the centre.

The opposing officials were, I am sorry to admit, almost entirely Indian – the "England-returned" variety. They considered the suggestion derogatory. "Was I trying to deprive the ward of the benefits of the University in order to keep him subject to authority? Let him take his B.A. degree, and we'd see about a Zemindari training after that." But the estate would be released when the boy was twenty one, and the B.A. degree meant living in towns, where he made the acquaintance very often of undesirable sycophants and acquired habits foreign to his race, with tastes which upon majority could be indulged only by living permanently in a town (as the lawyer and other professional Zemindars do) and neglecting his duties as a landlord. The "English-returned" ones would not see that; and I had to wait patiently till a more persuadable collector came to the district. Sometimes the Commissioner and the Member helped; but I was loath to antagonize the local authority by appealing to his superiors: since the ward is, after all, the business of the Collector. A better ally, when once convinced, was the Zenana. The objection of the Zenana to Agriculture was stated in terms of orthodoxy. I made it clear from the beginning that the ward would learn to plough and sow his land, and to do all the practical work of farming, as well as studying the science of agriculture, the use of machinery and the value of manures, etc.

"But – his hand on a plough – why, that would outcaste him!" they said. An inspiration helped me –

"I have read that the goddess Sita was turned up in a furrow. Do you believe that?"[30]

"But without doubt."

"Do you mean to tell me that the hand of an outcaste was on the plough?"

"No! *no!* Yes, *Sita* was turned up out of the earth by a ploughman, as he drove his plough. Agriculture is an occupation for caste folk truly." And the dear things gave me no more trouble. I will not say that I did not also point out that the occupation of an agriculturalist kept a Zemindar on his Zemindary among his people, and therefore more constantly with his mother. But it was really *Sita* in the furrow who turned the scale.

The acquiescence of the authorities and the Zenana did not, however, end our difficulties. There was really no suitable training-ground in India for the boys. I sent some to the Government Agricultural College at Sabour, and some to Dr. Higginbotham's American Training Station at Allahabad.

Dr. Higginbotham was nearer to our requirements than Sabour. "Sam"

Higginbotham, as everyone knew him, was an enthusiast. He made the worst bit of land burst with plenty. He boldly introduced American machinery and American (now world-wide) expedients – silage pits, deeper trenching, etc. He demonstrated how we could face four years of drought by wise use of trenching and percolation, and how the use of silage pits would improve the dietary of cattle. Best of all, he did propaganda work through his students. Every Sunday the boys visited the nearby villages and helped the peasants with their simple farming; getting thus the opportunity needed to persuade against the fatalistic submission of peasant farmers to disaster, e.g. showing them how pests and drought could be conquered: and urging the adoption of the newer methods, to observe the results of which they would carry the suspicious men back with them to the Agricultural Station – where conversion was speedy.

The expense of the new way was met by co-operative farming – contiguous farmers being persuaded to combine in the hire of machinery, or over silage pits.

But – the class of boy which went to these institutions was not of Zemindari standing. The wards were terribly lonely outside their hours of work, and terribly dependent on the kindness of their over-worked Principals and Professors.

What we really wanted was a training-ground designed primarily for Zemindars. Under our Act we assume responsibility for Zemindari training; but all we did (and still do) was to make a ward travel with his manager over his Zemindary for six months before the release of his estate. His manager, unfortunately, as a rule, had almost as little knowledge of agriculture and of estate management as the boy himself: for no more had been required of him in his turn (as qualification for his post) than that he should tour with an untrained manager (since these alone were as a rule available).

All that the manager really knew was how to collect rents and put in processes against the slacker, together with the office work in which his superior officers were chiefly interested. I do not want to suggest that there were not managers – mostly ex-planters – who did not know more than I have indicated: but they were exceptions.

What we chiefly needed primarily, then, was a well-thought-out training-ground for Zemindars and managers of estates over a sufficiently large and suitable area to demonstrate the chief crops of the country, in charge of an experienced officer fully trained and acquainted with local conditions. His nationality, as in other departments of service, would be of less account than his personality and equipment.

I have already whispered in this record my dreams about the materialization of such an area (p. 102). And may they indeed come true! For without such a centre, the Court of Wards cannot hope to fulfil its duties in this respect.

When there is only one son, the land may well be recommended to him as an objective. But it is not the only possibility open to wards. Several estates have been discovered, especially in Bihar, to offer development in mineral wealth. The Government has begun to recognize this fact, and young Zemindars are directed to Mining Schools where these are suitable to their needs.

Again, younger sons can always be released for the learned professions. But those responsible for shepherding ambition must for ever have as difficult a task as in a private family – indeed a more difficult task still than that. For one is without a guide as to inherited tendencies and has less chance than a parent for personal observation. When Dehra Dun Academy, the first Indian Military School, was started, I tried to inspire the Zenana with ambition for a military career for the younger boys.

"It would be unlucky," was the women's answer in Bengal. "We are not *Kshatriya* – not the mothers of fighters."[31]

When I appealed to Rajput (*Kshatriya*) Mothers –

"What! send our sons to Dehra Dun! It is said that sons of non-Rajputs may go there. The profession of a *Kshatriya* is degraded. It is unlucky to have anything to do with a scheme of that sort!"

"The first annual summary of important matters connected with the defence services of India 1933-34" was presented to the Central Legislative at Simla on September 7. It contains this passage as cabled by Reuter (*The Times*, 10 September, 1934):

> A special point has always been made of the fact that the Academy is open to all classes, castes, creeds, martial or non-martial, but statistics show that this invitation is little availed of by those for whose benefit its comprehensiveness was intended. In October last 200 candidates sat in open examination, and of those 86 were Punjabis, 30 came from the United Provinces, five from Bengal – the population of which is nearly double that of the Punjab – and seven from Madras. In March there were 44 Punjabis among 91 candidates, and of the total 19 were of the Kshatriya caste, to which Hindu fighting men mainly belong, 18 were Moslems, 16 Sikhs, and 12 Brahmins. No other caste or community provided more than five.

Might not the explanation of the failure of the Authorities to get a better response, both from the non-martial and from the martial classes, lie in just the "special point" about which the founders evidently took to themselves special credit in their ignorance of the views held by the people really concerned?

After all, the lawyers in the Assembly are – let us be frank about this – out of touch with the indigenous in every particular. These are the men who press for reforms and these are the men in the main who advise the Central Government. But (again as a rule) they themselves despise caste in its hold on "the superstitious" (who form the majority in India, for whom the Dehra Dun Academy was founded), and it will not be these lawyers who in the fullness of time will officer the Indian army for which they clamour.

The Army Councils Bill was passed in the Assembly the same final session of 1934, after fierce opposition from the left. H.E. the Commander-in-Chief, Sir Philip Chetwode, made a magnificent speech begging Indians not to weaken the morale of the Cadets by suggesting an "inferiority complex" to men who needed the great confidence which the profession of arms demands. And he won a notable victory.

But how much of that opposition was due not really to an "inferiority complex" in the usual sense of the word, but to the religious hold upon themselves (subconsciously) of the superstitions which Assembly lawyers overtly despise! I am inclined myself to think, in this case, not a little. In order to carry on and complete the good work initiated at Dehra Dun, and by the passing of the Army Councils Bill, there must surely be wise propaganda and house-to-house explanation made to the mothers, both of the martial and non-martial castes.

Broadcasting programmes might well include information about military training. And indeed I have long felt that a series of talks on *Careers* generally should be held to be imperative at this stage of our progress.

Indian mothers have yet to be taught what ambitions to hold in their hearts for their children. And you cannot get any politicians' (Indian or English) ideals of progress to materialize in India without the co-operation of the orthodox and illiterate mothers of indigenous India.

V THE LAST LAP

TRAVELS AND THRILLS – SOCIAL SERVICE AWAITING WOMEN IN INDIA – SOME VICEROYS

Travels and thrills! – the gods have been good to me in this as in much else. I've travelled by the flat-bottomed "green" boat, almost our only river transport in Warren Hastings' time, by river steamer, by "dug-out" in far water-ways – the crocodiles pointed out to me casually by a waterman who had got so *blasé* over them that he had light-heartedly sent my *chuprassis* to wade across their path! In the unsophisticated water-routes of Eastern Bengal I have tried vainly to capture sleep, under the wonderful dark-blue starlit sky, on my little camp-bed fixed up at one end of an open boat, while the *manjis* alternately rowed and poled, and sang songs without intermission throughout the night. I don't know that I resented being kept awake, for the stretches of jungle growth through which we passed were thridded with beauty and mystery, and seemed altogether unreal. Across country I've travelled in palanquins, on elephants, in the quaintest of ancient carrying-chairs and carriages; I've been offered every kind of beast to ride and drive; and in later years, motor-cars in every stage of dilapidation.

I became expert in riding elephants without fatigue, sitting close up behind the *mahout*. But the high lights of memory play upon the elephant on whose back I crossed a river in flood; and on the horse who had first to be harnessed face to the driver, that he might inspect her who held the reins, before he would consent to be driven through the dense unlighted jungle (this was always a midnight adventure), where "the spotted ones" were reported to prowl.

That experience was outdone by a ghastly drive in the Muzaffarpur Division (Bihar) during the rains when the floods were rising. I was bound for a distant Raj off the beaten track and had left my railway carriage at dawn, in a siding, to be attached to the midnight mail, which I must catch on a tour when adherence to my programme was essential.

The Raj motor-car had met me and taken me to my objective, and my work was happily concluded during the day. But before nightfall the roads had become impassable for a car; and there was nothing for it but to drive myself back in an ancient open dog-cart. We had no lamps; but a way-shower, girt to the loins, his bare legs swishing in the water, ran before us, carrying a lantern. A *sais* (groom) knelt on the back seat of the cart, holding an umbrella over my head – it was raining hard – and calling terrified directions – "to the right – no, no, to the left!" ... To miss the road meant worse than I would let myself imagine; the road ran beside the river and was under water. I concentrated on the way-shower and the smoky lantern, which seemed like the fast-closing eye of a malicious demon. It was a race between us and that descending eyelid, and we won by an eye lash; I settled into my waiting carriage shivering with ague, but triumphant.

A worse nightmare was a palanquin journey across seas of sand. My camp was pitched not far from a Burning Ghat during a cholera epidemic; and the death-chant, together with the smell of the burning – added to the pop of the heads when the flames had got there – was the worst possible atmosphere for an illness with which I was seized the evening we pitched camp.

I felt that the end might come any moment: and told my servants to despatch the telegram which they would find beside my bed – if I were not there next morning. I was there, of course, by a miracle, and laughed to read what I had drafted *in extremis*. It was a message to the officer in charge of the nearest police station, and read, "I'm sorry, but I died last night. Please see that I am not taken to the Burning Ghat". But Death is a gentleman, and never again "tapped me on the shoulder" with such grisly detail – no, not even when I was ferried, lying on a stretcher, across a river, with a temperature of 105∞, and had thereafter to ride an elephant across country to a Rajbari to hear the last wishes of an old *Purdahnashin*. And certainly not when one day, out in camp as I sat at tea in a shady cul-de-sac, near which we had camped, I looked up from the book I was reading to see the bare leg of a man slipping over a wall, followed by an arm bearing the naked blade of a Kathiawar weapon. His toes were feeling for a crevice; the wall was high and crevice there was none.

"There is no foothold," I said, "be careful" – and he dropped his sword, retrieving his limbs in haste. We never found him, though we did hear why he had wished to surprise me. Palace intrigue as usual – an attempt to remove the protector of a defenceless woman. It was not till many years later that I realized why experiences like those instanced above invigorated me.

The explanation was given me at a Washington dinner-party. I sat by the Chief Justice of the Supreme Court and we were talking of the Hon. O. W. Holmes, who had just retired from the Bench after a serious illness.

"Death has tapped me on the shoulder," wrote Mr. Justice Holmes to my neighbour, "and said, '*Live* – I am coming – '" That was just it. Hazards are invitations to a more joyous life.

It is not this way, however, that the orthodox Hindu looks at death. His indifference to death is indisputable; but it is not the "hurry-up-and-pack-in-all-you-can-while-you-may" attitude of my Western tale. It is the calm belief of one who holds that the house of this present body is only one of many houses in which he will live – of millions of houses. Why worry about the moment's tenancy?

"God has given me a lease of this house of my body," said my Wisest-of-the-Wise, "but it is undated." On another occasion, "Life", she said, "is a dream in the heart of a dream; Death is tomorrow's dream." The final objective, I gathered, is the loss of self, of personality, by absorption into God, the Great Soul.

I have met two Hindus, Mathaji Maharani Tapashwini, my "Wisest-of-the-Wise", and the old yellow-pink robed Swami, Sat Nam Singh – "Truth-named" – who have bought back for me all the degradations, the impositions, and the undesirable practices which are often the only form of Hinduism met by the alien. And what I learnt from them gave me the solution to much that was vital in my work among practising Hindus.

But I do not mean to suggest that, of Hindu Saints, I have met only two. The gentle faces of widowed *Purdahnashins* come before me as I write – humble little ladies who just simply would not have understood any suggestion that they were Saints or Devotees; but who, nevertheless, did keep alive the thought of God in the remote Zenanas where they "followed their rule".

One such was Rani-Ma, a widowed grandmother who spent hours in meditation in a "house of Gods" which contained no single image.

She adored a small granddaughter just married to a neighbouring Maharajah. The child sickened of enteric. They were distraught in the Zenana. They put in nurses and the Civil Surgeon (being our Wards, they knew what was advisable). But because she did not recover in a day, they sent to Calcutta for a Homœopathist, to whom they paid Rs.5,000 (£750) a day....

When I arrived, retrieved from tour, I found that this doctor, likewise being unable to cure enteric in a day, had been replaced, this time by a Hindu priest.

The nurses were turned out of the room, the patient was cast upon a mattress on the floor, her temperature was alarming, she was being fed on nuts and green mangoes, and the priest and his disciple were burning melted butter under her nose, snapping their fingers at all the pulses of her body, in order to drive out the devil with which she was possessed, and shouting at her to call on Kali.

Round the room were hung pictures of gods and goddesses, whom the waiting-women worshipped, blowing conch-shells.

It was a marvel that the child lived: but she was still there, moaning and turning her face away from the smelly butter.

I stood watching this scene from the verandah, Rani-Ma beside me, almost mad with grief. The priest, she said, was being paid twice as much as the Homœopathist; good must result.

"But you do not believe in idols – why do you not stop all this noise, and go and pray silently in your House of Gods?"

"That is for when things go well," said she. "But now, who knows what gods or demons should be propitiated?" She was taking no risks.

"The noise and discomfort are bad for little Chandi," I persisted. "Send the priest away." And I told her about the duties of nurses in enteric, and about the nature and probable duration of that illness.

"I dare not send the priest away. But she is your child. Do what you will."

Thus fortified, I went into that strange sickroom. The ringing of bells and invocations, the blowing of conch-shells, ceased. And I said to the priest:

"I hear that you are a powerful Magic Man."

"It is not for me to say."

"But I have heard. I know the fee that Rani-Ma gives you. I suppose you could work your cure sitting at Cape Comorin or in the Himalayas."

The idea was new to him – but he admitted that it was even so.

"Then I must apologize to you that they have brought you so close to your patient. This is a Zenana in my charge."

Yes, he knew that.

"Well! I've told them to prepare a room for you in 'the Outside'" (the buildings most distant from the Zenana), "and you will go there with your disciple, and burn your melted butter, and ring your bells; and the *Ji-s* will accompany you to blow their conch-shells and call on Kali…. And then when the poor sick Maharani is well again, I myself will bear witness that you were indeed as far removed as possible from the patient."

Without one word he departed; and his properties with him. The nurses put little Chandi back into her clean bed; and sponged her with vinegar and did the routine things. That night her temperature was down two degrees; and though we had an anxious time, she pulled through….

That is the only time I have ever got the better of a priest! He took the credit of the patient's recovery, together with Rani-Ma's largesse. Who cared? The child was alive. But my heart was sore for the numberless homes where scenes like these must be enacted without remedy.

Not long after, a Calcutta Zenana brought me another illustration – orthodox Hindu treatment in a maternity case.

I had known the child Kalidasi, the expectant Mother, since she was a darling baby of six, keeping wicket for her brother at cricket, which he was just learning to play in his distant Raj. She was now ten and a half years old, and her first baby was due.

The father-in-law sat outside the closed door of the room set apart for such happenings. He was reading aloud from a Bengali translation of an old Sanskrit book – specific directions to the Indian nurse within.

The terrified boy husband was the only other person admitted to that room. The Mother and grandmother, being widows, might not enter. They beat their heads on the stone steps outside, offering this self-flagellation to the gods, if haply it might avail.

As things seemed to be at their last gasp, the Rani had telephoned, begging me to come with whatever doctors and nurses I chose to bring. And I had brought them – only just in time....

The baby was a bouncing creature, and our anxieties lifted. It was now 2 a.m. The doctor had departed, leaving a competent English nurse in charge. The Ranis were sitting beside me in an adjoining room; the old father-in-law still read from his ancient book of the words, translating now into English for the English nurse.

"Now," he said, "it is high time to light a fire on the top of the Mother." The nurse hurried out to me, furious.

"Yes, I heard," said I. "What is it you really need?"

"Hot-water bottles, but there'll not be one in this house."

"I've brought two, they are in my trap; but we must first get Rani Sahiba's consent to use them."

"What is the Nurse *Mem* saying?" asked the Ranis.

"She says they'll kill my Kalidasi; they want to light a fire on a tin plate, and place it upon her."

"Yes, that is done – if it is her fate to live, she will live with a scar. If not –" and the two women fell to weeping.

"But why must you offer an oblation to Fire? My ancestors did that, not yours. You've got to remember Ganga Ma, the River Ganges.... Now listen – suppose we heat some Ganges water and pour it into these two bottles which I've brought" – and I showed them that they were quite safe, nothing outcaste-ing about them – "we can then place the bottles" (and I explained how they would retain heat) "on Kalidasi, instead of lighting that fire. So the Fire God and Ganga Ma can both be remembered; and the customary Fire offering we can still present on its tin plate; but in the window."

And thus it was done, without outraging the god of common sense, or any other god.

If one only knows enough, there is a way of getting round most of these centuries-old difficulties.

Thus, during an epidemic of black small-pox in remote villages in a fastness of superstition and ignorance – "a terrible one is visiting us," said the women; "he either takes us away, or leaves us with holes in our faces."

The disease was known as "the Kali-sickness" in that part of the country. So I said:

"It's the visit of Kali."

"Then she wants blood!" And wide-eyed, they wondered which little one would be claimed as a victim.

"But this time only a prick of blood will do," I said, "and I'll pay too."

So we got in a vaccinator, and saved the village.

In a Zenana in another part of the Province, small-pox had been recognized when it came.

"But we are doing everything that the books command –"

"What is that?"

"We have dressed all the women in red *saris*, and have dieted every one but the patient!"

Another instance of the value of a knowledge of superstitions to Social Service workers and doctors is set in one of my most poignant memories. A village woman unable to get ease of mind was brought to me with her story. After years of longing, she had given birth to a man-child. She adored him, but one day when he was seven or eight months old, a demon got into him, "Truly, Miss Sahiba, a demon. The child kicked his hands and feet at his own Mother. I could not stop him, I ran to my neighbours. 'It's a demon,' they said, 'we recognize it. The only thing to do is to *quiet* him, else he will kill his father.'

"But how could I do *that* to my little man-child for whom I had waited so long?

"I offered myself to the gods, if only he might be spared" ('Upon me be thy curse, my son,' – an Israelite Mother said that centuries ago). "And he did become still, the demon left him. But a few days later the demon came again, and there was no doubt this time, for the child's face began to change colour. 'Sit on him,' said the women, my neighbours, 'quick, lest the demon escape to kill the child's father.' And – we put him on the ground, and – I sat on him; how could I let his father be killed? – and my little man-child became very still, and very cold....

"I have no man-child now. But the child's father, he lives...."

Now when we go into the villages, we can say to the women – "When your child beats his fists and his legs into your face, you think he has a demon. We know that he has not. But this is the way to drive out the demon if you believe he is there." And we teach the requisite treatment for convulsions.

After years of experience, in untrodden ways, I conclude that the only way to help the illiterate and superstitious is to proceed from the known and accepted to the unknown; to base the enlightenment which you would bring upon the superstition; not to flout the superstition.

Very soon the women will begin to say, "Of course, it was not a demon," and to desire teaching. For that is another axiom which experience bought; you cannot help, however great the need, unless your help is desired. You have first to create recognition of a need for help, next a desire for help, and for help from you.

These reflections I put into a scheme – the League of Social Service – which planned for two kinds of workers, (a) the Forerunners, i.e. the indigenous or other worker acquainted with local superstitions who would go to the villages, accompanying a peripatetic clinic, so to speak, pitched under the village tree, demonstrating Infant welfare, Infant diet, giving talks about ante-natal care, a pure milk and water supply, etc.... all made attractive and complete with Magic Lantern and posters....

These visits were to be followed by the establishment in the villages of (b) our second battalion of fully trained workers, as specifically desired by the village for any of the subjects with which our Forerunners had acquainted them.

The finance of the scheme was also carefully worked out. Eventually the Districts were to pay for the workers sent to villages. And our dream was of expanding circles of control, the Division making the Clearing House for the District. But the kernel of the scheme and its primary necessity was a Central Training Institute located at Presidency Headquarters, where the "Practising Schools" for the various branches of training which we needed were already in existence. We were all for not overlapping; as also for reducing expenditure to a minimum. The Institute would provide specialized training in those subjects alone in which no training was already available at Welfare Centre, Hospital, or Teachers' College. Candidates would live at the Institute and instruction would be given under the guidance of an experienced Warden in the principles of Social Service and public work, in Civics, in the keeping of statistics, in the conduct of meetings, and in such matters as are indispensable to Social Service workers. This section of a Diploma Course would be obligatory, the workers branching off thereafter to specialize in the work which most attracted each one – Infant Welfare, Maternity and District Nursing, Factories and Industrial Social Service, Juvenile Court Work, or Vocational and the regulation School teaching...

From this Central Institute, then, the workers, both Forerunners and Trained Experts, would go forth to the surrounding villages as spokes from a wheel in – as I have said – ever-widening circles of influence.

My *Purdahnashins* were thrilled with the idea. Why should they not help, they begged, to raise the funds we needed, and yes – why not also with the work itself? This led to the suggestion – that they should "stage" the scheme as Voluntary Forerunners in villages. They knew the superstitions which had be combated; and were willing to learn how to present the new teaching.

No better pioneers could have been found. Their selflessness as to donations to the Fund was touching. They stewed in the Plains through the hot weather, giving to the League Fund the money they would have spent on their usual exodus to the Hills. They worked and gave gifts for a Fancy Fair held in purdah; they had a "Gold Mohur Day" (in imitation of Flag Day); they could not themselves sell flowers in the streets, but their English and emancipated Indian friends did this for them, and they drove round the city in purdah-ed cars, buying lavishly at each flower-seller's station....

For the village work they were invaluable. On Saturdays, they would come in purdah-ed cars to a village centre previously negotiated by myself. We began with the idea of a ten-mile radius round Calcutta, but invitations took us to villages, 18, 19, 20 and more miles away. Here they did the Forerunner's work, having previously learnt in a Zenana Centre, where regular teaching was begun, what was necessary for any individual talk. A small group of my girl friends – Parsee, Bengali, Moslem (not in purdah) accompanied us, and helped with the demonstrations. This co-operation, which took no thought of communal distinction, or of the division between Orthodox and Progressive – was one of the happiest incidents of our adventure.

Our village gatherings were held in strict purdah and grew in numbers from 150 to 500 women. Sometimes we met in the Purdah Courtyard of an influential Zemindar, sometimes in an enclosure made "purdah" with tent walls; once or twice outside the warehouses of Jute and Cotton Mills, seclusion being secured by the co-operation of the Mill Authorities, and shut gates.

It was essential to obtain the goodwill and approval of the villagers' male belongings in all that we did. And this, we had. Often they would vacate their own special courtyard for us as being larger and more airy than "the inside", making all secure with tent walls. But, cries of "*Shabaash*" (Well done!) or clapping betrayed them eavesdropping from behind the barriers, to the great amusement of the women.

It should be explained that only a few of the villagers were purdah. The precautions were chiefly in the interest of the *Purdahnashin* volunteers themselves.[32]

As I have said, voluntary work was designed to test the scheme while we were yet collecting funds for the Institute of our dreams and for its regular equipment. It fulfilled itself in many ways; not only giving us abundant proof that this was indeed the ideal way of working, but incidentally educating and interesting a class of women (the *Purdahnashin* proper) who had never before, in North-East India, been swept into Social Service activities.

But our League, upon the lines we conceived it, is, alas, now practically dead!

Bengal Congress Workers (as they called themselves, Terrorists as we believed them to be) threatened the life of the *Purdahnashin* President of the League Committee unless she would give them large sums of money "for political purposes to save the country". She was warned not to communicate with the police; she was assured that they would find out if she disobeyed them, and would "do her in" with her children and grandchildren.... She used a method of communication which they had overlooked. She telephoned the police, and her house was duly protected. But she did not dare go out of doors, and certainly not to the distant villages of our joyous itinerary.

She was a very great lady, a Begum, and it was she who had collected the *Purdahnashin* unit. Committee meetings were held at her house. It was from her house that the village workers started in their procession of purdah-ed cars....

There was nothing for it but to close down till the tyrannies of terrorism should be overpast.

But the Crusade of the Veiled Women has not been in vain. They have proved the League's point, and have lately been encouraged on realizing that a prominent group of workers in old Delhi has followed their lead in carrying its clinics out to the villages, instead of waiting for the village to come in to the town.

The work that is awaiting women in India calls with urgency in all directions; e.g. the investigation of our resources in natural-grown and manufactured food, and how to supplement these, so as to be self-sufficing: the study and revival of home-industries, not as a branch of Politics, but with a view to creating new careers for women, and teaching the appreciation of the beautiful in dress: the study of Labour conditions, and of the mills, again as divorced from Politics: the improvement of housing and living conditions: the establishment of crèches and schools in mill areas.... A Parsee woman, Dr. Tehmina Cama of Bombay,* the only Government Factory Inspectress in India, has done wonders in this last connection. Her tact and fearlessness, her ability and business capacity, the way she gets things done – appreciated alike by the mill-owners whom she has to persuade to *give* (money and accommodation) and the operatives whom she has to persuade to *accept* (her view of what is good for their children): all this, accentuated by her quiet unobtrusiveness, the perfume of personality, in short, of a woman who has found her vocation – fills me with joy in the hope for a future in which Indian women have entered upon their true heritage of Service.

I know how Dr. Tehmina would hate this pointing finger; but if she should ever chance to read these words, I crave her forgiveness. When sunburnt hearts are stirred, the tongue is apt to utter....

In some of our Presidency Towns, small children, mostly of the sweeper caste, are employed as sewer cleaners. I used to see them disappear down the manholes of a main street in Calcutta as I stood on my balcony, watching the Victoria Memorial, glowing like a pink and yellow opal in the reflected glory of the hour before sunrise. The children came out caked with filth. They haunted me; and I followed them up, through the courtesy of the municipal authorities. They are decent children, eager for education, and for a better occupation, but glad of this tunnelling work, as it is well paid. The parents keep them to it – "Soon a boy grows too big to go down the drains, then there is nothing for him to do but carry a broom and a basket."... Perhaps what I hated most was that the sweepers' quarters, where they lived, had no clean running-water taps, or bathing tank. The children had to bathe in the drain water which sluiced the streets.

Here, then, is another bit of worth-while work. And work which should be done, and is best done, without propaganda. It wants doing, not talking. House-to-house visiting in the sweeper areas, in Lower Circular Road, Calcutta, so as to get familiar with existing conditions; inspection of the children on their release from the sewers to ascertain how far health has been endangered – one knows about tetanus and what mud and dust can do to cuts and abrasions; then negotiation of the material municipal authority.... In Children's Courts, Reformatories and Prison-Visiting, Progressive Indian women have begun taking an interest. Through the efforts of Women's organizations, individuals are appointed Honorary Magistrates and Justices of the Peace; and are gazetted as "Unofficial Members" of Prison Visiting Committees. This is good as far as it goes; but until provision is made for the patient study of facts and conditions, for the training of Probation Officers and a system of Probation; with the necessary Clinics and all the marvellous machinery of the work done for the Juvenile offender as I have seen it in America, on the Continent and in England;

until women are taught something about crime and punishment, and the hope and scheme of reformation behind gaols and gaol discipline, can these appointments really be said to represent Progress?

We know that too often, alas, they represent stagnation, in so far as the recipients mistake the label for achievement; and that when Feminists of the West are deceived by the labels into urging wider enfranchisement and greater power without regard to local condition and circumstance, the result is like to be worse than stagnation.

I would not be misunderstood. I claim for my countrywomen no whit less, eventually, after our kind, than women enjoy in England; but after all, our chief right is to *reality*; to work, and to the necessary equipment for work – in terms of the needs and ignorances and sensibilities of our own so-different country.

What was it that King Faisal said to Gertrude Bell? She was assuring him that England wished to give his people freedom. "Lady," said he, "no one can free another. A man frees himself."

Sahi bat – a true word, worth consideration.

Six successive Viceroys of India have I known: and how different each has been from each!

Of Lord Curzon* Indians generally expected most – "Here at last," said they, "is someone who knows the East – and in him finally those who are articulate, expressed most disappointment.

For myself I admired Lord Curzon's demand for efficiency and his amazing capacity for work. That he should be remembered now only as the author of the Partition of Bengal, and by non-political Indians as "a mad Englishman who collected stones and piled them together, putting labels on them!" seems a tragedy.

The "Partition" was a great scheme, which thinking men are already saying should never have been recalled. And his Primary Education scheme put into the Bill drafted by my old tutor, Sir Thomas Raleigh, who was Law Member during Lord Curzon's time, is sponsored in its present form by the very politicians who opposed it.

It seems a paradoxical thing to say, but my own belief is that Lord Curzon failed because of the things which he did "as of grace". Indians understand an autocrat; he was a born autocrat: and had he been that, and nothing else, in India, I am inclined to think that he would have succeeded with the Indians who expressed their hatred of him. But "grace" made him repent of his autocracy: and he would apologize and explain to an Indian audience as if he were addressing an English constituency. Again he did not realize that Indians are like women in one respect. You may tell them their faults *tête-à-tête*, and go scatheless. You will never be forgiven if you accuse them (especially of that of which their hearts convict them) in public.

The most glaring occasion on which Lord Curzon ignored this rule was in his last much-resented Convocation speech. The fire, which had been smouldering, blazed at that: and Lord Curzon's successor entered upon a conflagration which it took a Lord Minto to keep from destroying the entire country.

"God must have loved India very much," as an orthodox Hindu friend said to me, of the Mintos, "to send us this Burra Lat and Lady Sahib." Indeed they were just what we needed. Lord Curzon's Viceroyalty had exhausted the country. Lord Minto* came among us as the perfect English gentleman and sportsman, never failing in firmness yet never failing in courtesy and graciousness: creating an impression of friendship, goodwill and fair play, without yielding one inch of principle or of the "*izzat*" of the British Raj: and ably seconded in all this by his charming wife.

Lady Minto was the first of the Viceregal Ladies to establish personal contact with the *Purdahnashin*. Her carefully secluded purdah parties were attended by more genuine secluded-women than have ever ventured forth in later years. They loved her. When King Edward died, it was to her Excellency that they took their sympathy, begging her to convey it to the Maharajah Bahadur's widow. The little Indian widows felt in the disaster which had overtaken Queen Alexandra a new bond; an alikeness in tragedy, from which they marvelled that such as she had not been preserved. A fresh string was plucked at in their hearts.

"We know how it feels: we want to say *that* to our Maharani Bahadurni."

And Lady Minto graciously sent their messages and received a beautiful letter in reply from Queen Alexandra – which she had lithographed for the signatories of the message of sympathy. I find the letter treasured to this day in the houses of orthodox *Purdahnashins*.

Of the political situation of 1907 in Bengal, I knew intimately from the inside. I had the amazing luck to observe it from an angle, ignored or despised by the Administrators of later years. The impression given and put into words by a *Purdahnashin*, speaking in all good faith during one of these later Administrations, could not have been given during Lord Minto's time.

We were discussing a rather difficult case in which her property was involved. I was comforting her with the assurance that the Government would see that justice was done. "No!" said she. "I will not get justice. I cannot prove that anyone in my family killed or tried to kill the British!"

Lord Minto's "reign" marked our first serious advance in visible "self-government": it gave their chance, I mean, to some of the most notable of Indians, who proved fitness by "making good". It was after Lord Minto's time that, as Lord Sinha said to me one day, the reward was not only to the efficient in the service of the country, whatever their race, but to the "expediently efficient" – i.e. to the man who must be noticed because it was a Hindu's or a Moslem's – or whomsoever's – turn racially to receive notice. Between 1907 and 1912 the pace at which we progressed was – just right.

These are memories: and my personal reflections will, on that ground, I trust be forgiven.

The change of capital brought back to my mind what an old general had said to me in London when I was a girl. "The early British," said he, "showed their wisdom in never making great any centre which would excite comparison with a past Empire. They made Calcutta the capital. Calcutta is British made."

I was at the opening of New Delhi, the magnificent buildings completed: and my sunburnt heart forgot its regrets at the desertion of Calcutta in the glittering scene of the Reception held by Lord and Lady Irwin.*

I tried to find justification. I could imagine – I told myself – a great proconsul who reasoned thus – "True, this city has been the grave of Empires: but I will build on its ruins that which cannot die, – in health and sanitation and true progress." Could that, I wondered, have been what Lord Hardinge* had said within himself, when he made the change. (For that the change was Lord Hardinge's personal "manifesto", backed by his Council, is generally believed.) But Lord Hardinge was there himself that evening and I asked him. The difficulty about Calcutta, I gathered, lay to Lord Hardinge's mind in the presence in that town of the Lieutenant-Governor. Spheres of authority overlapped to the detriment of Authority[xiv] [xiv Lord Hardinge's actual words – quoted with permission – are: "During my first six months in Calcutta, even from the very first day of my arrival, no action was taken by the local Government or the Lieut.-Governor without consulting me, with the result that I found myself involved in about half a dozen conspiracy trials inherited from my predecessor, and to a certain extent responsible for any action that was taken. This, with other reasons, convinced both Sir John Jenkins and me that the strengthening of the Government of Bengal by making it a Governorship was essential, and that with this change the removal of the Capital from Calcutta would be absolutely necessary. The correctness of this view has been proved by the history of the last few years."].... Presently I was given the conclusion of the whole matter from an unexpected quarter. The voice of an Indian Member of the Assembly

– a "Walker-Out" at many a debate when his party wished to show disapproval of Government measures – said in my ear:

"Very fine, no doubt. But we will change all this. These buildings will be turned into a University!"

It is odd, but the fact that Lord Reading had been Chief Justice of England commended him to law-breaking politicians. These were mostly lawyers themselves, accustomed to wriggling out of unpleasant situations, whether personally or vicariously. They argued that lawyers must be the same the world over; and congratulated themselves upon having for Viceroy a Super-Lawyer, *ergo* in their hopes, a Super-Wriggler who would bring sympathetic comprehension to the political difficulties referred to him!

Of dear Lady Reading it is difficult to write without emotion. Her courage was unmatched except by her graciousness. I can never forget the kindness shown me by their Excellencies both at Calcutta and at Delhi, where I stayed with them more than once.

It has been said of Mr. Gladstone that his religious ideals influenced his political actions in 1864. Would the like remark apply to Lord Irwin, whom, with Lady Irwin, those of us who were privileged to know, loved so whole-heartedly? I wonder. It is certain, at any rate, that Lord Irwin was too high-minded even to conceive the standards of men on lower levels: and that his personal dealings with Mr. Gandhi* had repercussions among the Red Shirts on the North-West Frontier of which I heard from themselves in 1933.

One sad consequence of Delhi Headquarters is that the Government is surrounded by politicians alone: and you cannot hear the voice of the inarticulate majority for their clamour. H.E. Lord Willingdon* can temper this disability, and has tempered it, by his earlier acquaintance with India in more than one Province. But the strain of listening for the unheard voice, of watching what cannot be seen at Delhi – must be greater than any man should be called upon to bear. I saw the Willingdons in Canada when H.E. looked as if he needed a long rest. Instead of resting he had to proceed from Canada to India. His amazing ability to cope with India in its present state, harassed by disruptive movements, can be understood only when one remembers that his Excellency has beside him an incomparable sharer of his burdens, one who creates the right atmosphere for the exercise of judgment – of right judgment and of courage to hold fast to the "vision" vouchsafed in times of panic and difficulty. The very thought of Lady Willingdon helps one to recapture a gaiety of spirit. Was there ever energy like hers? or friendliness?

A season or so ago in London I saw something which was to me a whole volume on International Relationships. A London hostess was entertaining her English and Indian friends. The company was distinguished, and to a stranger from India the glitter of clothes and jewels must have been dazzling. One of the guests was an elderly Indian lady who had not long renounced the seclusion of the women's quarters in her Northern home. It was her first visit to England. She was herself of a distinguished family; but wore, according to custom, only a simple white cotton *sari*. I saw her shrinking into herself in a corner, as if warding off the vision of diamonds and gleaming arms which met her eye. Suddenly Lady Willingdon walked towards the recess where she sat. Forgetful of everything, the dear old lady ran forward and threw herself upon Lady Willingdon, who embraced her with affection and with words of genuine greeting. And then turning to an English lady who stood by in a group of the supercilious ones, she said, "And I must greet you, too: it's long since I've seen you" – and embraced her also.

I loved that … perfect tact, perfect friendliness, perfect courtesy.

ECONOMICS AND POLITICS IN A
CHANGING INDIA

It sounds incredible, but I hold it truth that my *Purdahnashins* are primarily responsible for the Publicity Department of the Government of India, which materialized during the War.

I was in England on sick leave in 1914 – poignant memories.... The deferred State Ball in all its brilliance contrasted with the end of July and the days immediately preceding August 4th.

I spent a week-end at Ascot, with Lord and Lady Roberts,* hearing wonderful talk, realizing how that Great One was valued and consulted. The most crucial hours palpitating with anxiety I spent with the gracious friend of my Ceylon and Burmese journeys. The experiences of these days placed my fingers as it were on the pulse of the British Empire: the secret, as I realized when the four grisly years were over, of its stability, with Kings falling in ruins around it.... Shall I ever forget the patient crowds waiting for the sight of our King outside Buckingham Palace? Or the faces of the women at the moving service of Intercession at St. Paul's: or how British reserve dropped away as a disused garment; for the true-hearted recognized that the cloth-of-gold of Friendliness might now, for once, be exposed to the icy blasts of a common hazard.... I thank God that I was in England then. I can never forget.

But mine was a One-man job – I had orders to return to my post in India immediately: and could not join the Army of War-workers.

Till a boat was found, I filled in slips at the Duke of York's Headquarters in Chelsea.

And then, back I went across the waters.

I found my *Purdahnashins* all a-twitter, terrified, and longing for an interpreter.

"Why are the British sometimes so kind, and sometimes so cruel?" they asked me.

"Why do you say that?"

And then I discovered that the vernacular papers used the same word to denote the English and the Germans! No wonder the little women were puzzled! Again, "And why is there a War in Madras?" – the adventures of the *Emden* and the *Goeben*, mistranslated....

The relief of my questioners, on hearing facts, sent me straight to my Member. Would he allow me two more Clerks for two more *Vernaculars?* And would the Government print circular letters about the War, and the progress of the War, which I proposed to write to my *Purdahnashins?*

Permission was given. My Wards continued to write to me telling me the rumours afloat in their several vicinities, and I was able to deal with them in the circular letters. On their own initiative, the women then sent the letters to be read in the villages and bazaars – a practice which became general throughout the Court of Wards jurisdiction in my three Provinces. The Government of India, upon hearing of this, asked for copies of the Letters to be sent to Headquarters, and the need for propaganda being thus demonstrated, a Publicity Board was inaugurated to serve all India.

But the written word, I felt, was not enough for my illiterate charges. So I instituted War Talks at my house. The women in Calcutta and the neighbourhood came like the lizards of Eastern Legend to the hour of Prayer: but, unlike lizards, came strictly veiled – until they got safely inside my doors. Then, the only "veiled" visitor on the premises was the kind Principal of the School of Art, who – shut into the purdah of my little Hall – threw a series of War Pictures which I had collected for Magic Lantern slides on to a screen hung at the end of my long drawing-room. The questions which the women asked at these meetings were a revelation as to the necessity of full disclosure in any Indian crisis.

We all worked hard these years of war: and the responsibility of those, like myself, who were privileged to be in touch with a variety of needs, could not be neglected.

English stores were no longer imported – cornflour, oatmeal, macaroni, ground rice – numbers of things in daily use, had to be done without by people, often children and invalids, to whom they were necessities. It suddenly occurred to me that we ought to use the need to discover our own resources. And that was the origin of the Food Products Exhibition which we organized in March 1918, at the Town Hall, Calcutta; and which brought Rs.10,000 to the War Fund after all expenses, including prizes, had been met.

Letters were written to the Collectors of every District in India, asking for a list of natural-grown and manufactured food-products within their jurisdiction. The response was so generous, that the Survey made upon the data thus obtained was afterwards used as the basis of the Ministry of Food.

The Government gave me an extra office in the then Commerce and Industry Building, and with the help of a part-time Secretary and my two Brahmin head clerks, Gyanendranath Bhattacharjee and Surendranath Bannerjee, invitations were issued to agriculturists and fruit growers, to food manufacturers and food stores all over India – invitations to send exhibits to our Exhibition – the best to be awarded certificates and prizes.

I want to pay a tribute straightway to these two Bengali clerks. The circular letters gave us all extra work for the Wards, but they willingly volunteered to help with this, and with my other War work. It involved adding a minimum of three hours daily to their official duties. They were invaluable, keeping the Food-Products files and statistics as if they had been trained in London; and making many valuable suggestions.

Another lieutenant who was responsible for making from our books the Food Products Exhibition Catalogue – which we printed, and which was both survey and advertisement, giving prices and addresses for all locally manufactured Products – was Mrs. Biss, the wife of a man in the Educational Service.

British and Indians belonging to the Federation of University Women, of which I was the President, also dropped in to help from time to time. And we were a joyous company.

But there was need for investigation as well as enumeration. Cornflour grown in South India was sent to America to be tinned; rice grown in Patna came to England to be ground and tinned. When ships could no longer bring us back our home-grown food, ready to be marketed, the absurdity of this was apparent. Indian manufacturers were informed of the absurdity, and asked to rectify it.

The interest shown and the help given by the general public was most encouraging. A Director of Agriculture pointed out that the excellent green banana grown in certain tracts of Bengal was useless for even internal distribution, because it ripened so quickly. If we could find some means of preserving the banana, we would add considerably to the income of growers.

Every private letter I wrote thereafter to my family and friends began with – "Please discover how to preserve the banana!"

To my family I wrote daily, and they did indeed have occasion to swear at me. But search ended at last, through the efforts of my brother, at the Agricultural Station in Western India. And the Government of Bombay kindly lent us the services of an expert to demonstrate sun-dried bananas (a dessert delicacy) at our Exhibition.

Indian firms soon grasped our object, and used their brains. They essayed as exhibits crystallized Indian fruits, fruit juices, what not....

When visiting the Swadeshi (Gandhi) Fair at Delhi in 1931 – thirteen years later – I was amused at the stall-owners who ran after me to beg me to visit their section where our Food Products Exhibition Certificates were displayed.

The goods created by war necessities were soon regularly on the market.

Among private individuals who helped, mention must be made of an Italian priest, from a Jesuit Order in South India, who prepared and sent us macaroni. Manufacturers from South India were especially successful with their canned fish and fruits. Others experimented with substitutes for oatmeal. From Kullu, North India, fruit farmers sent the most wonderful consignment of pears, peaches and apples. The condition for display in our Exhibition was in all cases that the products should be sold for the War Fund. And this was willingly accepted.

But the Exhibition had its educational side also. At the Wheat Stall, the wheat grown by Mr. and Mrs. Howard at the Agricultural Station at Pusa was shown side by side with the bread which was made out of it, specially for the Exhibition. Farmers from the country came to see this wheat, and to hear how their own crops might be improved.

In another section, Mrs. Wiser of the American Mission, Allahabad, was demonstrating how to can fruits and vegetables – simply using the ordinary Indian *degchi* (or cooking vessel). She demonstrated valiantly, throughout the week, to visitors of all races, and to their servants.

The great difficulty here was over containers. Our supply in India had failed, and visitors and experts were experimenting with substitutes for the glass container. True, there were glass factories in India, but no one knew how to make a reliable stopper for glass jars. This had evidently been the department of German foremen. We tried coconuts, bamboos and other substitutes for glass containers, but either got a leaky stopper or one so tightly wedged in that it was useless.

The bigger firms had cooking stoves beside their stalls, and demonstrated with any food selected. It will be imagined how the entire show, being a novelty to us in Northern India, was appreciated, especially by women. Indeed the army of workers themselves enjoyed it. It was so beautiful – decorated with lanes of standards flying the colours of autumn, in which colours the stalls were also decorated.

The Women's Employment Bureau was another war-time necessity for the help of English women stranded in India; and, working at this through the Federation of University Women in India, we got many openings created which to this day continue for the benefit of Indian employees.

That Co-operation and Unity was one result of the War in India should never be forgotten. All races and all communities were drawn close together. We were one as a human unit, just as the British Administration of India had made us one as a political and geographical unit from the Himalayas to Cape Comorin.

Whence then came disruption – the disruption which has grown to-day to such sad dimensions?

This is not a history of politics. I will content myself with headlines.

Mr. Gandhi, on his return from South Africa, with his Indigo (rural) and Tea Garden riots; San Francisco and the Sikhs; Berlin and nefarious propaganda in the vernacular leaflets scattered over the country.[33]

But the Congress? Surely that existed long before the War? it will be asked. Yes, as far back as 1885.

But the Congress in its inception was only an attempt to secure more openings, easier competition, for Indians; to separate the Executive and Judicial services, etc.... It made no attempt to overthrow the Government. The anti-Government element came in with the Tilak* revival of Nationalism in the Maratha Country, in the eighteen-nineties.[34] The venue then changed to Bengal when the slogan was *Swadeshi*, "Own Country", the overt interpretation of which was the revival of Home Industries. The Partition of Bengal (Lord Curzon's Administration) gave this a new twist; and Gandhi started his *Khaddar* campaign – "Spin! Spin! Wear nothing but home-spun."[35]

Those of us who were in Bengal at the time saw amazing sights. It was a war by Indians upon, for the most part, the poorest of Indians. Trams were stopped, and men and women were dragged out of them, their clothes torn off their backs. Pedestrians were stopped, and equally maltreated. The shops of the little traders were raided, and such goods as were not hand-woven were burnt. When Lancashire-made goods were not burnt, schoolboys lay in wait for customers, armed with iron-bound sticks (*lathis*), and threatened the utmost penalties, beating those who defied them.

My clerk, S. N. Bannerjee, had an interesting experience, when his wits saved him. A machine-made pair of *dhotis* Lancashire stock cost Rs.2/8; its hand-woven equivalent at that time Rs.5/-. Babu S. N. Bannerjee wanted a pair of dhotis, and asked for the Rs.2/8 variety. I doubt if he knew whence it came. Instantly he was surrounded by the School-boy-Guard. "Don't you know Mahatma Gandhi's order? Buy home-spun *dhotis*. We will beat you to death if you disobey."

"I am a fearful man, Madam," said he, telling me the story, "and my heart was as water within me. But I said to them, 'Am I not an Indian, and a Brahmin, why should I not buy Indian *dhotis* if I can. But I can't – they cost Rs.5/-; I am a poor man. I have only Rs.2/8 to spend. Make up the rest, and I'll take the home-spun *dhotis*."

"Wait here!" commanded the boys, and went aside to consult with one another. They were in a predicament. For though they were Progressives, they were not past the superstitions of their race. He was a Brahmin. It would be difficult to keep their word about beating him to death. They came back to him. "This time we let you off. But if you spread this tale – beware!" and they shook their *lathis* in his face.

I visited the mills across the river in Calcutta, to ascertain the relative cost of production of hand-made and machine-made goods. I found that a mill could turn out 400 yards a day as against 4 yards on a hand-loom. In the Bengal Home Industries Committee (started with Government help) of which I was a member, we tried to standardize hand-woven *dhotis* (the men's ordinary wear), and a hand-woven *sari* (the women's garment); but even giving the workers their looms and raw material did not help. We could not get the cost down any lower than twice that of the machine-made article. The hand-woven production is a luxury the world over. But Gandhi will not see this. He wants India to keep her place among the nations (the fourth Trade-Centre in the World), by the use of handicrafts, in a machine-made age. His campaign was at that time against Indian mills, as much as against Manchester. The smaller Indian traders had for years stocked the cheap goods demanded by the poorer clients in town and village. They were expected to scrap their stock immediately, in response to a political slogan – even though home-spun was unmarketable. The situation was complicated by the fact that a large proportion of this home-spun was imported from Japan (and so stamped, as I have seen with my eyes).

And, with whatever genuine (if misguided) impulse the movement was started, it was here that unreality began to creep in, and upon unreality, in the face of facts, hatred. In 1930, 1931, 1932 the boycott of English goods was a deliberate campaign, not for internal industrial expansion (an absolutely legitimate object), but against England. And it has become more and more senseless. Benares weaves lovely silks shot with gold. Dacca weaves lovely muslins, famous since the beginning of England's connection with the East. Both these hand-loom industries had long been compelled to import – Benares its gold thread, Dacca its cotton yarn – because we could no longer produce these things by hand, sufficiently durably. The art seems to have disappeared with the master-workers whom the Moguls – so the legend goes – carried with them when they finally left India. The yarn and gold thread needed for the two purposes I have named, continued to be durably made, I am informed, till the families of the compulsorily migrated men died out, and the knack was lost....

The European machine-made output was then discovered and used (the lovely stuffs themselves have always been hand-woven). During his "Spin! Spin!" crusade, Gandhi heard of this substitution, and forbade his enthusiasts to sell or purchase Benares and Dacca goods.

I remember, even as late as January 1933, how terrified the Bombay shop-keeper (a humble creature in the Mangaldas Market) was, when I asked to see

Benares *saris* – "One of Gandhi's pickets may be about. She would burn down my shop," he said. And that same month, the Indian head of a Dacca muslin weaving industry came to see me in Calcutta, distraught about his business. Gandhi's taboo had put thousands of men, he said, out of employment. Mr. Mardy-Jones, M.P., happened to be staying at my hotel, investigating just such questions, and I turned the man on to him. Mr. Mardy-Jones went to Dacca to look into the matter and returned with a very sensible solution.

"Discover," said he, "how many men in Lancashire get employment through supplying that fine durable yarn for the Dacca muslin trade, and how many Indians are put out of work because of the taboo against using it. If the proportion tells heavily against India, get Gandhi to allow use of the importation."

Women picketers did the most harm to the Country, because they set back the clock of progress in the orthodox Hindu and Conservative regions where progress was vital, and where the move forward had but just begun. Moreover, that women should lie flat in the mud in public streets, should scratch the faces of Indian tradesmen, set fire to their shops; should picket liquor shops and bandy words with the intoxicated – all this was against tradition, and exposed the women to implications which were as a rule unjustifiable. "We had begun to think that Education was good," said orthodox Hindu *Purdahnashins*, "but if this is what it does to women, ignorance is better."

Boycott soon became a habit. A new slogan could be heard in the streets. *Swaraj* ("Own Rule"). Even schools, colleges and examinations were boycotted as the creation of the British Government – an absurd personal nose-cutting in despite. Parents were at their wits' end, losing all control over their children. Gandhi's "Monkey Army", as it was called, enrolled the babies as early as six and seven years of age. They paraded the streets singing slogans, and in English, too, which added to the absurdity! Older children were less harmlessly employed – burning the schools they had deserted and threatening the lives of those in control. Their Indian nationality did not save the masters suspected of loyalty to the established order; indeed, against these as "traitors" resentment boiled the fiercer.

Among the mothers who appealed to me for help was a Bengali widow, whose son, aged twelve, had defied her and gone off to attend one of the "National Schools", as they were called, founded by the Swarajists.

I asked him to tell me why he had left the Government School in the District where he was getting on so well. "I refuse," he said, "to have anything to do with the British. They bring nothing but evil upon us. Why, even the Plague was brought here from England."

"Tell me about that."

"It's in our National School history books, and the Masters explain it. We know that the Plague is carried about by rats. There was a Plague in London. And the English Government caught the Plague rats and sent them to India on P & O. boats. So the Plague is killing off thousands of us, as the British wish."

"I remember the first time that Plague appeared in India," I said, " it was about 1889. Do your 'National' history books tell you the date of the Plague of London?"

"No."

I told him the date ... and needed to say no more. He was a nice child. He burst out laughing.

But the new Educators were not content with perversion of history. This child and the boys belonging to other illiterate and orthodox Hindu families were given poisonous and misleading literature in the vernacular, which they were commanded to take home to read to their mothers.

Sometimes the Swarajists approached the Zenana directly. I will cite only one instance, a particularly glaring one, because the Zenana in question was under the protection of the Court of Wards.

It was on the eve of a marriage, and the Ranis had their jewels from the bank, and more cash than usual in the house. This must have been known outside the *Rajbari*, and it accounts for the timing of the incident.

The family priest approached the ladies with the news that certain widows who were on pilgrimage to shrines in Bengal were passing through the estate.

"Accommodate them in the Raj caravanserais," said the older Rani, "and see that they are cared for."

Next day he came again. "Those pilgrims of whom I spoke have heard of the devotion of the Rani Sahibas, and wish to talk with them about the things of religion." This had happened before, and, "Let them come in the 'Hour of Union' – the twilight hour," was the response.

In the twilight hour, that wonderful time when the sun drops into the sea, sending up stars for spray, the hour of Union between light and darkness, it was the habit of the women to sit on the roof terrace of the Zenana. They were usually there alone, their waiting women relieved from attendance, and it was an hour fitted to meditation and to talk of things religious.

Six veiled figures were ushered upstairs. They were slight, and wore the unbleached cotton *sari* of the countryside. They wore it, as was *de rigueur* for the widow and the traveller, pulled forward over shaved heads, covering their faces from observation. They spoke in low voices (that also was correct), almost in whispers.

After talk about the shrines for which they were bound, and the legends attaching thereto, they broached deeper topics – life, and death, and illusion. Then, perceiving probably by this time that they were alone with the women, "We want money," said the apparent leader of the group, "for *Swadeshi* purposes (Home Industries)."

"This estate is in charge of the Court of Wards," said Rani Thakur Ma, the older lady, quietly. "Tell the Manager Babu before you leave our Raj, and the Government will deal with your request."

But she told me afterwards that a sudden fear stabbed at her heart. How came orthodox Hindu widows on pilgrimage to talk of *Swadeshi?*

"We want the money *from you*," persisted the spokesman.

"I cannot give you any," said Rani Thakur Ma. "Some things are done in the name of *Swadeshi* of which we do not approve."

"We demand your keys, the keys of your safe," said the speaker, growing bolder.

Poor little Ranis! Their keys were tied to the end of their *saris*, and dangled over their shoulders for all to see.

"We refuse to give them!" – in a quavering voice which tried to be brave.

At a signal all the pilgrim "widows" stood up.

They pulled at their *saris*, which dropped to their feet, revealing – six young men.

"Very well then: we will proclaim to the world that your purdah has been broken and that the virtue of even old widow women, having a reputation for sanctity, does not prevent the reception of men in privacy, in the hour of Union."

The Ranis cowered together as if struck. They could not cry out. Their voices would not reach the guard at the foot of the Zenana stairs – three flights below. They had no voices; sound was frozen within them.

One of the men pushed into the Rani's bedroom which opened off the roof terrace. There was their safe, helpless to protect itself for all its iron bravery.

"Quick now, the key of that safe – or we go forth to proclaim what we have said."

Rani Thakur Ma threw them the key.

Two men kept guard on the palsied women, lest they should escape to find help. The rest rifled the safe; then they all resumed their *saris* and walked demurely downstairs. Thakur Ma had fainted, and her daughter-in-law was trying to revive her....

They did not dare tell even their priest this story. They wired for me and sobbed out the dastardly tale, begging that the Court of Wards should take no action against the men, lest their own honour should be blackened.

But the men were no fools; they had melted into oblivion, long before the Ranis could tell anyone about them![xv] [xv For other tales relating to the Zenana in this connection, see 'A Bengali Woman Revolutionary', *Nineteenth Century and After,* November 1933.]

In 1907 disaffection was confined to the *Bhadralog,* or English-educated classes. It made little way. This charge, made by loyalists, was greatly resented by the disaffected. The foundation of National Schools, and the propaganda to which I have referred above, was one answer to that charge. Another was to be found in the invention of the title "Mahatma" for Mr. Gandhi. I myself believe that Gandhi was genuine in his social service aspirations upon his return to India from South Africa, and that he was exploited by his disciples.

Gokhale, that level-headed and sincere reformer, realized Gandhi's danger, and put him under promise not to interfere in politics. While Gokhale lived, Gandhi obeyed his *Guru* (Master), as he called him. But after Gokhale's death, he was at the mercy of the body of clever young politicians. These men realized that the masses would respond to nothing but a call in the name of religion.

"A new Mahatma has arisen."

"Where is he," said the simple villagers, "that we might go and pay him reverence?"

"He does not allow you to visit his shrine, but he bids us collect alms in his name, and by us he will send you directions from time to time."

Now all this was begun in Bihar within my own area of work off the beaten track, so I speak of that of which I have personal knowledge.

Contributions were levied at the rate of two annas a man; and miraculous stories of the Mahatma were circulated by the best propagandists in the world.

The Agrarian Riots in Bihar, the Tea Garden Riots in Assam, were manufactured upon this religious embassage. To this day many of the village orthodox who believed in the Mahatma do not realize that he is not a Mahatma proper, nor an orthodox Hindu. To this day many do not identify him with the champion of the Untouchables, a connection which would instantly have revealed the fraud that had bought allegiance.

It was the *Temple Entry Bill,* permitting the entry of "untouchables" into caste Hindu temples, which stabbed the orthodox wide-awake, hounding the leaders into action; and the masses are now being fast undeceived.

But both in official India and in England those who have every excuse for taking pains to be better informed, still speak of orthodox Hindus as if they were disaffected (in the Governmental and political sense), and as if they formed the majority of the disruptive element in India.

During Gandhi's Salt-Tax campaign and Civil Disobedience (the attempt to secure non-payment of debts, taxes and revenue) which succeeded the *Swadeshi* and *Swaraj* slogans, a new illiterate element was roped in to the anti-Government movement upon other than the purely religious "prophet-among-us" ground.[36] These peasants, burdened with debt to the Mahajans (money-lenders) in a time of general economic depression, were lured by a millennium, in which all debts would be cancelled, all incomes quadrupled – but I doubt whether even these understood even the beginning of the Political Programme for which Gandhi and his movement stood.

I have seen and talked with the Civil Disobedience prisoners in gaols, all over India, and the answers given to my questions amounted to no more than "Mahatma Gandhi's orders", or, more generally, the confession that obedience was bought, and often bought very cheaply indeed.

("Whatever did you do that for?"

"*Huzur*, four annas"; or "*Huzur*, an empty stomach!")

After the Irwin-Gandhi negotiations, the released prisoners attacked Gandhi at meetings held openly in Bombay.[37] "You forbid boycotting and looting and Civil Disobedience. How are we to live? You must at least pay us the picketing wages." And Gandhi considered their requests, and announced what proportion of picketing wages would continue to be paid, although picketing must cease.

Mill strikes were organized on the same basis, the mills in the Ahmedabad area (Gandhi's "home town") escaping only by large subsidies to the Congress.

If success as success is to be counted to him for righteousness, Gandhi's name heads the poll of leaders of disruption in India.

Poor Gandhi! His truths were built upon deceptions, his loyalties upon verbiage.

One sees how it was with him. Does the like not happen in many lives? There is a moment when deception can be slain, false assumptions repudiated – hesitate and we are lost, smothered under admiration, saddled maybe with the responsibilities which homage, accepted, has brought in its wake.

His association with things revolutionary may have come about the same way. Who shall say? But the worst forms of disruption had justification when they sheltered behind his name and his world-wide reputation as a lover of peace and non-violence. A strict adherence to social service and social reform would have saved him and his country. But though he issued many manifestos to the effect that he had resolved to abjure politics, he broke his resolutions, when he saw power or leadership slipping from his hands.

His latest cry, the removal of "Untouchability" as a social service endeavour, has, however, undone him.

The Outcastes or *Harijans* – "the Life, the beloved of the gods", as he calls them – themselves point out to him that they are not hungering and thirsting after righteousness in the company of their betters; but after bread and water and the means of preserving their mortal bodies.

Of the Caste question in all its implications I have written elsewhere.[xvi] [xvi 'Temple Entry and Untouchability', *Nineteenth Century and After*, June 1933.] I do not propose to repeat myself. But it is enough to emphasize the fact that Gandhi has relied on the ignorance in the West, and indeed in Non-Hindu quarters in our own country, for support of his latest "disguise".

The Temple Entry Bill has been accepted by the ignorant in England and India as a genuine attempt to remove barriers, to set wide the door to "equal opportunity", the while astute politicians of the Hindu race, though not now of the Hindu religion, are using it as a Party "stunt" to capture the Legitimate Assemblies.

This is bad enough; but, if the Bill should go through in the Autumn Session of 1934, the orthodox Hindus apprehend that there will be bloodshed on a scale unknown since the British Occupation of India.[xvii] [xvii While this book is in preparation, *The Times* – August 24 – prints a message from Reuter that the Temple Entry Bill is withdrawn. The Government of India had wisely submitted it to the country for opinion, and the opinions against it were overwhelming.]

So much for Disruption on the surface. But ever since 1907 there have been underground forces at work – inspiration coming from outside India – from Berlin first, and since the end of the War from Soviet Russia. The movement is identifiable with the terrorism and communism which is sweeping the whole World.

Three hundred Indians trained at Moscow are, so far as certified information goes, back in India, plastering the country with their poisonous preparations. They represent an extremely well-organized body, acting with discipline, in secrecy, and capable of exacting obedience and a loyalty which defies fear.

Their expressed objective is just chaos – to bring about by violence a "smash down" of the (British till 1932) Government.

How far Gandhi himself was instrumental in suggesting a less drastic method cannot be known; but in March 1930 the Congress of which Gandhi is the official head, certainly made a compact – "the Three Years Pact", it was called – with the Terrorists to the effect that the Congress was to lead Disruption in India, upon a proposition that it would bring about the desired "smash down" by the "non-violent" methods of Civil Disobedience. If by March 1933 the Congress had not succeeded, it was to give over control to the Terrorists.

Now, by 1933, Disruption represented more than one independent body –

the Terrorists proper, the Congress, the Communists and the Red Shirts. A word must be said about the two latter.

The Communists are, like the Terrorists, a creation of Soviet Russia; and they are said to have materialized first in the Punjab, as a Peasants and Workers Movement, started with subtlety among the land-loving Punjabi peasants, based upon resentment against the Punjab Land Alienation Act. This Act was passed for the protection of the peasant against the *Mahajan* (money-lender); but the illiterate were persuaded that it was a measure designed to prevent the peasant holding land for himself.

But though begun here, and in this form, Communism has not been confined to the Punjab, or to the vestments of its *début*. Like Terrorism it is spreading all over the Country. When making an All-India investigation of prisons in 1932-3, I found Civil Disobedience and Political prisoners, both Professors and Students, armed with Communist literature, which they read avidly – the students only one-quarter understanding what they read, but exciting themselves to a great pitch in that they were part of a gigantic movement which was bound to capture the world. The professors, insolently vaunting the same confidence, and boasting that "India would see, presently, and the blind fools who had imprisoned them be sorry for it."

The Red Shirt Movement was started on the North-West Frontier by one Abdul Guffur, who got his initiation in the Soviet Centre at Tashkent, where his brother held some official post.[38] He crossed over into India, and collected men and boys whom he trained in the fastnesses and caves of the arid Mahmud countryside, in the use of weapons, announcing that his was a religious Pan-Islamic Crusade. The leaders of the Congress seeing here, in the fierce Border-men, an element of the kind of strength which the Congress lacked, sent many an emissary, and finally Jawaharilal Nehru himself, to suggest that the Red Shirts and the Congress should join forces.

But Abdul Guffur laughed them to scorn – "Join dogs of Idolaters? Not they! Their Movement was religious, and their political aims were their own concern."

But when the Irwin-Gandhi conversations were being held in Delhi in 1931, upon the return of the Delegates from the first Round Table Conference, the Congress sent again to Abdul Guffur – "You would not believe us, when we told you that India was going to be ruled by the Congress. But what of this? The Indian Delegates have returned from England with the Swaraj proposals of the King Emperor and the British Parliament. But not even the Viceroy may say whether we should accept them. Mahatma Gandhi had to be let out of prison to decide this question, because it is to the Congress that the British will transfer the Government of India."

And Abdul Guffur said to his followers, "Why the British should transfer Government to the Hindus, Allah alone can tell. Maybe the British are mad! But if it should be even as the messenger says, it is best to be in with them, so that when the British have left the Country we Moslems might swoop down and take back what is ours!"

And he consented to an alliance with the Congress, on condition that the Red Shirts kept their own identity and their name. They would be called "Khitmatgars of God", not "Volunteers", and their meetings would be "Jirgas", not "Congress" meetings.

The conditions were accepted. And the Congress has since then considered the Red Shirts part of the Congress. (Cf. the protest made to Government when Red Shirts were not included in the release of Congress Civil Disobedience prisoners in 1934.)

The facts which I have set down above were told me, personally, by the Red Shirts when I visited Mardan in 1933.

At the end of the prescribed three years, Civil Disobedience was proved to be an utter failure. It was represented almost entirely behind prison walls. The Congress had failed to "smash down" the British Government by the use of "non-violent" Civil Disobedience. It was forced to keep its Compact, and restore the leadership of Disruption to the Terrorists. This happened in March 1933. The Terrorists are now once more "in charge".

But two important differences from earlier tactics are to be noticed:

(1) Their objective is now against Law and Order, and stability, *as such*: against *any* Government, not against the British Government. Unlike the Congress, Terrorists have no political or party ambitions. Their policy and primary aim is to bring about chaos.

(2) They have decided that the killing of isolated individuals is to give place to mass murders, to which end they are mobilizing Revolutionary Armies all over India, and collecting money (through Dacoities, raids on Post Offices, attempted train wreckage), arms, ammunition and men.

The Indians returned from Moscow are detailed to work in schools and colleges, and through local movements and forces of disorder.

From headquarters, originally in Bengal, they now work through Provincial Revolutionary Armies, each Province evolving its own programme, though the aims and methods are similar. These programmes have lately come into the Courts as Exhibits, during the trial of Revolutionaries.

The Government under Lord Willingdon is facing this menace with efficiency, and without allowing itself to be deflected by it from the promise of immediate self-Government, as outlined in the Constitution under consideration while these words are being written.

The tale of what the Indian Police and Soldiery have together with their English comrades faced in this long-drawn-out combat, and faced so far in silence (since to disclose the full hazard of Terrorism to the public was believed against the interests of the country), has yet to be written. It braces one's heart with hope for the future.

Not equal support has the Government had, however, from the general public, as the Governor of Bengal has time and again reminded the citizens of that Province. But at last the despair of parents, at one promising boy (and girl) after another being swept into this cockpit of death, seems to have roused them to consider some sort of concerted action.

That Terrorism has appealed to the educated Indian woman, whom we older ones have relied upon for the work which so terribly needs doing for women and children, has its psychological explanation, but is, none the less, the most bitter drop in our cup.

This brings my summary abreast of August 1934. The Report on the White Paper has been presented to Parliament, and the India Bill is under consideration. There are two matters of great moment, from the angle of vision presented by this book, which seem to have been overlooked. The position of Orthodox Hindus, and the further enfranchisement of women. In the anxiety to consider minorities, including the English-educated, the reaction on the vast Orthodox Hindu majority abandoned to the Progressives who make no secret of using legislation to reform social ills – has been forgotten. I have discussed the hazard elsewhere.[xviii] [xviii 'An Indian looks at the Reforms', *National Review*, January 1935.] But it is real. And the remedy suggested by the Orthodox is simple enough – adherence to the policy pursued by the British since 1858.

Closely connected with this, is one aspect of the enfranchisement of women. Those of us who represent Construction have neglected the chance which has been ours since 1919, viz. education about the use of a vote. The Destroyers have been wiser. Parliamentary place and power have been emphasized to the detriment of service, and of the study of needs and conditions. Admirably indeed have Progressive women learnt to organize and speak at public meetings. But what saith wisdom speaking out of the Ancient East? "When your hearts are set on fire not for Power and Independence, but for the women and children who go neglected and sad, poor, sick, untaught and unloved in a world full of beauty, then alone shall ye be able to fulfil yourselves in every way… "

ENGLAND AGAIN – BACK TO INDIA – AMERICA – CANADA – JOURNEY'S END

I have thought it best to deal with Public questions in one breath; but that has naturally involved anticipation of my Time Chart, and I must now get back to my personal record.

At the end of 1918 blindness threatened, caused by over-use of my eyes during the War. I was compelled to return to England for attention; and, as my doctor feared for my eyes on the long journey round by the Cape, the Viceroy, Lord Chelmsford, kindly allowed me to travel through the Canal, a route at that time forbidden to women. Mrs. Macaulay, a Scotchwoman whose husband had come out to India to release a fighting man, was allowed a like privilege. We had the most thrilling voyage in a camouflaged P. & O. boat which was carrying soldiers and provisions; and from Port Said we went in a convoy of 21 ships, the whole line zig-ing or zag-ing to the blasts of the leader's syren.

We had orders to live in our belts, and to wear our heaviest coats when called to the boats.

We had three genuine summonses – terrible moments when you said to yourself, "What shall I save?" My mother's miniature was my only certainty, and it fitted into a breast-pocket.

At Aden we had heard rumours of an Armistice, which a wireless caught somewhere near France seemed to confirm. But it was harrowing having no certain news, indeed no news at all, that long all-sea journey to London.

When we got into the River on November 11th, the Officer on an Admiralty Boat, come to pass us, said casually, "Heard the news?"

"No!" from our Captain. They were talking through megaphones and we were crowded on deck listening.

"The Armistice is signed!"

It was not literally true; that was before the dawn hour. But we were stunned with joy. The news plucked at our tautened heart-strings. It seemed incredible that the guns were no more booming, mowing down our friends.

Our boat ran up all its flags – and we had a broom-stick on the mast. In harbour the noise of the sirens was deafening. We were the only P. & O. boat in, and the other boats saluted us. And such a din of rejoicing as there was from land and water I never expect to hear again.

We were delayed hours in landing; and the P. & O. express stopped at every station *en route* to Liverpool Street, munition workers and Tommies crowding on without tickets. In our carriage there were men all down the aisle.

"Let us in," said the Munitions girls.

A Tommy said, "Don't you see we're half out of the window here, Sally?"

"*Garn!*" said she. "Who won the War for you?"

And they let them in, laughing, to continue their banter. When they had all dropped out and there were only two Tommies left, one said to the other "I dunnow if those girls was right about winning the War for us. I thought that we'd had something to do with that ourselves. But I do know who'll win in a War of Words!" – which seemed to us of the ship, who had sat silent, listening, that this was an excellent summary of a possible future.

At Liverpool Street Station my old College friend, Eleanor Holland Martin, and Victoria Cholmondeley, were awaiting me. I was the only ship's passenger who got away in luxury. There was not a taxi to be seen anywhere.

On the long drive to Elvaston Place, S.W., through streets crowded with every variety of uniform, the faces of the men and women – chiefly the women – caught me by the throat. I'd seen the Mafficking after the Boer War, but this was different. Relief had tears at its heart....

My eyes were saved for the moment by my English doctor, and at the end of six months I was back again at work in India.

In 1919 the Bar was open to women, and the Allahabad High Court admitted me to the Rolls immediately upon application. Still I felt that I wanted to get back to England, and do Law Examinations there all over again, so as to get my real label – the label for which I had longed all my life.

But it was impossible to leave my work; and Ivy Williams of Oxford (how glad one was that she belonged to that beloved University!) has the distinction of being the first woman to be called formally to the English Bar. All who followed her must needs rejoice that it was she, for she took a brilliant First and is now professing Law at Oxford. She has never attempted to practise.

In 1922 I was allowed to take a year's furlough. Two spells of furlough were by this time under Civil Service Rules due to me. Through my long service I had only had snippets of "privilege" leave so far (except for my sick leave in 1918), three months every three years; and I was very tired.

But it seemed the best opportunity for taking my Bar Examinations, and because I was enrolled in India, I was able to fulfil all requirements in a year, reading at the same time in the Chambers of Mr. Lucius Byrne of Lincoln's Inn.

I was called at Lincoln's Inn (the Inn which had offered me asylum in the days of my youth) in Trinity Term, 1923.

Daily in my Inn, I passed the names in the New Hall which recalled those early days – Lord Hobhouse, Lord Mathew, Lord Macnaghten, Sir Edward Fry, and how many others? – names of men who had helped and inspired my ambitions close on thirty-five years previously … I knew they were glad that the door was now set wide for all women; and I knew that these "Watchers and these Holy Ones" would have advised me to travel back over the long road, and finish what was left undone.

It was that which encouraged an old woman who had never really been "examinable" to enter the lists with the young things who in these days do Examinations "off their heads".

While I was in England my Government revealed to me the fact I have already mentioned, that I was to have no successor in my Court of Wards job. This determined my retirement. I had by that date worked thirty years in India, and it seemed to me that I might well, after the manner of the ancient Indian, seek a hermitage of thought – might, in short, retire to the forest (of London) and meditate. There was much that could still be done here for my country, and with luck there might be Privy Council Junior briefs from India in the regions in which I had had opportunity to specialize. So I joined the Northern Circuit and did a second spell of apprenticeship, in Common Law Chambers this time, to Mr. P. B. Morle of the Temple. Going Circuit was fun, especially as I had for companion a young friend, Edith Hesling of Gray's Inn.

In London I lived in the most attractive of cottages in Gayfere Street, Westminster, maided by Mrs. Tabner ("Tabby"), aged seventy, erect and rosy-cheeked, the dearest old soul, a remnant of the Early Victorian type, whom anyone could ever have had at her glad or sick service. She deserves a monograph, and will have it some day.

Another joy at Gayfere Street lay in the fact that it adjoined a slum area, and the children who filtered into Smith Square and my street were my very good friends. They would stand in a body outside my door to see me to my friendly red bus for the Law Courts; and would wait at the corner of the Abbey to see me home again.

My first acquaintance with them was through two boys whom I found playing on the pavement just outside the Abbey; the elder had the younger at his mercy, and was pommelling him soundly.

I made him stop it.

"But, lydy, he's the Dragon, and I'm St. George. I must do it!" It was indeed an appropriate game to choose for that spot. I said I would watch them play it again with the small boy for St. George.

Friendship was inevitable after that; and those two brought the others. But there are too many stories about my Westminster Baby Friends to be told here.

And soon I had to say good-bye to my little cottage with its old furniture and its window-box; to my faithful "Tabby" and the little children.... My *Purdahnashins* wrote piteous letters – there was no one to help them, why had I forsaken them? Things were getting difficult in new ways. Reduced to specific cases, this last statement related, I found, to the spate of new Legislation which the Progressives carried through the Assembly at Delhi – beginning with the Act which, over-riding Hindu Law as represented by the Shastras and up to the present as administered in the British Courts, allowed the succession to family property of a daughter's or sister's son.

In the instance I have in mind my *Purdahnashin* was a sonless widow; after her death the property held in her husband's name would, under Hindu Law, go back to the next male branch of the old Joint Family. The Delhi Assembly allowed succession in the female line, i.e. of a daughter or sister and her descendants. Now property, in the conception of Hindu Law, exists for the benefit not of posterity but of your ancestors. That individual inherits who can buy most spiritual benefit for the deceased.

When a daughter marries, she adopts the gods of her husband. Prayers for her father no longer "reach the ears of the gods". And her sons are in like case bound to intercession for their father and his ancestors, not for their mother's family. A daughter and her progeny therefore could buy no merit for either her father or her brother, my *Purdahnashin's* husband.

As soon as the Bill became Law, the sons of my *Purdahnashin's* sister-in-law demanded recognition as heirs presumptive to their maternal uncle's property. My little *Purdahnashin* was distraught – "Were the souls of her father-in-law and her husband to be left in torment to live in Hell as caterpillars for 1,000 years – after she herself was dead?" (for a widow's prayers *are* efficacious, reaching the godly ears in safety).

"And why is the British Government interfering with our religion after all these years during which Queen Victoria's promise has been kept." ...

There was nothing for it but to pack up, and take the first boat out – the winter of 1924. And it seemed to me that maybe it was my duty to sample work at the Calcutta Bar, so as to make it easier for the women who would follow after. I therefore got enrolled in that High Court, and sallied forth, as before, from Headquarters at Calcutta at the call of my *Purdahnashins*. I gathered that politicians had been using the Act to try and persuade the orthodox that they had better join the forces which sought to overthrow the Government, because the British were now going back on their promise of personal law, "the Law of the Hindu for the Hindu in all matters of inheritance, marriage and succession".

Certainly the Bills being passed into Law by the Assembly did confirm this suggestion. But the orthodox generally had not realized that all such reforms emanated from Indians and indeed from Indians of the Hindu race.

As to the particular problem touching the estate of my client of the moment, we were able to extricate her. But all cases will not be so easy. And those of us who have lived among the orthodox, and know their reverence for the *Shastras* on which all personal law is based, must needs feel that there are difficult times ahead.

The professional work outside Calcutta now began to be as interesting as was my Court of Wards work. And I was glad indeed that I had returned, though I still hankered after that dream of sitting still and meditating....

In the autumn of 1930, when I was in England for our Calcutta High Court Long Vacation, visiting my friends in the country, a cable from America reached my hands asking me to go to the Institute of Politics at Williamstown to join in the discussions on India. It seemed there were several Indians set down to speak against the British control of India, none for it. There was only one answer to that invitation; and I sailed within two days from its receipt, terribly unsure as to my ability, but certain that it was right to go. All my life, bits of work have been found lying at my feet, and I have known that they must be attempted, and that it was not my business to worry about my lack of ability.

I had never wanted to go to America. But I came away loving it, and loving the American people.

My experience is that they are fair-minded. In regard to India, they never got a chance to judge. Anti-British propaganda has been deliberately carried on in that country for years; the British side was never represented. Americans have complained about this. "Why did not the British contradict the lies told?" My answer was, "Do you not know the British? It is not their habit to defend themselves. If you said of me, 'Miss Sorabji was found drunk and disorderly in Broadway,' do you think I would trouble to write to the papers and contradict it? I'd just laugh. It is that way with the British, and the absurd propaganda against them as a nation."

And they said, "Yes; but that is not fair to us, since our habit is different, and they know it. Besides, it's pride; being superior...."

I certainly did feel that more propaganda should be done; and after the

Williamstown Session, I accepted invitations to speak in several States, and to debate the Indian situation in public with Congress opponents.... In the winter of 1931-2 I was again asked to go to the United States, touring this time both East and West to continue the work already begun of stating facts and answering anti-British propaganda. On both these tours I visited Canada also, and received much kindness from Canadians, in the first instance because they were friends of my sister Susie, who during her life had travelled extensively in America and Canada, and was Regent of the Kaiser-i-Hind Chapter, the only branch in India of the Imperial Order of the Daughters of the Empire.

My sister died in March 1931. Her Canadian friends are putting up "in remembrance" a Memorial Building at St. Helena's, one of the Schools she founded at Poona in Western India.[xix] [[xix] *The Life of Susie Sorabji*, Humphrey Milford, Oxford University Press, 1932. [See the Editors' Introduction]]

On my first visit an amusing thing happened. My passport was visaed for the British Empire, and I naturally had no misgivings crossing into Canada from America. We were examined in the train. The Customs Officer passed my baggage, but the Emigration Officer refused to let me into Canada.

"Your passport is not visaed for Canada," said he.

" Do look at it, it is visaed for the British Empire. That lets in Canada all right."

"Excuse me, Madam, Canada is not in the British Empire. You go back to America, and get a visa for Canada."

Nothing I said would move him. He ordered my baggage out of the train; and I saw it depart with despair, for I was to be met, and was due at Toronto at a Banquet which the Daughters of the Empire were giving me that very evening.

The Emigration officer was also Station-master and I could get no attention from him till three successive trains – all that went by that line, the route which I wished to travel – had departed.

Then he returned to his office, where he had left me.

"Now, what's all this about Canada being in the British Empire?"

There was not a soul about to whom I could appeal for confirmation.

"Do you happen to have a boss?" I said. "Will you refer to him?"

He took up the telephone receiver.

"There's a lady here who appears to speak English all right; her passport is visaed for the British Empire, and on that she wants to get into Canada. I've detained her here to take a train back to-night to America."

I could not, of course, hear the answer. He said:

"There! The boss says you're quite wrong; and you must go back wherever you've come from and get a visa for *Canada*."

He would not let me use his telephone, or leave the station to find another, nor would he let me go to the telegraph office.

"How much money have you got with you?"

I said, "I don't know what concern that is of yours, but if you are afraid that I'll be on the rates if I go into Canada" (for it suddenly occurred to me that that might explain his procedure), "I can assure you you need not be anxious. Besides, as you see from my ticket, I am due back in America in two days."

He insisted, however, on seeing how much money I had in use and in reserve. And I was in a quandary. Was a tip all that he wanted? Or had he a confederate who would hold me up? But he did not look like a brigand.

"You'd better let me go on," I urged, "as I mean to report this senseless detention. Besides, I'm the guest at a Banquet to-night of the Daughters of the Empire. Your ignorance will furnish both apology and story for my after-dinner speech."

"Show me your invitation," said he. It was in my despatch-box, and I showed it him, telling myself that it was no use to waste good resentment!

"H'm! My wife belongs to the Daughters of the Empire."

"Then I must advise wives, to-night, to educate their husbands."

I had discovered that there was a train by another line which would take me to Toronto (too late for the Banquet) yet in time to see my hostesses, and to make my apologies. But I had to get past this wretched E.O. first.

"Would the Governor-General know if Canada was in the British Empire?"

"Yes!"

The Governor-General was Lord Willingdon.

"Well then, I'm going to telephone to his Excellency's Military Secretary to report that you are detaining me here, and why."

"Stop – you cannot use my official telephone."

"Then I'm going out to find a call-box."

"You may not leave this room. You've offended against the Emigration Laws.... But, I'll take you to the Head Office, myself."

I had to submit. There, I was denied speech of the Head, but after a time the E.O. came back with another underling who said, "We'll waive the question of Canada not being in the British Empire, but you can't go on, because you are an alien, and there is a law which prevents our letting you proceed."

"I'm not an alien in Canada. I was an alien in America. I come, as you know, from British India, and am equally with Canadians of the British Empire."

No persuasion availed here, either.

"Let me see the Law to which you refer."

"You would not understand it."

"I'd maybe understand it better than you. But I demand to see it, anyhow."

After consulting the E.O., he read me this, from what seemed to be a printed paper.

"'Emigration Officers are advised to use their discretion about admitting aliens into Canada, for purposes of trade.'"

"That does not apply to me. I'm not an alien, and I'm not going to Canada for purposes of Trade. I'm returning in two days, as you see from my ticket."

But my patience had run out to the very last grain, and I started to go downstairs.

"Where are you going?"

"To find a public telephone to report this detention to the Government at Ottawa."

But before I had reached the last step, the E.O. had caught up with me. "The Boss says we can waive both points this time, and that I am to accompany you to the —— Station where you can get a train to Toronto."

Here, I was at last able to telephone to my hostesses begging them to proceed with the Banquet, as timed, since that would cause least trouble; and adding that I would turn up in time to make the speech that was expected of me.

The kind Committee of the I.O.D.E. met me at a Station outside Toronto and motored me in.

The "Daughters" did have a laugh over Canada not being in the Empire; and I was really after all in debt to that E.O. for supplying me with a successful opening to my speech.[xx] [xx I did not report the E.O.; but the I.O.D.E., filled with indignation at the incident, looked into the matter officially on their own account, and I believe it reached Ottawa. I have since thought that the man, in haste, had at first mixed up British *Isles* and British *Empire*; they seemed generally to talk of "the Empire" without the prefix; and then stuck to it to save his face, after all he'd let all the trains on his line go without me.]

On my visit to Canada the succeeding year I saw this same E.O. at another Station.

"Hullo! Mr. ——, you here now?"

"You remember my name, Madam?" He was quite flattered.

"How could I forget the name of the Canadian who did not know that Canada was in the British Empire!"

He took my passport.

"Going to let me through?"

"If you'd had this passport, last year, Madam, there need have been no trouble."

"Do look at it. It's the identical passport which you examined and refused to pass a year ago."

That was fun!

There is an American story which I put beside this one.

On my first visit to the States, I was granted Free Entry – much to the envy of my American fellow-passengers who were returning from Paris, with trunks bursting with dutiable articles.

I should really have been the first to get clear of the docks. The Embassy had kindly sent to meet me, but I was delayed searching for my dressing-case, which contained what could not be abandoned.

Finally, we found it in the pen marked G.

The officer from the Embassy was furious – "Don't you see the S marked on it as large as life?" he said to the Customs man in charge. "What did you put the case in G for?"

"The Steward carried it and told me it belonged to the Indian lady" (I was the only Indian on board), said the man, "and told me to take care of it. I didn't look for the mark. I took it straight to her letter. Isn't she Mrs. Gandhi?"

I wonder why no one has ever told me of the beauty of America, of its riot of colour in the Fall, of its varying types – of humans as of landscape. The Red Indians in Texas might have come from Darjeeling.

I was hard-worked, but loved every moment of my tour, befriended royally by a people with a genius for friendship. My English friends have belovedly said that I have a heart with a double pulse beat – one for India and one for England. In the Great-West, I could distinctly hear a third!

My eyes began to fail me while I was in America, and I was fortunate in obtaining the advice and attention of the famous Dr. Wilmer at Baltimore, Maryland.

He ordered me into his clinic. I was operated on; but sight lasted only for the voyage back to England. And then, darkness began to descend upon me.

The doctor who had saved my eyes in 1918 said that no oculist could do anything for me now....

I thanked God that I was in a country where I could at least learn to be blind.

He was to reconsider this verdict in a month; my dim spark of sight, he thought, could not last longer.

I apologize for a reference which cannot be of general interest. I tell the story because of the wonderful experiences of that month under a sentence which, to me, was worse than death. It was a month vibrant with the joy of seeing; and I verily believe that, taken all round, it was the happiest month of my long and happy life. No one, except a single beloved and understanding friend, knew of the verdict; my experience was not blown upon, even by loving sympathy; and, in the secret of some inner heart-ward consciousness, I rejoiced to the full in a thousand things which could still be savoured and which, so far, one had taken as of right … in beauty, in day succeeding day, in night also; in the faces of little children, in the faces of my friends; in everything that Nature had to give, in colour (which has always intoxicated me), in form, in the way people moved – all "sweet things" – I seemed only just to have discovered how "sweet" they were.

My month up, I returned to the specialist. He confirmed his verdict. Hæmorrhage could not be stopped by an oculist. The trouble needed a different kind of specialist. He sent me to him. That I still see I owe, under God, to these two men. One result of the new diagnosis, however, was that India was forbidden me during the months of heat.

But, I have happily been able to return to my country in the winter, at the call of my *Purdahnashins* and of special needs. The latter included a study of Caste pursued to its fastness in South India; All-India Investigations of Prisons – our system as compared with the requisitions of Geneva, and the condition of political prisoners in British gaols: Terrorism, Communism, the Congress and disruptive forces generally: the relationship of the new legislation at Delhi to the people really affected by it, together with other studies in flesh and blood – the only way one can study Indian questions. That I have thus been enabled to keep in even closer touch with public questions than in the regularized pursuit of my profession, has been compensation indeed – one more instance of that "following goodness", of the fine gold thread, which this record has, I trust, revealed shining through the coarse warp and woof of its weaving.

Insofar as it relates to India, I have attempted no more in this record than a survey in human presentment of hitherto unexplored country – of the millions of women belonging to the Orthodox Hindu Community as opposed to the few thousand Progressives of whom alone the Public can know anything.

The problem is how to lessen the gulf between these two. The old way of reform was to ignore the need for reform. It was put into words by one of my charming Progressive Indian friends: "Let them come into the open, and take what we have, or die without."

The new way, proposed by this same body, is Legislation – compulsion to renounce the ties that bind. It has not succeeded, when tried: it has indeed pushed the Orthodox back upon an ancient and distorted Past, as into the only safe stronghold.

The way for which I would plead is, shortly, an understanding heart. Progress in *the Vernacular*, so to speak, not in the language of the Emancipated West: the study of the difficulties and bondages of a Community which has squeezed much that is beautiful out of ignorance and superstition; and is belovedly responsive when approached in this spirit of understanding. After all, the Emancipated have themselves been brought to the place where they stand, not by compulsory Legislation, but by personal conviction based on Education. Only, their progress has been rendered easy by the initial cleavage with ties of Religion. Where these ties remain, is not a different rate of progression indicated?

. . . .

And now – the sun is low on the horizon. It is time to put away my shuttles. I look around my work-room, and see scraps of silk and wool and cotton – bits of colour, glowing or dull, snipped off too soon, or never taken into use. I unroll the length which I have woven and see signs of carelessness, unfinished ends; here and there too much tension, or again too heedless a slackening … and the whole hanging "patchy and scrappy".

I can put my finger on the places I would change, making better use of my materials, or those others where I should not have used just those threads at all.... But there is no re-weaving it now. The Master Weaver, so I have heard, passes His hand over that which we bring Him – our poor workmanship – as we stumble into His presence across the threshold, in the dawn hour of the new day – all the failures and petty achievements of the day that is spent, forgotten; all the loves and goodnesses remembered for ever; and the names of our friends ringing a bell in our hearts.

Sometimes I dream of that hour; and I see it as the ghosts of blush-pink roses, floating in the air over a range of hills more wonderful than the Himalayas.

Appendix

WOMEN IN INDIA HOLDING LEGAL QUALIFICATIONS

UNIVERSITY	ON THE ROLLS
22 women:	20 women:
C.S. in 1897	C.S. in 1922
2 since 1911	19 since 1924*
19 " 1926	

*(Seven of these are Barristers; the rest are Vakils and Pleaders. Not all are practising.)

Glossary

Achkan:	A long coat, buttoned down the front.
Bahadur:	Brave: a hero: also used as a title.
Baithk-Khana:	Sitting-room.
Banawat:	A fabrication.
Bania:	A trader.
Basti:	A bazaar house: a village.
Brinjal:	Egg plant (*Solanum Melongena*).
Charpai:	"Four-legs", i.e. a bedstead.
Chhoti Hazri:	Little breakfast.
Degchi:	A cooking-pot.
Dhansak:	A Parsee dish, of rice, spices, etc.
Dhatura:	Thorn-apple (*Datura alba or fastuosa*): a narcotic; a poison.
Dhoti:	Loin-cloth.
Dhuli:	Litter.
Dumney:	Waggon.
Gadi:	(lit. Cushion): throne.
Gap:	Gossip: invention.
Guru:	Teacher: guide.
Huzur:	(*lit.* presence), a title of respect.
Izzat:	(difficult to translate) honour.
Kamar-band:	Waist-cloth.
Khabar-dar:	Take care: look out (warning).
Kincob:	(*Kam-khwab*) Brocade; cloth-of-gold.

Maulvi:	Learned man.
Nagawar:	Unlettered.
Pinjrapol:	Hospital for cattle.
Puja:	Worship (used by Hindus).
Puja Ghar:	Place of Worship: temple-chapel.
Pulao:	Rice boiled with flesh and spices.
Purdah:	Curtain; veil.
Purdahnashin:	The sitter behind the Curtain.
Rajbari:	Raj-house; palace.
Sanad:	Grant or deed of appointment.
Shastras:	Hindu Scriptures.
Stridhan:	Women's property: *peculium*.
Takht-posh:	Platform: a wooden "four-legs", used as a bed.
Tehsil:	The official headquarters of a Tehsildar.
Tehsildar:	Sub-Collector.
Thakur:	A title: in Gujerat and Kathiawar used as Raja is used elsewhere.
Thakurani:	Fem. of Thakur.
Tulasi:	A plant, sacred to the Hindus (*ocymum sanctum*).
Uth-bais:	Stand-sit; up-down (a form of punishment).
Zenana:	The women's apartment.

Editors' Glossary

A.D.C.	Assistant District Commissioner
basti	collection of slum dwellings or shanty town
chuprassi	messenger or attendant
dewan	Courtier and Finance Minister of a Native or Princely State
Guzerat	India's western state of Gujerat
I.C.S.	Indian Civil Service
Koran	The Qur'an, Islam's holy book, believed to have been revealed to the Prophet Mohammed
Maharajah Bahadur	(also known as Maharajah, Raja, Thakur, Thakuraja.) various styles for the title of King or Ruler in India's Native or Princely states
Mahommedan	Muslim
manji	steersman of a ferry or small boat
ryot	peasant labourer at the base of the feudal system
Shastras	ancient texts from which Hindu law derives, outlining

	religious duty and codes of behaviour
shikari	hunter
suttee	widow self-immolation (*sati*)
Thakurani	(also known as Rani, Maharani Sahiba, Rani Thakur Ma) various styles for the title of Queen in India's Native States
The Long	the long summer vacation at Oxbridge

Explanatory Notes

1. (p.9) Early eighteenth-century India witnessed the decline of the Mughal Empire (dominant since 1526), and an increasing devolution of power. This created a network of independently ruled kingdoms, known as Native or Princely States, and the vacuum in the remainder of the country was filled by the East India Company, which steadily widened its control from 1757. After the Rebellion or Mutiny of 1857, India was absorbed under the direct control of the Crown. The Indian Empire, or British India, was thus born, made up of existing administrative areas called Presidencies, and governed ultimately by Parliament via a Secretary of State in London and a Viceroy in India. 'Raj' ('rule' or 'control'), came to take on two meanings: the British Raj referred to the British Empire in India; as distinct from a Raj state, which denoted an independent princely kingdom.

2. (p.9) Multiple layers of religious influence make up India's ancient cultural traditions. Hinduism, the country's dominant religious and social order, exists alongside Islam, Christianity, Buddhism, Jainism, Zoroastrianism (whose followers are called Parsees), and the Sikh faith. Over the centuries many customs have migrated across religious boundaries, for example, the observance of *purdah* (the veil), originally a Muslim practice, which later became assimilated by the upper-class Hindu landed gentry: *purdah* was selectively adopted as a mark of status by upper-class Hindu women called *purdahnashins*. *Puja*, a prayer ceremony dedicated to individual gods, is intrinsic to Hindu worship, but the word is also used colloquially to describe a wide range of Hindu religious rites. Muslims are summoned to prayer by the call of the *muezzin* (priest), which takes the form of a recitation from the *Qur'an*, and is heard across the neighbourhood. Fire, the symbol of *Ahura Mazda* (the light and the truth), is central to Zoroastrianism.

3. (p.10) See note 2.

4. (p.12) For more on the Sorabji family background and their conversion to Christianity, see the opening to the Editors' Introduction.

5. (p.14) *Zenana* denotes the apartments of a house used exclusively by secluded women; it is also used to refer collectively to the women of a particular family. As they were unable to leave the *zenana*, widows were compelled to entrust their business affairs to estate managers or 'men-of-business'. As a rule, contact with men outside the immediate family was forbidden. See p.47 ff. for the author's explanation of the zenana.

6. (p.14) By 1857, co-educational universities were established at Bombay and

Madras, and before that at Calcutta, where the first women's college was inaugurated in 1849. Compulsory free primary education was first introduced in the Native State of Baroda by the Maharajah Gaekwar in the last decade of the nineteenth century. The wider government initiative to deliver primary education to the villages (the *halqabandi* system) was also established in this period. For more on Indian education, see the biographical notes on Maharajah Gaekwar and Macaulay.

7. (p.15) Although Hinduism is a multi-faceted religion, two defining characteristics are discernible: an acceptance of the ideology of *dharma* (religious duty), and a belief in the legitimacy of the caste system. In the late nineteenth-century, these formed the foundation upon which the socio-religious framework was based.

    Caste, believed to derive from ancient texts, the *Vedas*, classified Hindu society into a pyramid structure of four layers, with the *Brahmins* (priests) at the apex. *Kshatriyas* (warriors), *Vaishyas* (merchants), and *Shudras* (peasants) followed in descending order. Untouchables, considered so lowly that they fell outside the structure, were forbidden, along with *Shudras*, to have contact with the three upper castes, known as 'twice-born'. Not to be 'twice-born' was interpreted as a reflection of unmeritorious conduct in past lives.

    An immutable fact of birth, membership of a particular caste was hereditary and for life and, as Cornelia Sorabji was to discover in her personal contact with Hindus, an individual's religious duty was to obey the personal and social rules determined by caste relating to occupation, status, and social association. Adherence to these detailed codes was paramount to the Hindu way of life; any deviation threatened not only the spiritual standing of the transgressor, but also their caste, resulting in social disgrace. Serious violations culminated in expulsion from caste (outcasting) – tantamount to ejection from the entire socio-religious structure. For more on reincarnation, see notes 9 and 28.

8. (p.17) See note 5.

9. (p.20) Refers to the Hindu doctrine of reincarnation. This holds the soul to be eternal and inextricably bound to the circle of death and rebirth by the law of *karma* (action). Spiritual progress – which eventually emancipates the soul from this incessant cycle – is attained through good thoughts and deeds. Incorrect action is perceived to express limited spiritual awareness, and finds its consequence in rebirth lower down the scale of being, for example, as a dog. For more on the caste system, see note 7, and for more on rebirth, see note 28.

10. (p.25) Sorabji became the first woman in history to take Oxford University's

B.C.L. (Bachelor of Civil Law) examination in 1892, following the congregational decree permitting her to do so. Delay in returning to England for the ceremony, however, meant that she could not claim the distinction of being the first to be formally called to the Bar (Ivy Williams took that honour). Until 1919 women in Britain were barred by statutory law from qualifying, leaving Sorabji without a formal legal qualification to practice in India. Her early role as a roving *sanad* (special pleader in the Native States) was a self-created post that developed later into a more formal one. See note 13.

11. (p.27) Our upright foot-soldiers wander into your halls – Oxford!

12. (p.43) The word has multiple meanings, distinguishable by context. Generally, the *Durbar* refers to the Crown's interests and estates or to the royal household; or, collectively, it refers to the executive, legislative and judicial functions of a Native State. A *Durbar* Court is the state's court of law, but can also indicate an audience with the ruler or king (including the British monarch in the imperial *Durbar* of 1911); or a ceremonial state reception.

13. (p.46) See p.xiii for editors' explanation of Indian legal posts.

14. (p.46) Following 1857 those areas formerly administered by the East India Company were brought under direct Crown control, while the remainder continued to be governed by Indian rulers, each state with an independent executive and judiciary. The Agent, a British government employee, provided the vital link between the two legal systems: if cases could not be satisfactorily resolved within the *Durbar* Court of the Native State, legal provision existed for them to be heard under British Law by the Agent, even if they involved members of the royal household.

Denied a formal legal qualification because of her gender (see note 10), and unable to plead in government courts, Sorabji resolved to pursue her work in the *Durbar* Courts of Native States outside British India. Acting as the crucial interface between secluded upper-class women and the law, Sorabji's self-created role as a roving *sanad* (pleader) often brought her into conflict with the *Durbar* (Crown), when disputes of succession, inheritance and maintenance were involved. With the ruler of the state also his own High Court, this sometimes gave rise to the anomaly whereby, if the case was brought against the *Durbar*, the judge was also the defendant. In such instances, recourse to the Agency courts was crucial for the success of her work.

15. (p.50) The traditional practice of *sati*, the Sanskrit word for 'good' or 'true' wife, refers to the self-immolation of a widow on her husband's funeral pyre. In royal households when a king died in battle, the queen left a pigmented impression of her palm on a designated 'sati stone'. These can still be seen

at Junagarh Fort in Bikaner, and Mehernagarh Fort in Jodhpur. Controversial among Indian reformers from the early nineteenth-century, *sati* (abolished by the British in 1829) was widely accepted as the supreme act of fidelity. For an alternative reading, see p. 12 of *India Recalled*.

16. (p.50) Unlike monotheistic religions, Hinduism admits innumerable gods and goddesses within its cosmic structure, and even some zoomorphic ones. Although not considered to be personifications of the forces of nature, they are closely related to those forces, and do not have a fixed hierarchical structure.

As there is no congregational worship at temples other than for specific ceremonies, domestic worship forms a cornerstone of Hindu life. The *puja ghar* (small shrine) in every orthodox household contains an effigy of the family's principal god – the patron deity – as well as several secondary ones. The gods are worshipped at morning and evening prayers, and offerings of food (libations) are made to them. Baby Krishna is the playful child-god, often painted blue.

17. (p.60) Ancient texts from which Hindu law derives, the *Shastras* outline religious duty and codes of behaviour.

18. (p.60) Likely to be an equivalent to the post of Agent to the Governor-General (A.G.G.), a political adviser to the Native States and instrumental in exerting indirect control over them.

19. (p.71) Indian soldiers from a British Regiment. The vast majority of ordinary soldiers in the British Army in India were Indians.

20. (p.79) Sorabji seized the opportunity presented by the passing of the Court of Wards Act (Bengal, Bihar and Orissa, 1879; Bombay, 1905; Madras, 1902; United Provinces, 1912) to submit a scheme proposing herself in the official role of 'Advisor' to the Court, thereby continuing to act as liaison between secluded women and the law, but this time in a formal role. She took up her post in Calcutta in 1904. See note 14.

21. (p.85) Hindu goddess of Destruction.

22. (p.88) The Elephant-headed god, son of Shiva.

23. (p.98) Benares or Varanasi on the Ganges is one of Hindu India's foremost holy places and centres of pilgrimage. To die there is considered especially auspicious.

24. (p.117) Lord Curzon's Partition of Bengal was a deeply unpopular and highly controversial measure that sparked the Swadeshi Movement of resistance (1905-08). See the biographical note on Curzon and notes 35 and 36 for more on Indian resistance.

25. (p.118) Until 1919 women in Britain were prevented from qualifying for the Bar. See note 10.

26. (p.119) The 1829 abolition of *sati* (widow self-immolation) by the British signalled a change in the policy of non-interference in Indian religious affairs. See note 15 on *sati*.

27. (p.124) The marriage situation described here correlates closely with that in Tennyson's poem 'Enoch Arden' (1864), as Sorabji herself notes in a subheading to the first edition.

28. (p.124) Refers to the three upper castes of Hindus: *Brahmin, Kshatriya*, and *Vaishya*. Membership of one of these castes signifies a second birth, hence the term 'twice-born'. For a fuller explanation of the caste structure, see note 7; for more on reincarnation, see note 9.

29. (p.125) Religious rituals are central to Hinduism, often marking different life-stages. Initiation ceremonies like rice-taking mark the transition to weaning an infant, and the chalk-in-hand signals the beginning of learning to read and write.

30. (p.140) In the Hindu epic, the *Ramayana*, the goddess Sita was Rama's exemplary wife. She embodied the virtues of fidelity and devotion to duty.

31. (p.142) The warrior class, second after the *Brahmin* (priestly) class in the Hindu caste system. For more on caste, see note 7.

32. (p155.) The observance of *purdah* (the veil) was a mark of status among Hindus, and its use was confined largely to the aristocracy and gentry. It was, however, widely observed by Muslim women in general. See note 2.

33. (p.167) In the late 1910s, the Gandhi-led Non-Cooperation Movement was marked by a new defiance that also informed several violent peasant revolts, like the Indigo riots (1917). Throughout the nineteenth century, forced cultivation of indigo culminated in persistent unrest among peasants who worked for little or no remuneration from European planters. Although the system was overthrown in Bengal in the 'Blue Mutiny' (1859-60), resentment continued in the neighbouring state of Bihar until 1917, when Gandhi took up the cause, leading to riots that signalled the end of a hated and repressive structure. For more background to M.K. Gandhi, see biographical note.

As the independence movement gathered pace, Indians all over the world began to advocate the nationalist cause. Under the leadership of a Sikh political exile called Har Dayal, the Ghadar movement was initiated in San Francisco in 1913, with the aim of instigating armed revolt against British rule in India. Its influential monthly bulletin provided a powerful ideological critique of colonial rule.

34. (p.167) By invoking parallels with the seventeenth-century Maratha victory over Mughal invaders, Tilak played a pivotal role in igniting anti-imperial, nationalist sentiments in the 1890s. For more on B. G. Tilak, see biographical note.

35. (p.167) The Swadeshi (own country) Movement of resistance (1905-08) was initiated as a response to Curzon's deeply unpopular Partition of Bengal (1905), and was distinguished by increasingly confident aims and strategies. Advocating self-help and home industries, the movement mounted a boycott of British imports, institutions and education. Although fairly successful, unscrupulous mill owners seized the opportunity to inflate the price of local cotton goods. This arguably led to coercive tactics being employed by swadeshi activists in an effort to achieve compliance from the masses.

By 1919, these early efforts had grown into the Non-Cooperation Movement (1919-22) and the first all-India agitation. This last was piloted by Gandhi in response to the disappointing Montagu-Chelmsford reforms, the Rowlatt Acts, which permitted the imprisonment without trial of individuals suspected of subversion and the Amritsar massacre where a British General Dyer fired on an unarmed crowd, leaving hundreds dead and injured. The boycott of foreign goods and institutions was now accompanied by Gandhi's campaigns in favour of local khaddar cotton. Spinning became synonymous with resistance, and khaddar cloth the badge of dissent. Vast bonfires of foreign cloth became another potent symbol of anti-Western defiance.

36. (p.173) Triggered by British rejection of dominion status for India, the new Civil Disobedience campaigns (1930-31 and 1932-34) were characterised by a more trenchant brand of resistance. With considerable nationwide co-ordination, several anti-government offensives were launched. Of these, the most powerful articulation of national defiance was embodied in the Salt March (1930), which initiated the Civil Disobedience campaign. Arguing that the government monopoly on salt had the effect of artificially inflating the price of a necessity, Gandhi and a group of followers led a 240-mile march to the sea, culminating in the symbolic collection of salt. It was a dramatic gesture that encapsulated the meaning of independent action. Other offensives were mobilised all over the country: boycotts of alcohol, foreign cloth and other taxable goods; and the refusal to pay land and other taxes.

37. (p.173) In early 1931, after a year of civil disobedience, negotiations between Gandhi and the Viceroy, Lord Irwin, delivered a truce: the Gandhi-Irwin pact. This secured Congress participation in discussions towards a new constitutional plan. Congress also agreed to halt civil disobedience and the

government reversed ordinances in the much-hated Rowlatt Acts. Crucially, Irwin also capitulated on the salt laws.

38. (p.175) A non-violent communist resistance movement active in the North-West Frontier Province, the 'Khudai Khitmatgars' (Red Shirt Movement) was led by Ghaffar Khan, and inspired by the Russian Bolshevik revolution of 1917 which brought Lenin to power.

Appendix: Biographical Notes

Herbert Henry ASQUITH (1852-1928): British Liberal statesman who served as Home Secretary (1892-95) and Prime Minister (from 1908), and enacted important social reforms. He headed a war coalition government in 1915, and was ousted by David Lloyd George's Conservative coalition in 1916.

Arthur James BALFOUR (1848-1930): Philosopher, statesman, and Conservative Prime Minister (1902-1905), Balfour presided over Curzon's (q.v.) Partition of Bengal. As Foreign Secretary (1916-1919), he was responsible for the controversial Balfour Declaration (1917) in which Britain established a homeland for the Jews in Palestine. His famous clarification of Dominion status (1926) as a state of complete autonomy in domestic and external affairs represented a watershed in British colonial history.

Stella BENSON (1892-1933): British novelist of unusually independent spirit, she had a rich and varied life, working in London, the USA, and China. Of her many works, the acclaimed *Tobit Transplanted* (1931) combined wit and tragedy, fantasy and realism.

Mary Elizabeth BRADDON (1835-1915): Prolific British novelist who published about seventy-five novels including *Ishmael* (1884). The thriller, *Lady Audley's Secret* (1862), propelled her to fame.

Dr. Tehmina CAMA (n.d.): Daughter of the prominent Parsee family Cama, committed to religious and social reform, and to women's education in particular.

Mary CHOLMONDELEY (1859-1925): Novelist and daughter of a clergyman whose most well-known work is *Red Pottage* (1899), a melodramatic and witty critique of clerical life.

George Nathaniel, Lord CURZON of Kedleston (1859-1925): Widely respected as a leading authority on Asia, Lord Curzon became Viceroy of India (1898-1905), aged only 39 years. He is largely remembered with opprobrium, however, for his Partition of Bengal, a miscalculation that triggered the Swadeshi Movement of Indian resistance. Partition left Curzon vulnerable to Kitchener's (q.v.) political and military intrigues and he resigned during his second term. He later served in Lloyd George's war cabinet in 1916, and as Foreign Secretary in the Liberal coalition government of 1919.

(Sir) Francis FORD (1828-1899): Diplomat who began professional life in the British army in India; adoptive father of Cornelia's mother Francina Santya.

Edward Augustus FREEMAN (1823-1892): Empirical English historian and Professor of Modern History at Oxford (1884-1892), after which the position passed to Froude (q.v.).

James Anthony FROUDE (1818-1894): Renowned English historian and man of letters, he became Professor of Modern History at Oxford in 1892 and published the impressive twelve-volume *History of England from the Fall of Wolsey to the Defeat of the Spanish Armada* (1856-70). Later works revealed blatantly racist sentiments, for instance, *England and her Colonies* (1886) and *The Bow of Ulysses* (1888).

Maharajah GAEKWAR III of Baroda (1863-1939): Progressive ruler of one of India's foremost Native States, Maharajah Gaekwar III was dedicated to education and social reform. He introduced compulsory free primary education in his state in the late 1890s, an unprecedented step in India. An ardent supporter of the Indian National Congress and a staunch nationalist, he harboured several resistance leaders during the struggle for independence.

Mohandas Karamchand GANDHI (1869-1948): A barrister, social reformer and revered resistance leader, he initiated *satyagraha* as a method of non-violent resistance against the British. He was impassioned in his abhorrence of all injustice, not only denouncing colonial rule, but also social iniquities like caste. After spending twenty formative years (1893-1914) in South Africa initiating legal and political protests and reforms, he became, on his return, leader of the Indian National Congress (1915-1948), transforming it into a mass resistance movement. Although largely successful, critics (like Cornelia Sorabji) indict him for the indiscipline and violence prevalent in the movement.

An individual of indomitable courage and vision, Gandhi was repeatedly imprisoned during the struggle, and lived in poverty and abstinence, convinced that India's destiny lay in a return to a non-Western agrarian society. He was deeply distressed by the prospect of the partition of the country, and laboured to conciliate extremist Hindu and Muslim factions. His assassination in 1948 by a Hindu fanatic triggered an unparalleled outpouring of national grief. See note 35 on the Swadeshi Movement; note 36 on the Civil Disobedience Movement; note 37 on the Gandhi-Irwin Pact.

William Ewart GLADSTONE (1809-1898): Distinguished Liberal statesman, brilliant orator, and four times Prime Minister of Britain, who started his public career as a Tory and concluded it a Liberal. A strong proponent of free trade ideas, he played a crucial role in delivering political and economic freedoms, achieving universal male suffrage and a system of national education, and a reduction in tax levels. His controversial support for Irish Home Rule irrevocably split the Liberal Party.

Gopal Krishna GOKHALE (1866-1915): A teacher, politician and moderate voice in the Swadeshi Movement, and the Indian National Congress leadership, he was a believer in constitutional methods and advocate of social reform.

(Sir) Mountstuart GRANT DUFF (1829-1906): Author and Liberal statesman who served in Gladstone's (q.v.) first government as Under-Secretary of State for India (1868-1874).

Charles, Lord HARDINGE (1858-1944): Viceroy of India (1910-16) after Lord Minto (q.v.).

Arthur, Lord HOBHOUSE (1819-1904): English judge of strong liberal sentiment, advocate of legal reform and law member of the Council of the Governor-General of India (1872). During his tenure, he clarified several points in Hindu law regarding adoption and inheritance.

Mrs HUMPHRY WARD (née Mary Augusta ARNOLD) (1851-1920): British novelist and one of the first women magistrates in England, married Thomas Humphry Ward, a Fellow of Brasenose College, Oxford in 1872, and became Secretary of Somerville College, Oxford (1879-1881). She registered her antipathy to the burgeoning suffragette movement by becoming the first president of the Anti-Suffrage League in 1908. Her novels, all on social or religious themes, include the popular *Robert Elsmere* (1888) and *Marcella* (1894).

Edward Wood, Lord IRWIN, Earl of Halifax, (1881-1959): During his term as Viceroy of India (1926-31), he strove to quell widespread discontent following the constitutional review held by the Simon Commission (1927). Establishing an unprecedented working dialogue with M. K. Gandhi (q.v.), he initiated a Round Table conference to discuss reform, and secured the Irwin Declaration of 1929, recognising eventual dominion status for India.

Benjamin JOWETT (1817-1893): An outstanding English scholar of Greek and Latin who rose to prominence with astonishing speed. He was elected a

Fellow of Balliol College, Oxford (while still an undergraduate), then a Tutor, later Master of the college in 1870, and eventually Vice-Chancellor of the University in 1882, and Regius Professor of Greek. His formidable energy and liberal influence permeated deep into the ethos of Balliol, and indeed the university as a whole. An independent thinker deeply committed to reform, he encouraged the foundation of scholarships for poorer students and supported initiatives in music and drama. He was a great liberal spirit who was tried and acquitted by the Vice-Chancellor's court for his essay, 'The Interpretation of Scripture'. Consulted on the question of the Indian Civil Service examinations, he developed an abiding interest in India, and in the training of imperial administrators generally, helping to establish a school of Oriental languages at Oxford.

Horatio Herbert, Lord KITCHENER (1850-1916): A foremost imperialist, Kitchener distinguished himself in conflict and rose to the highest military and political echelons: Commander-in-Chief during the final year of the South African War (1901-02) and in India (1902-09), and Secretary of State for War (1914-18).

Alfred LYTTELTON (1857-1913): Barrister and statesman.

Thomas Babington MACAULAY (1800-1859): Eminent early nineteenth-century historian who also played a significant colonial role in India, he framed the Indian Penal Code (1860) and initiated the use of English as the medium of instruction in Indian education. In his influential 'Minute on Indian Education' (1835), he endorsed English over Oriental languages, arguing for the need to create a class of westernised Indians able to act as an interface between rulers and their subjects.

H.H. Princess MARIE-LOUISE (1872-1956): Grand-daughter of Queen Victoria, married Prince Aribert of Anhalt in 1891 (marriage dissolved in 1900).

Friedrich MAX MÜLLER (1823-1900): Eminent German Orientalist and philologist who pioneered the British study of comparative mythology, religion, and philology. One of the most brilliant, prolific and versatile scholars of the nineteenth century, he became Professor of Modern European Languages at Oxford in 1848, and Chair of Comparative Philology in 1868. Max Müller's output was formidably wide in range and depth: he became the first editor of the *Rg Veda* (1873); and published the highly acclaimed *History of Ancient Sanskrit Literature* (1859). *The Sacred Books of the East* (1875-1900), under his editorship, provide English translations of important Oriental religious texts, thus building an unprecedented, rigorous basis for the study of comparative religions. *The Science of Thought* (1887) expounds his thesis of the inseparability of thought and language.

Gilbert John, Lord MINTO (1847-1914): Prominent colonial administrator who became Governor-General of Canada (1898-1904) and succeeded Curzon (q.v.) as Viceroy of India (1905-10). His defining legacy, together with that of the renowned Liberal Secretary of State John Morley (q.v.), was to heed public opposition to the Partition of Bengal, and to initiate policies to extend self-government in India. In aiming to secure greater representation of Indian interests (including those of Muslims), the Morley-Minto Reforms of 1909 effectively served to introduce the principle of communal representation in India. As such, they are widely regarded as the destructive seeds of the Partition of the country in 1947.

John, Lord MORLEY (1838-1923): Greatly influenced by J.S. Mill's Liberalism, a biographer and distinguished Liberal statesman and a vociferous exponent of humanitarian rationalism. As Irish Secretary in Gladstone's (q.v.) governments of 1886 and 1892, he was an ardent advocate of Irish Home Rule. During his tenure as Secretary of State for India (1905-10), he presided over significant reforms initiated by the Viceroy, Lord Minto (q.v.), known as the Morley-Minto reforms of 1909.

(Sir) Frederick POLLOCK (1845-1937): English Jurist and Professor of Jurisprudence at UCL (1882) and Oxford (1883).

Frederick, Lord ROBERTS, Earl of Kandahar, Pretoria, and Waterford (1832-1914): Lord Roberts served as Commander-in-Chief (1885-93) and enjoyed military successes on India's northern frontier; later he served as Field Marshal in the early period of South Africa's Anglo-Boer War.

Raja Rammohan ROY (1772-1833): Prominent Bengali intellectual, he was a member of a small Calcutta-based group of educated Indians who advocated religious and social reform. He founded the Brahmo-Samaj, a monotheistic Hindu reform movement which denounced practices like child marriage, widow burning (*sati*), and the worship of idols, arguing that they were not sanctioned by the ancient texts, the *Vedas*. Simultaneously, he encouraged the spread of Western education.

(Sir) Henry Morton STANLEY (1841-1904): The ruthlessly determined English explorer whose accounts of his adventures served to fuel the burgeoning imperial spirit. His most renowned expedition is described in the volume *How I Found Livingstone* (1872); a subsequent adventure is portrayed in *Through the Dark Continent* (1878).

Margot TENNANT (1864-1945): Artistically gifted, intelligent and feisty, Margot Tennant became an influential society hostess, leading a group of young intellectuals and aesthetes called the 'Souls' who championed greater freedoms for women. She married Herbert Asquith (q.v.) in 1894 and wrote two notoriously indiscreet autobiographies following his resignation.

Bal Gangadhar TILAK (1856-1920): Prominent Indian resistance leader, advocate of a more advanced nationalism and a militant member of the radical wing of the Indian National Congress, Tilak resolutely called for full independence for India, and was twice imprisoned. He helped to establish the Home Rule League in 1914, just as M.K. Gandhi (q.v.) returned from South Africa. An astute politician and an inspiration to Gandhi, he was innovative in harnessing old religious symbols to convey new messages in the 1890s. Invoking a parallel with the Maratha victory over Mughal invaders in the seventeenth century, he urged Indians to reject British imperialism. Implicit in his overtly Hindu nationalism was an anti-Muslim edge that polarised Hindu and Muslim India.

(Sir) George Otto TREVELYAN (1838-1928): The renowned Trevelyan family played an important role across two generations in the Indian Raj. Sir George Trevelyan, nephew of the prominent historian Thomas Babington Macaulay, was a politician, historian and writer. *The Competition Wallah* (1864), written following his long visit to India, vividly portrays Anglo-Indian life after 1857.

Freeman, Lord WILLINGDON (1866-1941): Governor of Bombay (1913-18), he later followed Lord Irwin (q.v.) as Viceroy (1931-36). Although lacking Irwin's sensitivity, Willingdon helped establish the Government of India Act (1935), giving virtual autonomy to the provinces.

(Sir) Robert Samuel WRIGHT (1839-1904): Respected judge and outstanding legal thinker educated at Balliol College, Oxford, under Benjamin Jowett (q.v.). Called to the Bar in 1865, and became a Bencher of the Inner Temple in 1891.